Steven Mann
Chuck Rivel
Ray Barley
Jim Pletscher
Aneel Ismaily

Microsoft®
SharePoint®
2010 Business
Intelligence

UNLEASHED

SAMS | 800 East 96th Street, Indianapolis, Indiana 46240 USA

Microsoft® SharePoint® 2010 Business Intelligence Unleashed

ISBN-13: 978-0-672-33551-8

ISBN-10: 0-672-33551-4

Library of Congress Cataloging-in-Publication Data is on file.

Printed in the United States of America

First Printing: May 2011

Trademarks

Warning and Disclaimer

Bulk Sales

Pearson offers excellent discounts on this book when ordered in quantity for bulk purchases or special sales. For more information, please contact:

U.S. Corporate and Government Sales
1-800-382-3419
corpsales@pearsontechgroup.com

For sales outside of the U.S., please contact:

International Sales
+1-317-581-3793
international@pearsontechgroup.com

Editor-in-Chief
Greg Wiegand

Executive Editor
Neil Rowe

Development Editor
Mark Renfrow

Managing Editor
Kristy Hart

Project Editor
Andy Beaster

Copy Editor
Keith Cline

Indexer
Erika Millen

Proofreader
Charlotte Kughen

Technical Editor
Mark Meyerovich

Publishing Coordinator
Cindy Teeters

Book Designer
Gary Adair

Composition
Gloria Schurick

Contents at a Glance

Table of Contents

Contents   v

15   Integrating Visio and Excel Services   271

Part VII   Troubleshooting

16   Reporting Services Issues   281

17   PerformancePoint Services Issues   287

About the Authors

Steve Mann was born and raised in Philadelphia, Pennsylvania, where he still resides today. He is an Enterprise Applications Engineer for Morgan Lewis and has more than 17 years of professional experience. Steve was previously a Principal Architect for RDA Corporation where he worked for over 13 years.

For the past 8 years, he has primarily focused on collaboration and business intelligence solutions using Microsoft technologies. Steve managed the internal BI Practice Group at RDA for several years. He was also heavily involved within RDA's Collaboration/Search Practice Group.

He has authored and co-authored several books related to the subject of SharePoint Server 2010. Steve's blog site can be found at www.SteveTheManMann.com.

Chuck Rivel is currently employed at RDA as a Principal Architect which involves scoping, designing, developing and delivering custom data warehouse projects for many different industries. He has over 14 years' experience working with MS technologies and the last 8 years have been focused on DW\BI development. Currently, he is the BI Technical Lead for RDA, which is responsible for the technical direction of the BI team within RDA and for creating training programs for existing RDA employees to learn the BI toolset.

Ray Barley is a Principal Architect at RDA Corporation and has worked as a developer, analyst, project manager, architect, trainer and independent consultant. He has been focused on architecting and delivering Business Intelligence solutions since 2005. Ray helps to run the Baltimore SQL Server User group, is a frequent speaker at local user group meetings, and a frequent contributor to MSSQLTips.com.

Jim Pletscher is a Senior BI Consultant with RDA and has worked in the IT field for more than 15 years. Jim first began exploring OLAP technologies with SQL Server 2000, and has worked extensively with SQL Server 2005 and 2008, developing Reporting and Analysis solutions for numerous clients in a variety of industries over the past 8+ years. He is originally from Pennsylvania, and lives there now, but has also lived in Northern California as well.

Aneel Ismaily was born and raised in Karachi, Pakistan and then moved to the United States at the age of 18. Since then he has lived in Atlanta, GA. Aneel joined Georgia State University in 2001 and finished his BS degree from there in Computer Science. He is currently enrolled in a professional MBA program at Georgia State University and expecting to graduate in Dec, 2012. Aneel brings over eight years of experience to RDA in designing, developing, deploying, and supporting Business Intelligence Solutions. He currently holds Sr. Software Engineer Position with RDA. Prior to RDA, Aneel was employed at BCD Travel as a BI Solution Developer and previously as a Database Administrator. You can learn more about Aneel at http://www.linkedin.com/in/aismaily.

Dedications

To my family, especially my wife Jen, for being so excited for me on getting the opportunity
to write the book and then pushing me to get it done.
—Chuck Rivel

To my wife Karen, and our children Katelyn, Jessica and Joshua.
To my dad for teaching me the value of perseverance.
—Ray Barley

I'd like to thank RDA and my colleagues there for creating an environment where we can learn together and encouraging me to take on new challenges. I'd also like to thank Ralph Ceseña and Dominic Eve who first got me interested in Business Intelligence technologies many years ago.
—Jim Pletscher

I dedicate this book to each and every member of my family for their unconditional
support in all aspects of my life. I love you all!
—Aneel Ismaily

Acknowledgments

Special thanks to Deepak Gupta from RDA for pitching the idea to me for a SharePoint BI book. In addition to Deepak, I really appreciated my colleagues' efforts and assistance in authoring this with me - I wouldn't have had enough time or energy to complete this on my own. Thanks to Neil Rowe and Sams Publishing for allowing us to produce a focused authoritative guide within the *Unleashed* series.
—Steve Mann

I want to thank all of the colleagues that I have worked with over the years. Because you shared your knowledge to me on the different technologies we have worked with over the years, those experiences gave me the confidence to want to share my thoughts in an effort to help others learn in the same way as I have learned from all of you. In addition, I want to thank Sams Publishing for providing this vehicle to me and my fellow co-authors. Lastly, special thanks to Steve Mann for asking me to come on board.
—Chuck Rivel

Thanks to Steve Mann for asking me to participate in this project. Thanks to all of my colleagues who over the years have shared their knowledge.
—Ray Barley

To my parents, who bought me my first computer, a Commodore64, and started what has become my career with computers. To my wife, Treva, and kids, Rebecca, Colin, and Hayden, who keep life fun and exciting and remind me not to sweat the small stuff.
—Jim Pletscher

Thanks to Steve Mann, Chuck Rivel, Ray Barley and Jim Pletscher for giving me this opportunity. I also thank the entire team of Sams Publishing for their support during the book review.
—Aneel Ismaily

We Want to Hear from You!

As the reader of this book, you are our most important critic and commentator. We value your opinion and want to know what we're doing right, what we could do better, what areas you'd like to see us publish in, and any other words of wisdom you're willing to pass our way.

As an associate publisher for Sams Publishing, I welcome your comments. You can email or write me directly to let me know what you did or didn't like about this book—as well as what we can do to make our books better.

Please note that I cannot help you with technical problems related to the topic of this book. We do have a User Services group, however, where I will forward specific technical questions related to the book.

When you write, please be sure to include this book's title and author as well as your name, email address, and phone number. I will carefully review your comments and share them with the author and editors who worked on the book.

Email: feedback@samspublishing.com

Mail: Neil Rowe
Executive Editor
Sams Publishing
800 East 96th Street
Indianapolis, IN 46240 USA

Reader Services

Visit our website and register this book at informit.com/register for convenient access to any updates, downloads, or errata that might be available for this book.

Introduction

Business intelligence (BI) has been around for many more years than you might think. *Decision support systems* (DSS) and *executive information systems* (EIS) from the 1970s and 1980s, along with *artificial intelligence* (AI) systems from the 1990s, can now all be considered as part of what BI comprises today.

In brief, BI refers to the aggregation of all relevant business information, put together such that correlations and metrics may be monitored and analyzed, and the making of decisions based on trends and the results of the analyzed information.

In the early 2000s, when economic conditions became rough, companies began focusing on their businesses more closely. This produced the essential need for BI solutions. Many organizations began building data warehouses using SQL Server 2000 and Analysis Services 2000. Microsoft recognized this need and approached the development of their SQL Server 2005 product with BI in mind.

The release of SQL Server 2005 brought BI to the forefront of Microsoft solutions. Although this took care of the data and reporting components, it did not address the core monitoring and planning aspects of a BI solution. To fill this gap, Microsoft began developing Office *PerformancePoint Server* 2007 (PPS) in conjunction with the acquisition of ProClarity. At the same time, *Microsoft Office SharePoint Server 2007* (MOSS 2007) was being promoted as the main delivery mechanism for BI solutions using Microsoft technologies, and was at this point being referred to as the Microsoft BI stack. The Microsoft BI stack fulfilled the business needs, but the solution was made up of various separate components. Enter Office 2010.

With the releases of SharePoint Server 2010 and SQL Server 2008 R2, the convergence of the BI stack is more evident. Once-separated components (MOSS and PPS) are now combined within the same architecture, and tighter integration now exists between SharePoint and Reporting Services and Analysis Services.

The Office 2010 platform forces technological change within skillsets and roles. The BI specialists who may be considered SQL Server experts now need to understand SharePoint and its role within a BI solution. Conversely, SharePoint experts and developers need to be able to use SharePoint as a delivery mechanism for BI solutions.

Previously, if you needed to understand BI solutions using SQL Server, you referred to a SQL Server or data warehousing publication. If you needed to understand SharePoint, you referred to SharePoint-related material. With the tighter integration of the Microsoft BI Stack, we believe there is a need to combine the components of BI and SharePoint into one reference book for this integration. This book bridges the gap between the two worlds of database technology and portal solutions.

How This Book Is Organized

▶ Part I, "Getting Started," explains how to prep SharePoint 2010 for the deployment of BI solutions. The Business Intelligence Center is described, and you learn about Excel Services.

▶ Part II, "Reporting Services," focuses on the integration and use of Reporting Services within SharePoint, including uses of the Report Viewer web part.

▶ Part III, "PerformancePoint Services," discusses the configuration and development of PPS (which is now part of SharePoint 2010 as an application service), along with security aspects of PPS.

▶ Part IV, "PowerPivot," explains how Analysis Services and SharePoint 2010 have been integrated to produce a mechanism for business users to publish analytical information via Excel.

▶ Part V, "Visio Services," explores how the visualization of BI data is becoming as important as the information it provides. Leveraging Visio Services within SharePoint adds an interesting component to BI solutions.

▶ Part VI, "End-to-End Solutions," covers how all the components and services all fit together (in contrast to earlier chapters where these components and services are examined from discrete perspectives). This part provides two scenario-based end-to-end solutions that explain how to construct a BI solution.

▶ Part VII, "Troubleshooting," outlines resolutions to common problems so that you do not have to search the Internet for guidance with regard to currently known issues and errors.

What This Book Does Not Cover

This book explains the integration and uses of SQL Server 2008 R2 components with SharePoint Server 2010. It does not discuss the processes of building a data warehouse, dimensional model, or Analysis Services cube. These are separate core topics that need to be explored on their own.

Some BI specialists consider *Business Connectivity Services* (BCS) an extension of business solutions. Although BCS does provide access to external data sources (which could include data warehouses or central repositories), this book focuses more on the commonality of SQL Server components in SharePoint 2010. To really understand BCS and the various capabilities, you should refer to publications that deal specifically with that subject; general SharePoint 2010 books just scratch the surface.

Another extension possible through the leveraging of BI data within SharePoint is InfoPath 2010. By creating forms with InfoPath 2010, you can leverage data from BCS, external data sources via Web Services, or from direct database connections. However, this subject area is beyond the scope of this book. To explore the possibilities of InfoPath 2010 within a SharePoint environment, refer to *InfoPath with SharePoint 2010 How-To* (Sams, 2010).

Expanding Your Knowledge

We hope that this book provides a solid foundation of understanding about potential BI solutions via SharePoint and SQL Server and that you find everything you need here. However, business requirements and changing needs usually require custom solutions that cannot all be possibly documented in one location.

So, to stay current and find additional answers if needed, consider the following resources a good investment of your time and attention:

- ▶ **Microsoft BI site:** http://www.microsoft.com/bi/

- ▶ **Microsoft Office Developer Center:** http://msdn.microsoft.com/en-us/office/default.aspx

- ▶ **Microsoft SharePoint 2010 site:** http://sharepoint.microsoft.com/

- ▶ **RDA BI/SQL Server Practice Group Blog:** http://bisqlserver.rdacorp.com/

PART I

Getting Started

IN THIS PART

CHAPTER 1

Introduction to the Business Intelligence Center in SharePoint 2010

The Business Intelligence Center is a prebuilt site collection and site template that you can use to get started with your integration of *business intelligence* (BI) solutions and SharePoint 2010. Although you can build solutions into other sites or site collections, the Business Intelligence Center provides a foundation of features and SharePoint components that enables you to quickly create a central location for the presentation of BI information.

Planning for Your Business Intelligence Center

This section provides some preliminary thoughts and actions for organizations interested in implementing BI functionality to provide end users a vehicle for gaining insight into business performance. Planning aspects are covered in this section, although from a fairly high level because of the wealth of information provided by Microsoft on these topics (for which links are given). To start, it is recommended that you review the business intelligence planning section from Microsoft TechNet, located at http://technet.microsoft.com/en-us/library/ee683867.aspx.

Server Prerequisites and Licensing Considerations

SharePoint Server 2010 Enterprise is required to use the BI services provided by SharePoint. From the SQL Server side, SQL Server 2005 and 2008 are supported options for Excel Services, PerformancePoint Services, and Visio Services. However, SQL Server 2008 R2 64-bit is required for Reporting

Services and PowerPivot when integrating with SharePoint 2010. Therefore, it is recommended that you use SQL Server 2008 R2 64-bit within your SharePoint farm architecture.

Choosing BI Tools

SharePoint 2010 and SQL Server bring together various services and tools that enable you to build out business intelligence solutions. The various services and tools covered in this book are as follows:

- ▶ Excel Services
- ▶ Reporting Services
- ▶ PerformancePoint Services
- ▶ PowerPivot
- ▶ Visio Services

You can use all of these tools either separately or together to provide an organization with its desired business performance solution. Each tool has its own purpose and role within a BI solution. Therefore, it is important to understand each one and determine how it might fit within an organization. (See http://technet.microsoft.com/en-us/library/ff394320.aspx for more help in this area.)

Another way to understand how you might use these tools independently or together is by reviewing already constructed solutions, case studies, and business scenarios. Microsoft has compiled a helpful list of these, shown in Table 1.1.

TABLE 1.1   Solutions and Scenarios Provided by Microsoft

Title	Link
Corporate Dashboards: Sales Solution	http://technet.microsoft.com/en-us/bi/ff643005.aspx
Self-Service Analytics: Sales Solution	http://technet.microsoft.com/en-us/bi/ff770841.aspx
BI Reporting: Reports and Subscriptions Scenario	http://technet.microsoft.com/en-us/bi/ff769487.aspx
Configure Excel and Excel Services with SQL Server Analysis Services	http://technet.microsoft.com/en-us/library/ff729457.aspx
Configuring Extranet Access for PerformancePoint Services 2010	http://technet.microsoft.com/en-us/library/gg128954.aspx
Dynamic IT and Self-Service BI Case Study	http://www.microsoft.com/downloads/en/details.aspx?FamilyID=9a2d40e3-3340-4074-baf8-6c093275aa57&displaylang=en

Creating and Configuring Your Business Intelligence Center

The Business Intelligence Center is available as a site collection template and as a site template. By default, the Business Intelligence Center site template is not available from the SharePoint 2010 front end when creating a new site, and therefore you must create your Business Intelligence Center as a site collection from SharePoint Central Administration. After the Business Intelligence Center site collection has been created, the Business Intelligence Center site template is available to create subsites that integrate with the site collection. Once created, the new site collection (or site) contains various SharePoint components and has features deployed and activated. This section steps through the creation process and review of the Business Intelligence Center components.

Creating a New Site Collection Using the Business Intelligence Center Site Collection Template

The following steps walk through the process of creating a new site collection using the Business Intelligence Center template. Complete the following steps to create your Business Intelligence Center:

1. From within SharePoint 2010 Central Administration, click the **Create Site Collections** link in the Application Management section.
2. Select the web application you want to create the site collection.
3. Provide a name for the site collection (for example, Business Intelligence Center).
4. Select a managed path or use the link provided to generate a new managed path. For this example, the /sites/ managed path is used.
5. Enter the URL for the new site collection (for example, BICenter).
6. Select the Business Intelligence Center template from the Enterprise tab, as shown in Figure 1.1.
7. Enter a primary administrator for the site collection.
8. Optionally, enter a secondary administrator for the site collection.
9. Optionally, select a quota template.
10. Click **OK**.

SharePoint creates the new site collection using the managed path and URL entered. Upon successful completion of the process, a successful creation screen is presented along with a link to the new site collection, as shown in Figure 1.2. Click the link to open the new Business Intelligence Center.

Reviewing the Business Intelligence Center

When you navigate to the new Business Intelligence Center site collection, you see that the main page of the top-level site contains four quick launch links, as shown in Figure 1.3:

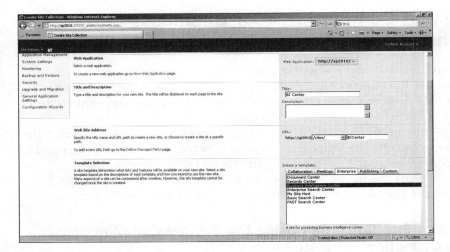

FIGURE 1.1   Selecting the Business Intelligence Center site collection template.

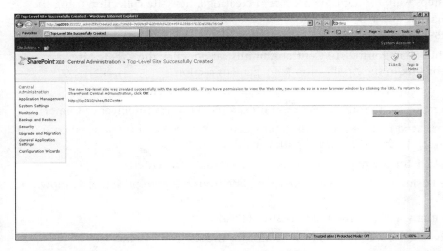

FIGURE 1.2   Successful creation of the Business Intelligence Center site collection.

▶ Dashboards

▶ Data Connections

▶ Libraries

▶ PerformancePoint Content

The Dashboards link takes you to the Dashboards library, which is essentially a page library that allows you to store web part pages and dashboard pages. Data Connections is a link to the Data Connections library, where all the data connections for your BI solution should be stored. The Libraries link displays all the SharePoint libraries within the Business Intelligence Center site collection, as shown in Figure 1.4. Finally, the PerformancePoint Content link displays the PerformancePoint Content list, which stores PerformancePoint objects deployed to the Business Intelligence Center via Dashboard Designer. (See Chapter 7, "PerformancePoint Services Development," for more information on using Dashboard Designer.)

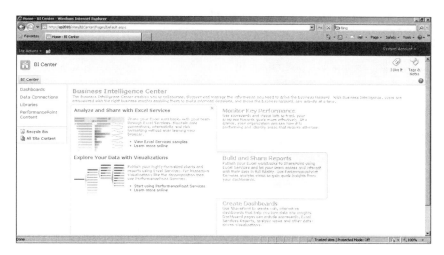

FIGURE 1.3   Main page of the Business Intelligence Center.

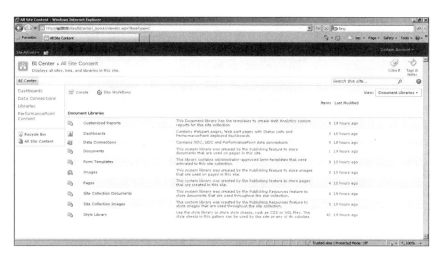

FIGURE 1.4   Libraries available within the Business Intelligence Center site collection.

Reviewing Features Enabled for BI

Assuming the previous steps were followed and the Business Intelligence Center site collection created, you need to review the site collection features to make sure the appropriate items are enabled.

Follow these steps to verify the features are enabled at the site collection level:

1. Navigate to the site settings page for Business Intelligence Center site collection from the Site Actions menu.

2. Click **Site Collection Features** in the Site Collection Administration section.

3. Locate the PerformancePoint Services Site Collection Features entry, as shown in Figure 1.5.

FIGURE 1.5   PerformancePoint Services site collection features.

4. If the feature is not activated, click **Activate**.

Follow these steps to verify the features are enabled at the site level:

1. Navigate to the site settings page for Business Intelligence Center site collection.

2. Click **Manage site features** in the Site Actions section.

3. Locate the PerformancePoint Services Site Features entry, as shown in Figure 1.6.

4. If the feature is not activated, click **Activate**.

FIGURE 1.6   PerformancePoint Services site features.

Creating a New Subsite Using the Business Intelligence Center Site Template

The Business Intelligence Center site template is available as a site-creation option within the main Business Intelligence Center site collection. You can use this site template to generate subsites within the Business Intelligence Center. Although by activating features on other site collections the Business Intelligence Center site template may be available, it becomes useless unless the site is generated within the Business Intelligence Center site collection.

> **NOTE**
>
> Creating a Business Intelligence Center site under a different type of site collection does not generate the appropriate libraries and lists. Although you can create most of these manually, there is no place to store PerformancePoint content.

To create a Business Intelligence Center subsite, follow these steps:

1. Navigate to the main Business Intelligence Center site collection in which you want to create a subsite.

2. From the Site Actions menu, select **New Site**. The Create dialog appears.

3. Select **Data** in the Categories section on the left side of the dialog.

4. Select the **Business Intelligence Center** site template, as shown in Figure 1.7.

5. Enter a name and URL name for the site. (Optionally, click **More Options** to enter initial settings.)

6. Click **Create**.

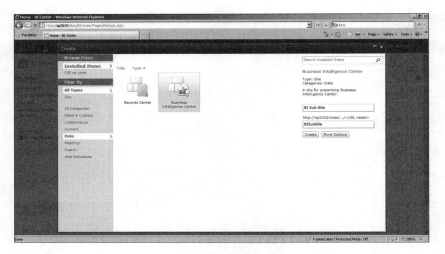

FIGURE 1.7   Creating a subsite using the Business Intelligence site template.

NOTE

If Silverlight is not installed, the Create dialog will appear differently than shown.

SharePoint creates the new site under the current Business Intelligence Center site collection using the URL entered and integrates the subsite into the Business Intelligence Center. The subsite appears in the top navigation and within the quick launch of the top-level (parent) site, as shown in Figure 1.8.

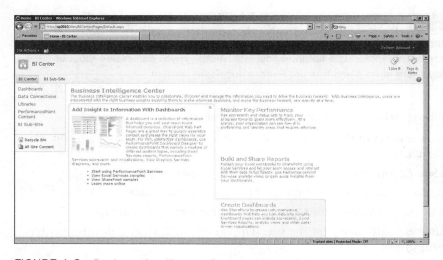

FIGURE 1.8   Business Intelligence Center with a subsite.

TIP

The appearance of the subsite in the top and left navigation is part of the standard site collection functionality. Use the navigation settings within the top-level site settings to control where subsites appear (or if they should appear at all).

Summary

This chapter covered prerequisites for implementing BI with SharePoint 2010 and topics to consider when planning BI solutions within an organization. As discussed throughout this chapter, the creation and configuration of the Business Intelligence Center is the first step in getting started; it provides a central location for presenting performance and company data using the tools discussed throughout this book.

Best Practices

The following are best practices from this chapter:

▶ Review the BI planning section from Microsoft TechNet, located at http://technet. microsoft.com/en-us/library/ee683867.aspx.

▶ Use SQL Server 2008 R2 64-bit within your SharePoint farm architecture to take advantage of all BI tools on the 2010 platform without limitations.

▶ You can use all the tools covered in this book separately or together to provide an organization with its desired business performance solution. It is recommended that you become familiar with each of these components and understand how they might fit into various solutions. See http://technet.microsoft.com/en-us/library/ ff394320.aspx for more information.

▶ A great way to understand how you can use the Microsoft BI tools independently or together is by reviewing already constructed solutions, case studies, and business scenarios. Microsoft has compiled a helpful list of these, available at http://technet. microsoft.com/en-us/sharepoint/ee692578.aspx.

▶ Use the Business Intelligence Center site template within a Business Intelligence Center site collection only when creating BI subsites. Although by activating features on other site collections the Business Intelligence Center site template may be available, it becomes useless unless the site is generated within a Business Intelligence Center site collection. This method does not generate the appropriate libraries and lists within the site. Although you can create most of these manually, there is no place to store PerformancePoint content.

CHAPTER 2

Configuring and Using Excel Services in SharePoint 2010

Excel Services is a shared service application within SharePoint 2010 that allows for the sharing and presentation of Excel spreadsheets and workbooks within SharePoint via the web browser. Excel Services was first introduced in Microsoft Office SharePoint Server 2007 and continues to evolve within the 2010 platform. A SharePoint Enterprise license is required to deploy and implement Excel Services.

Excel Services may be used to present business data to the enterprise and can be considered a piece of the *business intelligence* (BI) puzzle. However, because it is not one of the main tools provided by the integration of SharePoint and SQL Server, this chapter covers the basics for configuring and using Excel Services.

Excel Services is actually made up of three core components: Excel Calculation Services, Excel Web Access, and Excel Web Services. The Excel Calculation Services component is the main component and enables the loading and calculations of the spreadsheets, and the Excel Web Access component provides the delivery mechanism for the Excel workbooks. The Excel Web Services component enables customizations of Excel solutions by providing web methods hosted within SharePoint that can be exploited by custom-coded applications.

Configuring Excel Services

The Excel Services configuration is performed at the service application level within SharePoint Central Administration. Managing Service Applications provides access to all the service applications running on the SharePoint farm, including Excel Services, as shown in Figure 2.1. Managing the Excel Services Application provides various groups of settings, as shown in Figure 2.2. This section covers each of these areas.

FIGURE 2.1   Managing Service Applications in Central Administration.

FIGURE 2.2   Managing Excel Services Application.

Global Settings

In the Global Settings section, you can modify and configure overall settings for the Excel Services application, including security, session management, and various cache settings.

Security

The Security settings determine how Excel Services handles authentication, as shown in Figure 2.3. The File Access method is used when accessing trusted Excel Services locations that are not hosted within SharePoint. If you set the method to Impersonation, Excel Services impersonates the current user when accessing the non-SharePoint location. To access the locations using the service account that is running Excel Services, just set the method to Process Account.

> **NOTE**
>
> Whether you choose Impersonation or Process Account, either the logged-in SharePoint user or the Excel Services service account needs access to the non-SharePoint location.

The Connection Encryption setting determines whether the communication between Excel Services components within SharePoint and the user's local machine should require encryption. Requiring encrypted communication ensures that the *Secure Sockets Layer* (SSL) protocol is being used and data is secured. Leaving this option as Not Required leaves your data less secure.

Allowing cross-domain access enables Excel Services to render Excel workbooks and components that are located on different domains. These locations still need to be registered as trusted file locations, which are explained in the next section.

FIGURE 2.3   Security settings of the Excel Services application.

Load Balancing

The Load Balancing settings determine how the *Excel Calculation Services* (ECS) feature manages its processing of user requests. You have three options: Workbook URL, Round Robin with Health Check, and Local.

The Workbook URL option ensures that the same ECS process handles requests from the same workbook at all times regardless of the user. This allows for a workbook to be loaded into memory only once. When ECS is running across multiple web front ends, this method provides a more efficient use of hardware.

If you select the Round Robin with Health Check option, each request to open a workbook goes to the next ECS in line. Even if another user selects the same workbook that someone else has already opened, the next ECS opens it again. This balances the requests and limits *central processing unit* (CPU) and *input/output* (I/O) strain. The health check portion ensures that CPU and I/O usage do not overpeak, which could occur when opening workbooks with long-running calculations. This option is good for balancing traffic and server resources.

Selecting Local ensures that the workbook is processed by the same ECS that received the open workbook request. To use this option, ECS must be running on each web front end. This option provides performance to the end user by streamlining server communication; however, in this configuration, the same workbook could be open by multiple ECS processes.

Session Management

The Session Management setting is the maximum number of sessions in which a user can invoke Excel Services, namely the ECS. Each open workbook instance produces a session. If the maximum number of sessions is reached, older sessions are removed such that new ones can be generated. Typically, each user should have just a handful of sessions at one time. The default of 25 maximum sessions does seem a bit excessive. To keep your SharePoint farm performing well right from the start, reduce the maximum session setting to 10.

Memory Utilization

The Memory Utilization settings assist in configuring the physical memory consumption by Excel Calculation Services. There are three settings: Maximum Private Bytes, Memory Cache Threshold, and Maximum Unused Object Age.

The Maximum Private Bytes setting determines how much of the server memory that the ECS process may use exclusively if needed. The default of –1 indicates that up to 50% of the server memory can be allocated. Again, this default seems a bit excessive and could reduce memory available for other processes. If your organization will use Excel Services heavily, the default might be warranted. Otherwise, you might want to start out with a number closer to 25% of the server memory. So if you have the minimum of 8GB, the setting here should be around 2048MB. You can always increase this value if users complain of nonresponsiveness.

The Memory Cache Threshold determines what percentage of the available memory (determined by the Maximum Private Bytes) can be used to maintain inactive objects. If there are many users using a small number of workbooks, it is important to keep the cache up so that repeated instantiation of similar objects is not necessary and user experience is very responsive. The default is 90%, which might be valid if Excel Services is heavily used within your organization with a small amount of distinct workbook instances. Otherwise, you can ensure that at least 25% of the maximum memory can be used for new sessions and objects by reducing the threshold to 50% to 75%.

The Maximum Unused Object Age determines how many minutes need to transpire before unused objects are released. The default entry of –1 indicates that there is no limit. Depending on the usage and performance of Excel Services in your farm, you might want to modify this setting such that the maximum age is only a few days. To account for weekends, set this value between 4320 and 5760 minutes (3 to 4 days).

Workbook Cache

The Workbook Cache settings enable you to configure how temporary files used in rendering and processing workbooks are handled on the server. It is important to take note of these options because they affect both memory and disk usage.

The Workbook Cache Location defaults to a nonentry that tells Excel Services to use the system temporary directory for writing temporary files to disk. This is probably not the best option. Having too many disk hits on your system drive could cause performance issues within your farm. The system drive is being used to run the web front ends and other services, and so it is warranted to use a separate drive for caching the workbooks. Doing so keeps the disk I/O isolated to the specified drive and reduces the number of hits to where the system is operating. You can use the separate drive for other purposes, too, because the workbook cache uses only the amount of space allocated by the next setting: Maximum Size of Workbook Cache.

The Maximum Size of Workbook Cache setting determines how many *megabytes* (MB) of disk space can be used for the temporary workbook files. The default value of 40960 equates to 40GB of space. This is a large amount of disk space but may be warranted depending on the size and complexity of the workbooks being used by Excel Services. If you have an allocated drive for the workbook cache, set the maximum size to 75% to 80% of the drive capacity. If server disk space is limited, set this value to 25% to 50% of the available space on the drive that houses the workbook cache location.

The Caching of Unused Files check box determines whether files should remain in memory if they are no longer being used. Depending on the memory available on your web front-end servers, you might want to uncheck this box. Although this could reduce the performance of Excel Services, if server memory is limited, keeping the box checked could affect overall SharePoint performance.

External Data

The External Data settings determine how external connections are managed and authenticated. The Connection Lifetime value determines how long a connection to an external system should remain opened. The default is 1,800 seconds, which equates to 30 minutes. Depending on external data usage and Excel Services usage, this value may be reduced to limit potential pegging of the system housing the external data.

The Unattended Service Account is used to authenticate with external systems to retrieve external data accessed by Excel Services. You must set up this account using the Secure Store Service in SharePoint. The application ID for the account should be entered into the Application ID entry within the External Data settings.

NOTE

If an unattended service account is not used, users are prompted for authentication when accessing the external data. The unattended service account must have access to the external system.

Trusted File Locations

The Trusted File Locations determine the locations where Excel workbooks may be loaded from within Excel Services, which include SharePoint locations or locations accessible via *Universal Naming Convention* (UNC) or *Hypertext Transfer Protocol* (HTTP). The default location entry is configured as a SharePoint location set to http://, which means that Excel Services can render any workbook within your SharePoint instance. (This is also because the default entry states that children locations are trusted.) When editing the default location entry or creating a new trusted file location, you must configure many settings.

Location

The Location section defines the actual location that should be trusted. Enter the address or path into the Address setting. The type of location can be SharePoint, UNC, or HTTP. Select the appropriate type in the Location Type area. The Trust Children check box determines whether folders, directories, or libraries located underneath the entered location should also be trusted (so, in other words, whether everything under the path inherits the trust).

Session Management

For each location, you can configure Session Management settings that determine the tolerance of the Excel Services requests and interaction with workbooks in the specified location, as shown in Figure 2.4.

There are several timeout settings. The Session Timeout is the overall setting that determines how long an inactive ECS session can remain open. The Short Session Timeout is a threshold for new sessions that never receive any activity. This could happen if an error occurs or if a user navigates through pages and never interacts with the workbook. The New Workbook Session Timeout determines the number of seconds in which a new workbook session can remain open while being inactive.

The Maximum Request Duration is similar to a timeout setting but is a stop measure to prevent long-running requests or processes. This could happen if requests get hung or become unresponsive. Similar to this setting is the Maximum Chart Render duration, which determines how long the ECS should spend rendering any chart within a workbook. The default is 3 seconds. So, if any complex charts take several seconds to render, you might need to increase this value to somewhere between 5 and 10 seconds.

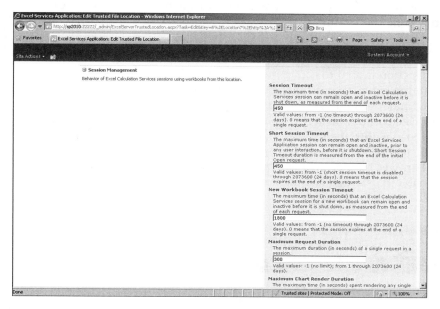

FIGURE 2.4   Session Management settings of a trusted file location.

Workbook Properties

In the Workbook Properties section, you can limit the size of the workbook and any chart or image that may be embedded within the workbook. The settings are in megabytes and default to 10 and 1, respectively. Although typically workbooks and images should be well under these settings, the workbook properties are used to limit or manage network traffic and bandwidth from the trusted file location.

Calculation Behavior

The Calculation Behavior settings determine how calculations are handled within the workbook when being rendered via Excel Services.

The Volatile Function Cache Lifetime setting determines how long Excel Services waits before it recalculates worksheets that contain volatile functions for new sessions. The volatile function cache stores the results of previously calculated values such that when a new session is activated the values are not recalculated (until this lifetime setting is reached).

TIP

Volatile functions are functions that cause a recalculation of a cell when a spreadsheet is recalculated. These are similar to nondeterministic functions in SQL Server.
Examples of Excel volatile functions include RAND() and NOW().

The Workbook Calculation Mode determines how the workbooks are recalculated when being rendered by Excel Services. The default is File, which means however the recalculations are configured within the actual workbook is how Excel Services recalculates the workbook. The other settings, which configure manual calculations or automatic calculations, override the workbook settings.

External Data

The External Data section is used to configure how the workbooks on the trusted location interact with data from external sources, as shown in Figure 2.5. The first setting, Allow External Data, determines whether external data can be used at all in the first place. The default is to allow data connection access from trusted data connection libraries and any connections embedded within the Excel workbook. To manage workbook data connections appropriately, it is best to remove any embedded connections and only use the connection files that have been created within trusted data connection libraries. This reduces overall troubleshooting and administration of connectivity to external sources (by allowing them to be centrally managed).

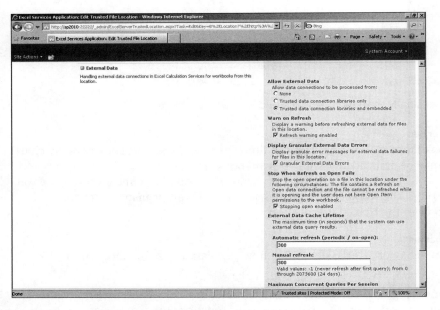

FIGURE 2.5   External data settings of a trusted file location.

The Warn on Refresh option notifies users that external data is being refreshed within the workbook. It is a good idea to leave this checked. If data changes after the refresh, users need to understand why. If there are any errors within the external data retrieval, leaving the next option (Display Granular External Data Errors) checked propagates the error to the workbook and notifies users of an issue.

The Stop When Refresh on Open Fails setting prevents workbooks from being opened if a refresh of external data needs to occur during the opening of the workbook and the retrieval of the data is not successful. This prevents older cached values from being displayed. The explanation in the setting is a bit confusing as to users having access to open the workbook. If they don't have access to open the workbook, the workbook will not open regardless of whether the refresh of external data fails.

The External Data Cache Lifetime determines how long Excel Services should use cached data results from external data sources. This is broken out into two refresh settings: Automatic and Manual. The defaults are set to 300 seconds, equating to 5 minutes. If the data does not change too frequently, increasing this number limits the number of queries that need to occur against the external system. This reduces network traffic and bandwidth usage. So, for example, if the external data source performs updates only overnight, the same queries throughout the day produce the same data results (and so 5 minutes or 5 hours does not make a difference from a data refresh perspective).

The Maximum Concurrent Queries per Session setting determines how many data requests can occur concurrently within a given session. The default setting of five is probably good for most organizations. Standard workbooks accessing external data typically contain one to three data requests, whereas more complex workbooks could require three to five requests that occur simultaneously. It all depends on the actual use and requirements of the workbook itself.

The Allow External Data Using REST option is unchecked by default. This option determines whether the REST *application programming interface* (API) can be used to refresh the external data within the workbook. The REST API, a new feature in SharePoint 2010, allows access to Excel Services objects and resources.

The User Defined Functions option determines whether the Excel workbooks in the trusted file location can run user-defined functions. User-defined functions are created by coding functions within managed code that gets built as an assembly (*dynamic linked library*, or DLL) deployed to the SharePoint farm.

Trusted Data Providers

Trusted data providers determine what types of data connections can be implemented within Excel Services. The most common data providers are provided out of the box. When editing or adding a new data provider, you have only a few settings, as shown in Figure 2.6.

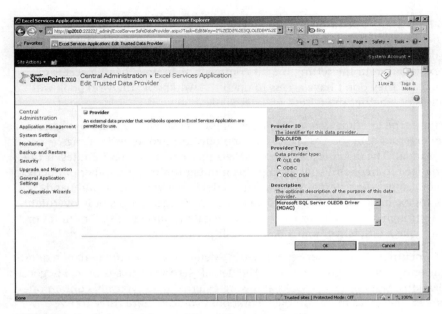

FIGURE 2.6   Trusted data provider settings.

The Provider ID is the data provider identifier. This is the value used within a data connection string. When creating a new provider entry, review sample data connection strings for the provider to determine how it is identified.

Three types of providers are supported: OLE DB, ODBC, and ODBC DSN. Determine what type of provider is being added and select the appropriate option.

TIP

OLE DB = *Object Linking and Embedding*

ODBC = *Open Database Connectivity*

ODBC DSN = *Open Database Connectivity with Data Source Name*

The Description is an optional entry used to identify the trusted data provider. When adding a new provider, it is probably a good idea to explain what it is and why it was added.

Trusted Data Connection Libraries

The Trusted Data Connection Libraries are the locations of the data connection libraries that Excel Services is allowed to use to obtain external system connectivity information. Adding a new entry is as simple as providing the URL address of the data connection library, as shown in Figure 2.7.

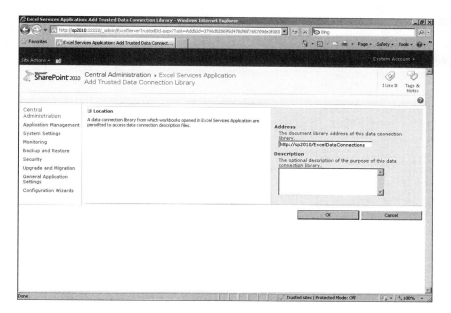

FIGURE 2.7   Adding a trusted data connection library entry.

User-Defined Functions

If user-defined functions are going to be used within Excel Services workbooks, the assemblies containing the managed code for the functions need to be registered with Excel Services.

Adding a new user-defined function entry is performed by entering the assembly details, as shown in Figure 2.8. It is recommended to strongly name the assemblies and deploy them to the *global assembly cache* (GAC) within the farm.

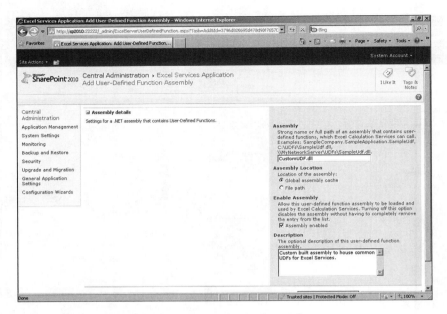

FIGURE 2.8   Entering assembly details for UDF support.

Using Excel Services

Using Excel Services is easier than configuring the service application. The overall process is creating or uploading Excel documents to a specified (and trusted) library and then using web parts to display the Excel workbooks on pages within a site.

Creating a Library for Excel Workbooks

For each site that may display Excel workbooks, you should create a library to house the documents. Although this can be a standard document library, the report library is set up to handle Excel documents (.xlsx).

To create a library for your Excel workbooks, follow these steps:

1. Navigate to the site collection or site in which you want to display Excel workbooks.

2. From the Site Actions menu, select **More Options**. The Create dialog appears.

3. Select **Library** in the Filter section on the left side of the dialog.

4. Select the **Report Library** template, as shown in Figure 2.9.

5. Enter a name for the library. (Optionally, click More Options to configure other settings.)

6. Click **Create**.

NOTE

The Report Library template may not be available until the SharePoint Server Enterprise Site feature is activated at the site level.

TIP

Add the new library as a trusted file location in the Excel Services service application settings.

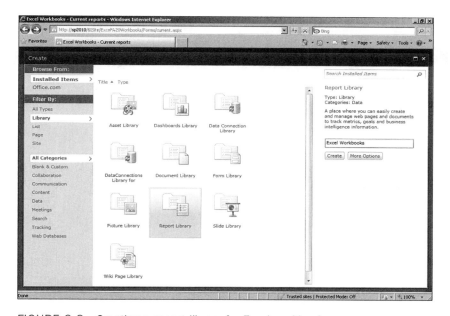

FIGURE 2.9   Creating a report library for Excel workbooks.

Adding Excel Workbooks to the Library

Excel workbooks may be added to library by creating a new document or uploading an existing one. Navigating to the library and selecting the Documents tab from the ribbon provides the options available.

To create a new document, follow these steps:

1. From the Documents tab of the ribbon, select the pull-down from the New Document button, as shown in Figure 2.10.

2. Select **Report**. The New Report screen appears.

3. Enter the name, title, and description of the report.

4. Optionally, enter the owner of the document.

5. Select the report category and status using the drop-downs.

6. Click **OK**.

The new Excel document is created within the library.

TIP

Change the available report categories or report statuses by accessing the Library Settings of the library and editing those columns.

FIGURE 2.10   Creating a new Excel document.

To upload a document, follow these steps:

1. From the Documents tab of the ribbon, click the **Upload Document** button. The Upload Document dialog appears.

2. Click the **Browse** button and locate the Excel document.

3. Select the file and click **Open**.

4. Optionally, enter version comments.

5. Click **OK**.

The Excel document is uploaded to the library.

Accessing Excel Workbooks from the Library

Users may simply navigate to the library and click the Excel document to open the workbook. The workbook is launched using the SharePoint Excel Viewer and renders within the browser. It is presented in a read-only fashion and is designed to display data and calculation results within the spreadsheets of the workbook.

Using the Excel Web Access Web Part

The other common reason to access Excel workbooks stored within a SharePoint library is to display them on a page using web parts. The web part that enables you to render Excel workbooks from a trusted file location using Excel Services is called the Excel Web Access web part.

To add the Excel Web Access web part on a page, follow these steps:

1. Navigate to the page that you want to use for the Excel Web Access web part.
2. From the Site Actions menu, select **Edit Page**.
3. Click the **Web Part** button from the Insert tab on the ribbon.
4. Select the **Business Data** category, and then select the **Excel Web Access** web part, as shown in Figure 2.11.
5. Click **Add**. The web part is added to the page.

FIGURE 2.11   Adding the Excel Web Access web part.

After the web part has been added, the selected workbook information is rendered within the web part contents. The web part needs to be configured to access an Excel workbook.

To configure the Excel Web Access web part on the page, follow these steps:

1. Select **Edit Web Part** from the Web Part drop-down menu or click the **Click Here to Open the Tool Pane** link. The web part tool pane is displayed, as shown in Figure 2.12.

2. Enter the location of the workbook. Click the ellipsis (...) button to navigate through the SharePoint site and locate the workbook location.

3. Enter a named item if you want to show only a specific piece of the selected workbook.

4. Modify the other options as desired.

5. Click **OK**.

The web part renders the workbook selected.

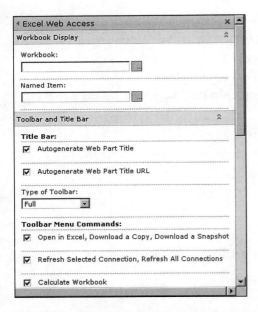

FIGURE 2.12   Excel Web Access web part tool pane.

TIP

Don't forget to save the page by using the Page tab of the ribbon and clicking the **Save & Close** button.

Summary

This chapter covered the configuration and usage of Excel Services within SharePoint 2010. Excel Services can be exploited to provide business data interaction to end users using a familiar end-user tool. Many configuration settings affect the behavior and usage of Excel Services within your SharePoint farm, and each one should be carefully analyzed.

Best Practices

The following are best practices from this chapter:

▶ Requiring encrypted communication ensures that the SSL protocol is being used and data is secured. Leaving this option as Not Required leaves your data less secure.

Allowing cross-domain access enables Excel Services to render Excel workbooks and components that are located on different domains. These locations still need to be registered as trusted file locations.

▶ The Workbook URL load-balancing option provides a more efficient use of hardware when ECS is running across multiple web front ends, where the Round Robin with Health Check option assists in limiting traffic and CPU utilization.

To keep your SharePoint farm performing well right from the start, reduce the maximum session setting from 25 to 10.

▶ Set the value of Maximum Private Bytes to a number closer to 25% of the server memory if your organizational usage of Excel Services is not considered heavy.

▶ Reducing the Maximum Cache Threshold to 50% to 75% ensures that at least 25% of the maximum memory can be used for new sessions and objects.

▶ Set the Maximum Unused Object Age to a value between 4320 and 5760 minutes (3 to 4 days). This takes weekends into account.

▶ If you have an allocated drive for the workbook cache, set the maximum size to 75% to 80% of the drive capacity. If server disk space is limited, set this value to 25% to 50% of the available space on the drive that houses the workbook cache location.

▶ The Caching of Unused Files check box determines whether files should remain in memory if they are no longer being used. Depending on the memory available on your web front-end servers, you might want to uncheck this box. Although this could reduce the performance of Excel Services, if server memory is limited, keeping the box checked could affect overall SharePoint performance.

▶ The Connection Lifetime value may be reduced to limit potential pegging of external systems (depending on external data usage and Excel Services usage).

▶ To manage workbook data connections appropriately, it is best to remove any embedded connections and only use the connection files that have been created within trusted data connection libraries. This reduces overall troubleshooting and administration of connectivity to external sources.

▶ Increasing the External Data Cache Lifetime setting can help reduce network traffic and bandwidth usage if the data on the external system does not change too frequently.

▶ User-defined functions should be compiled into a strongly named assembly that is deployed to the GAC within the SharePoint farm.

PART II

Reporting Services

IN THIS PART

CHAPTER 3

Reporting Services Setup and Configuration

There are two options for installing Reporting Services: native mode and SharePoint Integrated mode. Native mode includes the Report Manager web application that can be used to manage all aspects of managing, deploying, and executing reports. Reporting Services can be installed in native mode completely independent of SharePoint. With SharePoint Integrated mode, the Report Manager is disabled and all report management and execution functions are provided in SharePoint. The considerations and steps for installing and configuring Reporting Services in SharePoint Integrated mode are the topic of this chapter.

Reporting Services uses a SQL Server database to store reports, subscriptions, and so on. This database is named ReportServer by default. The contents of the database are different depending on how it is created; i.e. whether it is created for Reporting Services running in native mode or SharePoint Integrated mode. The creation of the appropriate database can be handled by running the Reporting Services Configuration Manager or during the installation of Reporting Services and the database engine.

After installing or configuring Reporting Services to run in SharePoint Integrated mode, the Reporting Services Add-In for SharePoint must be installed and configured. The Add-In is a SharePoint feature that is activated at the site collection level and provides the infrastructure for storing, running and managing reports within SharePoint.

There are a number of advantages to installing Reporting Services in SharePoint Integrated mode versus native mode. First and foremost is the fact that the integration of Reporting Services with SharePoint is seamless. Reports are stored in SharePoint document libraries, allowing users to interact with them from the familiar SharePoint web interface. Report security is handled in SharePoint rather than in the Report Manager, which implements its own security scheme.

Installing Reporting Services

Reporting Services is one of several features that can be installed from SQL Server setup along with the relational database engine. There are two steps during the setup that are important to highlight to allow the setup to do the majority of the work in getting Reporting Services running in SharePoint Integrated mode. First, as shown in Figure 3.1, choose the **SQL Server Feature Installation** option. The SQL Server PowerPivot for SharePoint option is not relevant to this discussion. The All Features with Defaults option is normally a good choice, except that it installs and configures Reporting Services in native mode, which is of no benefit.

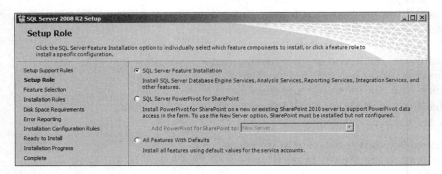

FIGURE 3.1   Configure service application associations.

The second step to highlight is Reporting Services configuration, as shown in Figure 3.2.

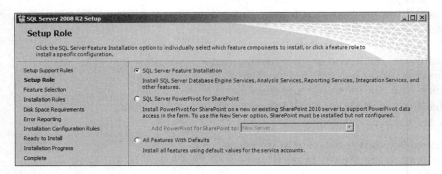

FIGURE 3.2   Reporting Services configuration.

Choose **Install the SharePoint Integrated Mode Default Configuration**. This creates the Reporting Services database in SharePoint Integrated mode. There are some scenarios where the integrated mode default configuration option may not be available; for example you have to install both the database engine and Reporting Services. If the option is not available then the alternative is to choose **Install, but do not configure the Report Server** and then use the Reporting Services Configuration Manager to create a new Reporting Services database in SharePoint Integrated mode.

Installing the Reporting Services Add-In for SharePoint

In addition to getting Reporting Services set up and configured for SharePoint Integrated mode, the Reporting Services Add-In for SharePoint needs to be installed and configured. The add-in is a SharePoint Feature that provides the infrastructure to seamlessly integrate Reporting Services within SharePoint. Beginning with SharePoint 2010, the Reporting Services Add-In for SharePoint is included in the software prerequisites for SharePoint, as shown in Figure 3.3.

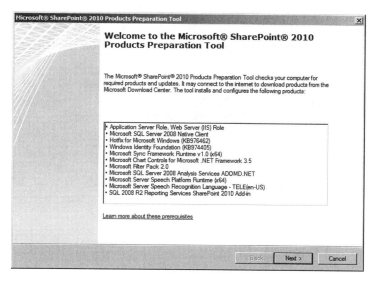

FIGURE 3.3   Microsoft SharePoint 2010 Products Preparation tool.

You can install any of the necessary software prerequisites by selecting **Install Software Prerequisites** from the SharePoint 2010 setup. The Reporting Services Add-In for SharePoint is also available as a separate download from the Microsoft website. (Just search for SQL Server 2008 R2 Feature Pack). Note that the version of the Reporting Services Add-In for SharePoint is based on both the version of SQL Server and the version of SharePoint. There are versions of the add-in for SQL Server 2005, SQL Server 2008, and SQL Server 2008 R2, and versions for SharePoint 2007 and SharePoint 2010.

After installing the Reporting Services Add-In for SharePoint, you see the Report Server Integration Feature in the Site Collection Features gallery.

Configuring the Reporting Services Add-In for SharePoint Integration

After getting Reporting Services set up for SharePoint Integration and installing the Reporting Services Add-In for SharePoint, the next step is to configure the Reporting Services SharePoint Integration in SharePoint Central Administration. To do so follow these steps:

1. Launch SharePoint Central Administration from the Start menu. (It should be pinned to the Start menu; if not, select it from the All Programs, Microsoft SharePoint 2010 program group.) The SharePoint Central Administration home page is displayed, as shown in Figure 3.4.

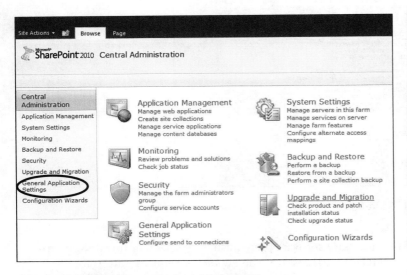

FIGURE 3.4   SharePoint Central Administration.

2. Click **General Application Settings** to display that page, as shown in Figure 3.5.
3. Click **Reporting Services Integration** and fill in the form, as shown in Figure 3.6

FIGURE 3.5   SharePoint Central Administration General Application Settings.

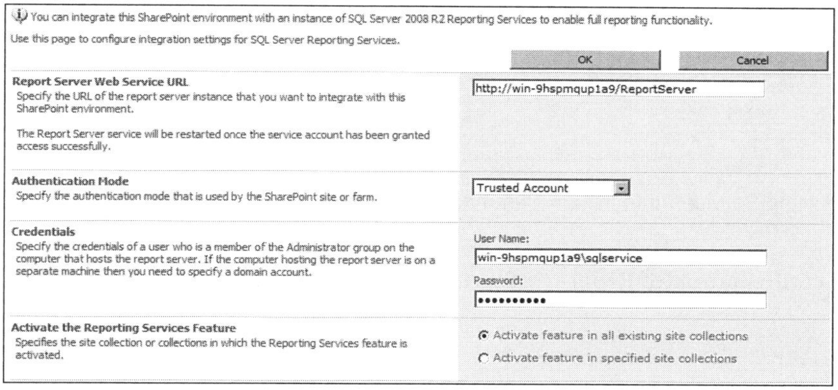

FIGURE 3.6   Reporting Services Integration in SharePoint Central Administration.

The following are the main points about the entries on the form:

▶ You can find the Report Server Web Service URL by opening the Reporting Services Configuration Manager and navigating to the Web Service URL page, as shown in Figure 3.7.

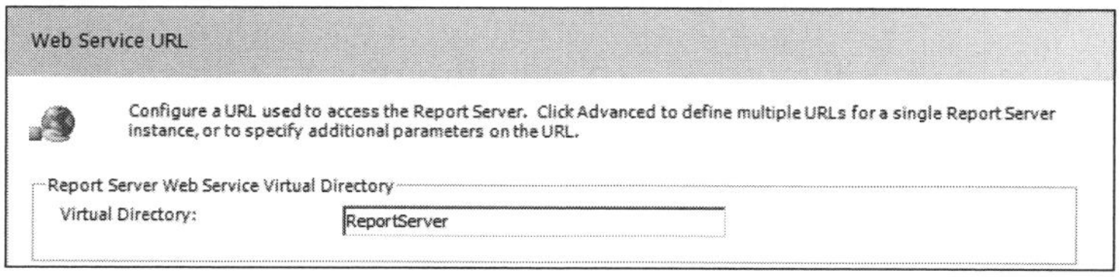

FIGURE 3.7   Reporting Services Configuration Web Service URL page.

▶ Choose **Windows Authentication for Authentication Mode** if Kerberos is configured; otherwise, choose **Trusted Account**.

▶ Enter a domain account for the credentials; this account must be in the Administrators group on the server where Reporting Services is installed.

▶ Specify to activate the Reporting Services feature for all existing site collections or specific ones as appropriate. As a general rule, it is a good idea to choose all existing site collections.

After you enter the required information and click **OK**, the Reporting Services Integration Summary is displayed, as shown in Figure 3.8.

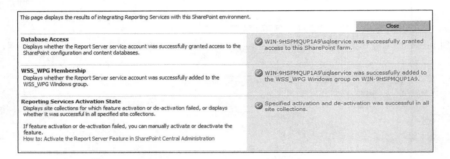

FIGURE 3.8   Reporting Services Integration Summary.

At this point, the configuration of Reporting Services in SharePoint Integrated mode is complete.

Adding Content Types to a Document Library

A Content Type in SharePoint is a collection of settings that describe a piece of content such as a document, task, contact, report, and so on. If you set up Reporting Services in SharePoint Integrated mode, you can then store reports, report models, and shared data sources in SharePoint document libraries. For a given document library, the appropriate content types for these artifacts must be added and the New Document menu customized to specify the types of documents that can be created when the New Document button is clicked. Follow these steps to add the appropriate Reporting Services content types to a document library and customize the New Document menu:

1. Navigate to (or create) a document library and click the **Library** tab, as shown in Figure 3.9. (The Library tab is underneath Library Tools.)
2. Click **Library Settings** on the ribbon to display the Library Settings page, as shown in Figure 3.10.
3. Click **Advanced Settings** to display the Advanced Settings page, as shown in Figure 3.11. (Only the relevant portion of the page is shown.)

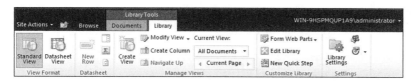

FIGURE 3.9   Document library.

FIGURE 3.10   Document library settings page.

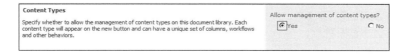

FIGURE 3.11   Document library advanced settings page.

4. Click **Yes** to allow management of content types (that is, to allow multiple content types in this document library).

5. Click **OK** to return to the Library Settings page. Navigate to the Content Types, as shown in Figure 3.12.

FIGURE 3.12   Document library content types.

6. Click **Add from Existing Content Types** to display the Select Site Content Types from, as shown in Figure 3.13.

7. Select the **Report Builder Model**, **Report Builder Report**, and **Report Data Source**, as shown in Figure 3.13, and then click **Add**.

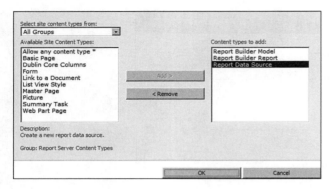

FIGURE 3.13   Add content types.

8. Click **OK** to return to the library settings page.

9. Navigate again to the Content Types and click **Change New Button Order** and **Default Content Type**, as shown in Figure 3.14.

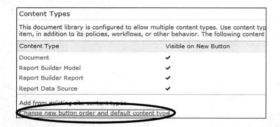

FIGURE 3.14   The new button order and default content type.

10. The Content Type Order form is displayed, as shown in Figure 3.15. Edit the Content Type Order, as shown in Figure 3.15.

FIGURE 3.15   Content type order.

11. Click **OK** to return to the library settings page, and then navigate back to the home page for the document library (refer to Figure 3.9, earlier in this chapter).

12. Click the **Documents** tab underneath Library Tools.

13. Click **New Document** to display the drop-down menu, as shown in Figure 3.16.

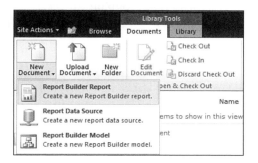

FIGURE 3.16   New Document drop-down menu.

The drop-down menu shows Report Builder Report, Report Data Source, and Report Builder Model choices. Selecting Report Builder Report launches Report Builder, a user-friendly tool used to design a report. This completes the setup and configuration of Reporting Services in SharePoint Integrated mode. The steps required to create a data source and a report are covered in the End-to-End Solutions chapter later in the book.

Summary

The setup and configuration of Reporting Services in SharePoint Integrated mode is a somewhat tedious process, but the advantages are many, and the integration is seamless. Business users get the benefit of being able to do everything in SharePoint without having to resort to the Report Manager web application. Report security leverages SharePoint, which also reduces complexity.

Best Practices

The following are best practices from this chapter:

▶ Choose the **SQL Server Feature Installation** option on the Setup Role step in SQL Server setup. This creates the Reporting Services database in SharePoint Integrated mode and makes it ready for the SharePoint configuration.

▶ Run **Install Software Prerequisites** for SharePoint to install the Reporting Services add-in for SharePoint (rather than downloading it).

▶ Add the Report Builder Report, Report Data Source, and Report Builder Model content types to any document library that will store reports. Customize the New Document menu to show these content types as choices.

▶ Choose Windows Authentication for Authentication Mode if Kerberos is configured, otherwise choose Trusted Account.

▶ Use a domain account that is a member of the Administrators group on the server where Reporting Services is installed.

▶ Activate the Reporting Services Feature for all existing site collections. If you choose not to do this, you can selectively activate the feature in the appropriate site collections.

CHAPTER 4

Report Management

When Reporting Services is running in SharePoint Integrated mode, reports are stored in a SharePoint document library. Reports are essentially documents, and the document management functions provided by SharePoint are automatically available (for example, properties, versioning, check in, and check out). In addition, a number of report management functions are applicable only to reports that are also integrated into SharePoint. Most of the report management functions are available via a drop-down context menu (referred to as the *document context menu* in the rest of this chapter) accessible by clicking the glyph next to each report in the SharePoint library, as shown in Figure 4.1.

This chapter covers deploying reports to a SharePoint library and the following report management functions:

▶ **Built-in SharePoint functions:** Functions available in all SharePoint document libraries.

▶ **Shared schedules:** Schedules that can be reused for multiple report management functions, like expiring a cached report or generating a report snapshot.

▶ **Processing options:** Specify whether a report is run with live data, cached data, or rendered from a report snapshot.

▶ **Data sources:** Define the source of data for a report.

▶ **Shared datasets:** Define a query or specify a stored procedure that is executed to retrieve the report data from a given data source. The shared dataset can be used in multiple reports.

▶ **Parameters:** Specify default value and prompt for parameters defined in a report.

▶ **Subscriptions:** Generate a report periodically based on a schedule and output format.

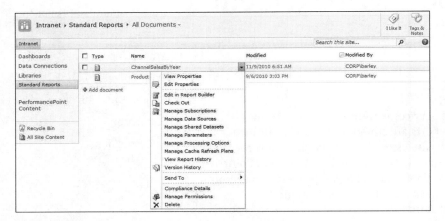

FIGURE 4.1   Document context menu.

Deploying Reports

Reports can be deployed to a SharePoint document library by any of the following actions:

▶ Upload to the document library

▶ Deploy from SQL Server *Business Intelligence Development Studio* (BIDS)

▶ Save from Report Builder

BIDS is included with SQL Server; it is a subset of Visual Studio (the developer tool for building applications), and it provides project types to develop reports, SQL Server Integration Services packages, and SQL Server Analysis Services cubes. Report Builder is a user-friendly tool for developing reports and is available for download as part of the SQL Server 2008 R2 Feature Pack.

Upload Report to Document Library

Follow these steps to upload a report to a SharePoint document library:

1. Open your browser and navigate to the document library

2. Click the **Documents** tab, and click the **Upload Document** icon on the ribbon bar or the **Add Document** hyperlink beneath the list of reports, as shown in Figure 4.2.

3. After you click Upload Document or Add Document, the Upload Document dialog is displayed, as shown in Figure 4.3.

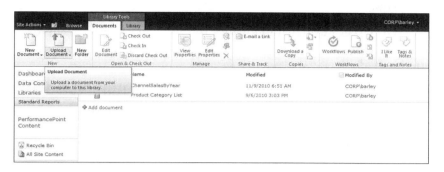

FIGURE 4.2   Upload a document.

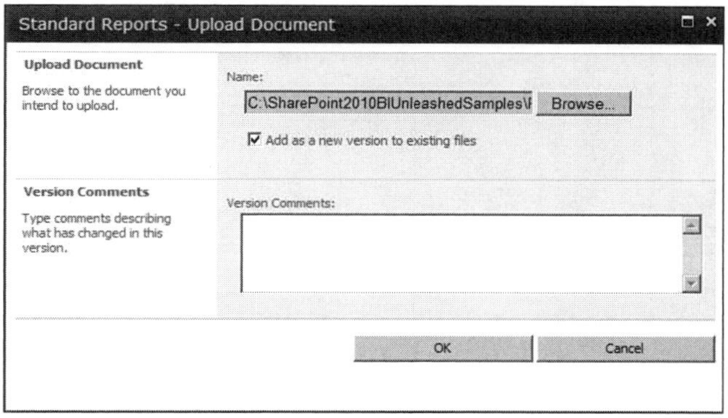

FIGURE 4.3   Specify the report to upload.

> **NOTE**
>
> The document library used in Figure 4.3 has Versioning enabled, which retains a version of the document for each change that is made. If your document library does not have Versioning enabled, you will not see the Version Comments text box; you will see an Overwrite existing files check box and a link to upload multiple files.

4. Enter the full path of the report to be uploaded or navigate to the report by clicking the **Browse** button. If the report already exists in the SharePoint library, click the **Add as a New Version to Existing Files** check box to retain the version history of the report; leave the check box unchecked to overwrite the report.

Deploy Report from BIDS

Follow these steps to deploy a report from a BIDS report project:

1. To launch BIDS, click the **Start** menu, navigate to the SQL Server program folder, and then select **SQL Server Business Intelligence Development Studio**, as shown in Figure 4.4.

2. Navigate to the project that contains the reports to be deployed.

3. Right-click the project in the Solution Explorer to display the project Properties dialog, as shown in Figure 4.5. Fill in the properties with the appropriate values for your environment.

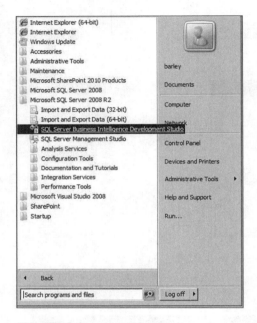

FIGURE 4.4   Launch BIDS.

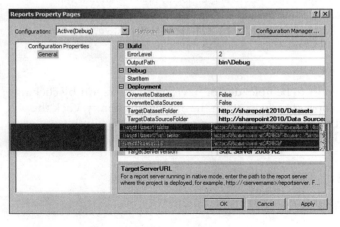

FIGURE 4.5   Report project Properties dialog.

Several important properties are directly related to deploying reports and their dependent artifacts to a SharePoint document library:

▶ **TargetServerURL:** The URL of the SharePoint site. This should be the root site in the site collection (for example, http://SharePoint2010).

▶ **TargetDataSourceFolder:** The URL of a SharePoint library where shared data sources will be stored.

▶ **TargetDatasetFolder:** The URL of a SharePoint library where shared datasets will be stored. Shared datasets are a new feature in SQL Server 2008 R2 that allow a query to be defined once and then reused in multiple reports.

▶ **TargetReportPartFolder:** The URL of a SharePoint library where report parts will be stored. Report parts are a new feature in SQL Server 2008 R2 allowing portions of a report to be published and then reused in other reports (for example, a chart, table, or tablix).

▶ **TargetReportFolder:** The URL of the SharePoint document library where reports will be stored.

Note that except for the TargetServerURL property, each property detailed here requires the full URL of the SharePoint library. If the SharePoint library does not already exist, it is created automatically when reports are deployed. After setting the properties, as shown earlier, deploy an individual item in the project by right-clicking it in the Solution Explorer and selecting **Deploy** from the context menu. To deploy everything in the project (that is, reports, shared data sources, shared datasets, report parts, and so on), right-click the project in the Solution Explorer and then select **Deploy** from the context menu.

Save from Report Builder

Follow these steps to deploy a report by saving it to a document library from Report Builder:

1. To launch Report Builder, click the **Start** menu and select **Microsoft SQL Server 2008 R2 Report Builder**, as shown in Figure 4.6.
2. To set the deployment options in Report Builder, click the icon in the upper-left corner of the window to display the drop-down menu, as shown in Figure 4.7.
3. Click the Options button to display the Report Builder Options dialog, as shown in Figure 4.8.
4. Fill in the settings as appropriate for your environment.

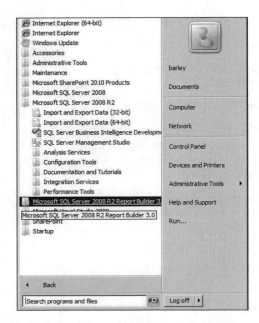

FIGURE 4.6   Launch Report Builder.

FIGURE 4.7   Report Builder settings.

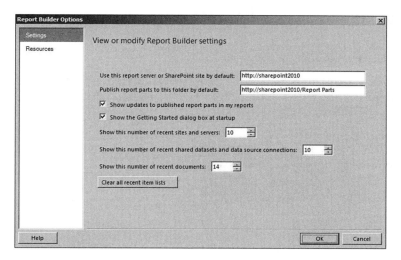

FIGURE 4.8   Report Builder options.

There are two important settings for deploying reports in the dialog shown in Figure 4.8:

▶ **Use This Report Server or SharePoint Site by Default:** Fill in the SharePoint site where reports will be published. This must be the root site in a SharePoint site collection.

▶ **Publish Report Parts to This Folder by Default:** Fill in the SharePoint library where report parts will be deployed. The URL for the report parts library is the SharePoint site plus the report parts folder.

Built-In SharePoint Functions

SharePoint provides a number of built-in functions to manage documents; a report deployed to a SharePoint library is essentially a document. SharePoint provides properties for a document. For a report, the properties can be viewed or edited by selecting **View Properties** or **Edit Properties** from the document context menu. An example of the report Properties dialog is shown in Figure 4.9.

The report Properties dialog also provides access to a number of other built-in SharePoint document management functions, such as the following:

▶ **Edit Item:** Provides a dialog to edit the report properties.

▶ **Delete Item:** Removes the report.

▶ **Version History:** Shows the change history for the report (if document versioning is enabled for the document library).

▶ **Manage Permissions:** Specifies the access levels of individuals and groups for a report.

▶ **Alert Me:** Enables an email or text message when a report is modified.

▶ **Check Out:** Locks the report while changes are being made. Another user will be blocked from checking out the report until it is checked in or the checkout is cancelled.

▶ **Manage Copies:** Creates linked reports.

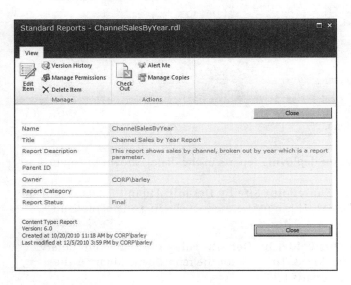

FIGURE 4.9   Report Properties dialog.

With the exception of Manage Copies, each of the report management functions available from the View Report Properties dialog is built in to SharePoint and is available in any document library.

In addition to the report management functions available from the document context menu, SharePoint provides customizable library settings. To navigate to the library settings, click the **Library** tab in a SharePoint library, and then click **Library Settings**, as shown in Figure 4.10.

The Library Settings page will display, as shown in Figure 4.11. The General Settings and Permissions and Management settings are available in any SharePoint library. There is nothing special for a library that contains reports, so there is no discussion of these items here other than to say that you can use them to customize various aspects of a SharePoint library, and this is relevant to a library that contains reports.

For more information about customizing the content types for a SharePoint library that contains reports, see Chapter 3, "Reporting Services Setup and Installation."

FIGURE 4.10   Library settings.

List Information		
Name:	Standard Reports	
Web Address:	http://sharepoint2010/Standard Reports/Forms/AllItems.aspx	
Description:		

General Settings	Permissions and Management	Communications
Title, description and navigation	Delete this document library	RSS settings
Versioning settings	Save document library as template	
Advanced settings	Permissions for this document library	
Validation settings	Manage files which have no checked in version	
Column default value settings		
Manage item scheduling	Workflow Settings	
Audience targeting settings	Enterprise Metadata and Keywords Settings	
Rating settings	Information management policy settings	
Form settings		

Content Types

This document library is configured to allow multiple content types. Use content types to specify the information you want to display about an item, in addition to its policies, workflows, or other behavior. The following content types are currently available in this library:

Content Type	Visible on New Button	Default Content Type
Report	✔	✔
Report Builder Model	✔	
Report Builder Report	✔	
Report Data Source	✔	

FIGURE 4.11   Document Library Settings page.

Shared Schedules

A number of report management functions can be scheduled, such as generating report snapshots and setting a time for a cached report to expire. When configuring these items, you can specify a custom schedule or a shared schedule. A shared schedule can be created once and then used for more than one report management function. Follow these steps to create a shared schedule:

1. Make sure that the SQL Server Agent service is running. You can start the service from the SQL Server Configuration Manager, which is available from the SQL Server 2008 R2 program group in the start menu.

2. Click **Site Actions** (available on any SharePoint page) to display the drop-down menu, as shown in Figure 4.12.

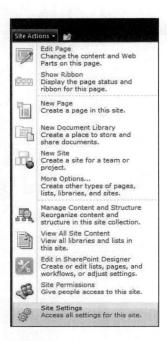

FIGURE 4.12   Site Actions menu.

3. Click **Site Settings** to display the Site Settings page, as shown in Figure 4.13.

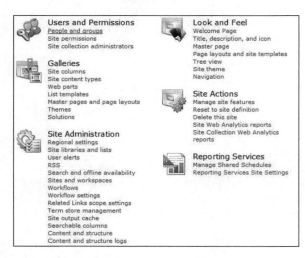

FIGURE 4.13   Site Settings page.

4. Click **Manage Shared Schedules** under the Reporting Services category to display
   the Manage Shared Schedules page, as shown in Figure 4.14.

FIGURE 4.14   Manage Shared Schedules page.

5. Click **Add Schedule** and fill in the values, as shown in Figure 4.15.

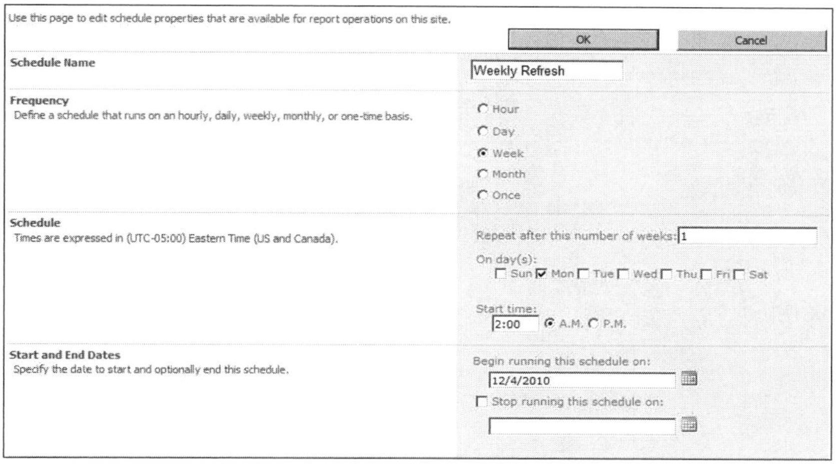

FIGURE 4.15   Add Shared Schedule page.

The preceding example is a shared schedule used for any number of report management functions where things need to be available first thing Monday morning. This could be used to schedule the generation of report snapshots, expire cached reports, and so on. The schedule is now displayed, as shown in Figure 4.16.

FIGURE 4.16   Shared schedules.

NOTE

If you see an error message that the SQL Agent service is not running when you try to add a schedule, go to the SQL Server Configuration Manager in the SQL Server 2008 R2 program group and start the service.

By default the schedule status is set to Ready. You can disable the schedule by clicking the check box and clicking **Pause Selected Schedules**. You can enable the schedule by clicking the check box and clicking **Run Selected Schedules.**

Processing Options

Processing options provide settings for data refresh options, processing timeout, and report snapshots. The Processing Options page for a particular report is available from the document context menu and is shown in Figure 4.17.

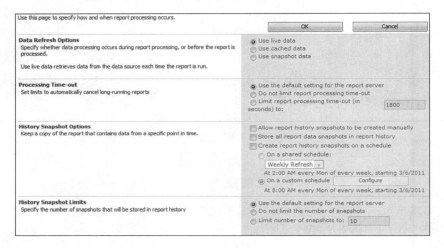

FIGURE 4.17   Report processing options.

You have the following three data refresh options for specifying when data shown on a report is retrieved:

▶ **Use Live Data:** Retrieves data from the data source every time the report is executed. This is the default and ensures that the report always uses current data.

▶ **Use Cached Data:** Retrieves data from a cache on the report server instead of querying the underlying data source each time the report is executed. When the cache expires, the data is retrieved from the data source and then cached for future use.

▶ **Use Snapshot Data:** A copy of the report is stored on the report server. This report copy is rendered when the report is executed. When the snapshot expires, the report is run with live data, and a new snapshot is created.

When you select the data refresh option **Use Cached Data**, the Cache Options are displayed below the data refresh options as shown in Figure 4.18.

The cache options enable you to specify when the cached copy of a report expires. The choices are a number of minutes, a shared schedule, or a custom schedule.

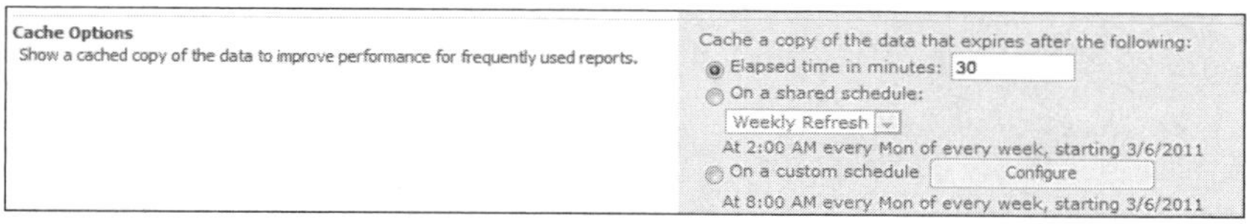

FIGURE 4.18   Cache options.

When you select the data refresh option **Use Snapshot Data**, the Data Snapshot Options are displayed below the data refresh options as shown in Figure 4.19.

A snapshot is a copy of a report generated at a point in time. It is especially useful to archive a report at the end of a reporting period, such as a week, month, quarter, or year. Data snapshot options enable scheduling of data processing based on a shared schedule or a custom schedule, and an option to create or update the snapshot after completing the page.

FIGURE 4.19   Snapshot options.

TIP

When you choose the data refresh option **Use Snapshot Data**, the report cannot be executed if a snapshot does not exist. You can check **Create or update the snapshot when this page is saved** so that a snapshot will be generated. Otherwise you would not be able to run the report until the shared schedule or custom schedule creates the snapshot.

The processing timeout option provides for limiting the amount of processing time it takes to run the report. If the allotted time is exceeded, processing is aborted, and the report is not generated. The setting on this page could override the server default, but choosing the server default is probably best in most instances.

The history snapshot options determine whether to allow a snapshot to be created manually, to store all snapshots in report history, and schedule snapshot generation. Allowing manual snapshot generation provides users with the flexibility to archive a copy of a report at any time. To generate a snapshot manually, select **View Report History** from the document context menu, and then click **New Snapshot**, as shown in Figure 4.20.

The initial snapshot shown here was created after completing the processing options page for the report and checking the option **Create or update the snapshot when this page is saved**.

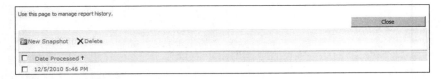

FIGURE 4.20   Report history.

Data Sources

A data source defines information needed to be able to retrieve data for a report. A report may use one or more data sources. A dataset defines the query or stored procedure to be executed to retrieve the necessary data; a dataset is associated with a particular data source. Select **Manage Data Sources** from the document context menu for a particular report to edit the data source information. The Manage Data Sources page is displayed showing the data sources used by the report, as shown in Figure 4.21.

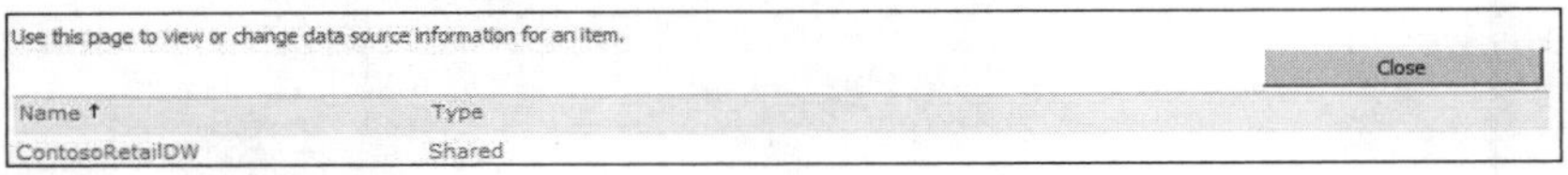

FIGURE 4.21   Data sources.

Click the data source name to display the data source properties page, as shown in Figure 4.22.

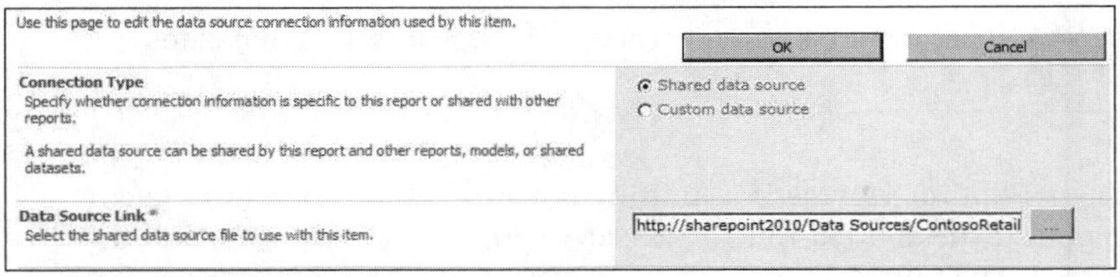

FIGURE 4.22   Data source properties.

A shared data source is one that can be reused in multiple reports. A custom data source is embedded in a single report. As a general rule, using shared data sources is a best practice, allowing the data source details to be defined once (and changed if necessary) and then used in multiple reports. The Data Source link points to the actual data source definition.

A data source can be created or edited from a SharePoint document library. Follow these steps to create a data source:

1. Click the **Documents** tab in a SharePoint library.
2. Click **New Document**, and then select **Report Data Source**, as shown in Figure 4.23.

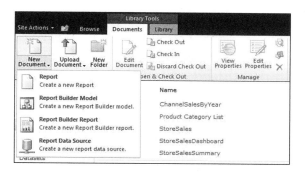

FIGURE 4.23 Create a data source.

Note that for the report options to be shown in the drop-down menu in Figure 4.23, the appropriate content types need to be added to the document library. See the "Add Content Types to a Document Library" section in Chapter 3 for details.

After you click Report Data Source on the New Document menu, the Data Source Definition dialog displays. Fill in the details, as shown in Figure 4.24.

Note that Enable This Data Source must be checked before it can be used by a report.

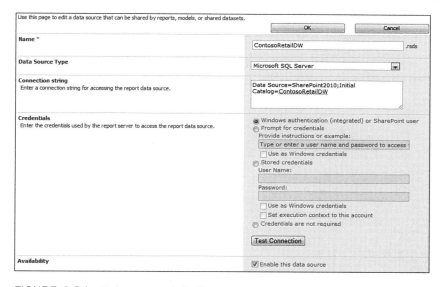

FIGURE 4.24 Data source definition.

TIP

Your Information Systems department should create data sources since they typically can supply the appropriate settings for the credentials section.

An existing data source can be changed by clicking the glyph next to the data source in the document library and then selecting **Edit Data Source Definition** from the context menu, as shown in Figure 4.25.

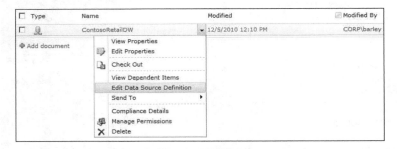

FIGURE 4.25   Edit data source definition.

Shared Datasets

A dataset is a query definition (or the name of a stored procedure) that retrieves data to be rendered on a report. A shared dataset is defined once and can then be used in multiple reports. For instance, a dataset used to populate the list of states is a good candidate for a shared dataset because the same parameter drop-down might be used in many different reports. To view or manage the shared datasets used by a report, follow these steps:

1. Click the glyph next to the report and select **Manage Shared Datasets** from the document context menu, as shown in Figure 4.26.

FIGURE 4.26   Manage shared datasets.

2. The dataset information page is displayed, as shown in Figure 4.27. Click the dataset name to view or edit it.

3. The dataset information is displayed, as shown in Figure 4.28.

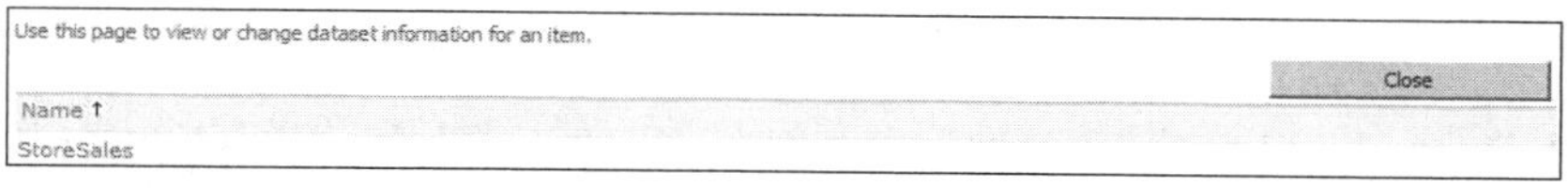

Use this page to view or change dataset information for an item.

Close

Name ↑

StoreSales

FIGURE 4.27   Shared datasets.

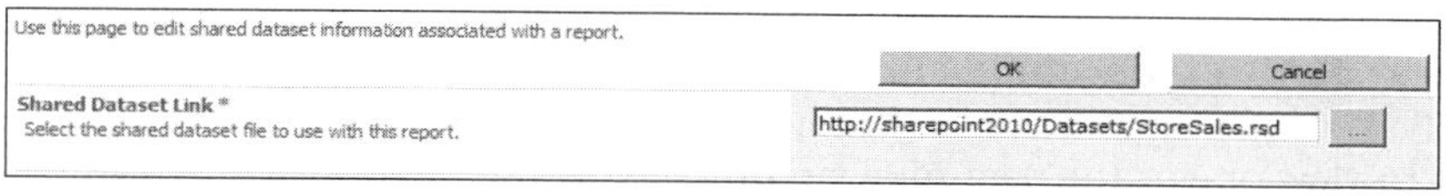

Use this page to edit shared dataset information associated with a report.

OK   Cancel

Shared Dataset Link *
Select the shared dataset file to use with this report.

http://sharepoint2010/Datasets/StoreSales.rsd

FIGURE 4.28   Shared dataset properties.

The dataset link is the only property available, and it is the file that contains the dataset definition.

To edit a shared dataset, follow these steps:

1. Navigate to the document library where the dataset is stored.
2. Click the glyph next to the dataset and then select **Edit in Report Builder**, as shown in Figure 4.29.
3. Report Builder opens and allows changes to the dataset, as shown in Figure 4.30.

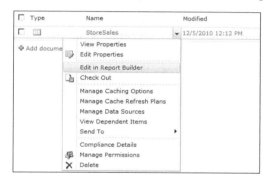

FIGURE 4.29   Edit a shared dataset.

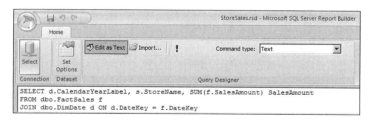

FIGURE 4.30   Edit a shared dataset in Report Builder.

Report Builder allows editing the data set query by using the familiar query designer or by entering the query as text. The default for editing the dataset query is based on how the query was created. Figure 4.30 has the Edit as Text button selected and the dataset query is displayed for manual editing because this is how the dataset query was saved. Edit the query as necessary and then save it by clicking the disk icon on the top of the Report Builder window.

The other options available for fine-tuning the shared dataset are as follows:

▶ Click **Select** to view or edit the data source properties.

▶ Click **Set Options** to view or edit the fields, options (collation, case sensitivity, and so on), filters, and parameters.

▶ Click **Import** to navigate to a .SQL file or report and copy an existing query.

▶ Click the exclamation point (next to the Import button) to execute the query.

▶ Select **Text** or **Stored Procedure** from the Command Type drop-down and edit the query as appropriate.

Parameters

Reports can include parameters that can be set at runtime to filter the data rendered in the report. Parameters can be defined only in the report itself. After a report is deployed, some changes can be made to the existing parameters. To edit or view report parameters, follow these steps:

1. Navigate to a report in a document library.

2. Click the glyph next to the report, and select **Manage Parameters**, as shown in Figure 4.31.

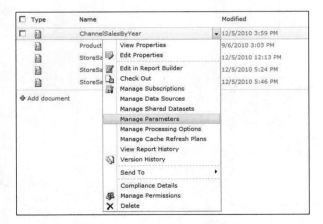

FIGURE 4.31   Manage parameters.

3. The Manage Report Parameters page is displayed, as shown in Figure 4.32.

4. To edit a parameter, click the parameter name to display its properties, as shown in Figure 4.33.

FIGURE 4.32   Report parameters.

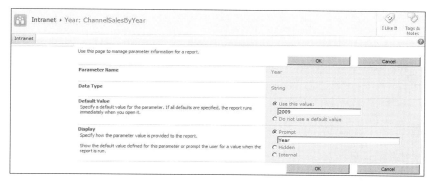

FIGURE 4.33   Report parameter properties.

You can use the parameter properties to set a default value for the parameter and set its display status. If a parameter would always have the same value, specify a default value and change the Display option to Hidden or Internal so that users are not prompted for it.

Subscriptions

A subscription provides the capability to execute a report based on an event or a schedule, select the output format for the report, and select the report delivery mode (for example, email, store in a Windows file share, or store in a SharePoint document library).

Follow these steps to create a subscription for a particular report:

1. Select **Manage Subscriptions** from the document context menu, as shown in Figure 4.34.

2. The Add Subscriptions page is displayed, as shown in Figure 4.35.

3. Click **Add Subscription** and then fill in the Subscription properties page, as shown in Figure 4.36.

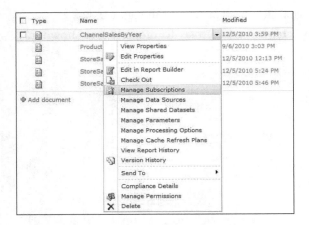

FIGURE 4.34   Manage subscriptions.

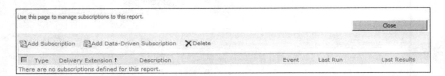

FIGURE 4.35   Add subscriptions.

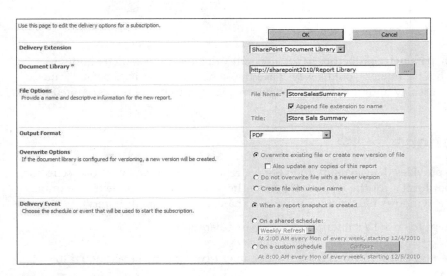

FIGURE 4.36   Subscription example.

This example executes the report whenever a snapshot is generated and stores the report as a PDF in a SharePoint document library.

Another option is the data-driven subscription, which enables you to specify a query to retrieve the values for the various subscription settings. Each subscription option can be specified by retrieving the value from the query, selecting from a drop-down list, or entering a static value.

Follow these steps to create a data-driven subscription:

1. Click **Add Data-Driven Subscription** on the Manage Subscription page and fill in the Create a Data-Driven Subscription page, as shown in Figure 4.37.

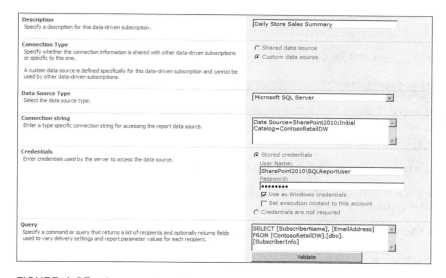

FIGURE 4.37   Create a data-driven subscription.

2. Click the **Validate** button to check that the query executes successfully.

3. After completing this page, click **Next** to proceed to the Parameters page where you can enter any parameter values required for running the report. The Parameters page is always displayed even if the report does not require any parameters.

4. Enter the parameter values (if any) and click **Next** to proceed to the Delivery Options page and fill in the values as appropriate for your subscription.

The Delivery Options page has more settings than can be easily shown in a single screen shot. For many of the settings, the choice is to either specify a static value or get the value from a column in the query (defined on the previous page). Figure 4.38 has the Delivery Type and To: settings.

The following delivery types are available:

▸ **Windows File Share:** Saves the report as a file in the folder you specify

▸ **E-Mail:** Sends the report as an e-mail attachment

▶ **SharePoint Document Library:** Saves the report as a document in a SharePoint library that you specify

▶ **Null Delivery provider:** Runs the report but does not save it anywhere; use this option to execute a report and update the cache

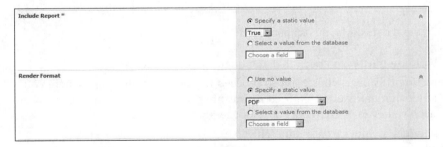

FIGURE 4.38   Delivery Type and To: options.

If the E-Mail option is not shown in the delivery types drop-down, go to the Reporting Services Configuration Manager and fill in the E-mail Settings page.

Note that the To: setting gets its value from the EmailAddress column in the query.

Figure 4.39 shows the settings for whether to include the report as an attachment to the email and the render format for the report.

Figure 4.40 shows the settings for the email subject.

FIGURE 4.39   Include Report and Render Format options.

FIGURE 4.40   Email subject options.

Figure 4.41 shows the setting for the delivery event, which is the trigger for executing the data-driven subscription. The delivery event can be when a snapshot is created or on a schedule. Daily Refresh is a shared schedule that executes at 5 a.m. on the days noted; it is used to execute report subscriptions that are to be available when people arrive each day.

FIGURE 4.41   Delivery event options.

After you complete the data-driven subscription setup, the manage subscriptions page is displayed as shown in Figure 4.42.

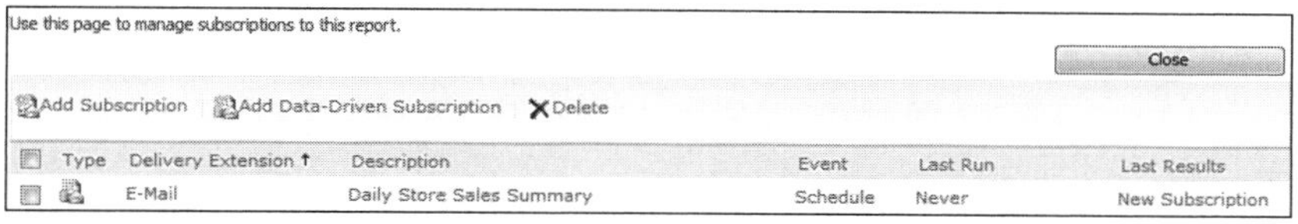

FIGURE 4.42   Manage subscriptions.

Summary

A number of report management functions are integrated into SharePoint when Reporting Services is configured in SharePoint Integrated mode. In addition, the built-in document management functions provided by SharePoint are available (for example, versioning, check in, and check out). This simplifies report management and provides an intuitive user interface that business users can easily master.

Best Practices

The following are best practices from this chapter:

▶ Use shared data sources to store this information in one place rather than embed it in each report. If the data source information changes, the data source can be updated rather than each individual report.

▶ Use shared schedules so that a single schedule can be defined and used to trigger multiple report management functions. If the schedule needs to change, only the shared schedule needs to be updated, not the individual report management values.

▶ Use shared datasets to define reusable queries and then reference them in multiple reports.

▶ Take advantage of subscriptions to schedule report generation during off hours to reduce the load on servers and to provide information to users automatically.

CHAPTER 5

Using the Report Viewer Web Parts

W̲eb parts are one of the most useful features of SharePoint. They encapsulate functionality that a user can add to a page and customize by setting various properties. There are many examples of useful web parts, such as Lists and Libraries, Business Data, and so on. From a *business intelligence* (BI) standpoint, there are web parts for rendering a Reporting Services report on a page, which is the focus of this chapter.

There are different Reporting Services web parts depending on how Reporting Services is configured. The SQL Server Reporting Services Report Viewer web part is used to render reports when Reporting Services is running in SharePoint Integrated mode. For Reporting Services running in native mode, there are two web parts: Report Explorer displays the list of reports in a particular folder in the Report Manager, and Report Viewer renders a report. Report Viewer can also render the selected report in the Report Explorer web part.

Configuring the SharePoint Integrated Mode Web Part

When Reporting Services is configured to run in SharePoint Integrated mode, the SQL Server Reporting Services Report Viewer web part is available to render a report in a web part page. The SQL Server Reporting Services Report Viewer web part is included with the Reporting Services Add-In for SharePoint installation. This is currently the only way to install the web part. The installation and configuration of the Reporting Services Add-In for SharePoint is covered in Chapter 3, "Reporting Services Setup and Configuration."

Follow these steps to add the Report Viewer web part to a page and configure it to render a report:

1. Create a new page (Click **Site Actions** and select **New Page** from the drop-down menu) or navigate to an existing page.

2. Click the **Insert** tab under Editing Tools, and then click **Web Part** on the toolbar ribbon, as shown in Figure 5.1.

FIGURE 5.1   Adding a web part.

3. Select **SQL Server Reporting** from the Categories list, and then **SQL Server Reporting Services Report Viewer** from the Web Parts list, as shown in Figure 5.2.

FIGURE 5.2   Select Report Viewer web part.

4. Click the Add button to display the web part on the page, as shown in Figure 5.3. All web parts have a drop-down menu that is used to modify the web part properties. The menu is accessible by clicking the glyph that appears when the mouse hovers over the title bar of the web part. The Report Viewer web part also has a Click Here to Open the Tool Pane hyperlink that you can use to configure the web part.

FIGURE 5.3   Report Viewer web part added to page.

5. Click the **Click Here to Open the Tool Pane** hyperlink or hover the mouse over the web part title bar, click the glyph, and select **Edit Web Part**, as shown in Figure 5.4. The report to be displayed must be specified in the web part properties.

Report Viewer

Actions   ⊕ |◀ ◀ [   ] of 0 ▶ ▶| ⊕   [   ] Find Next   100% ▾

                                        Microsoft SQL Ser[   ]ces

📄   Select a Report

You must first select a report to display in this Web Part. Do this by opening the tool pane and specifying the pat[
Reporting Services report that you would like to show. Alternatively, you can connect the Web Part to another Web Part on the page that
provides a document path.
Click here to open the tool pane.

Minimize
Close
✕ Delete
📝 Edit Web Part
Export...

FIGURE 5.4   Web part menu.

6. The web part properties form is now displayed, as shown in Figure 5.5. The Report property is used to specify the report to be rendered by the web part. Click the button next to the Report text box to display the Select an Item dialog, as shown in Figure 5.6.

7. Navigate to the folder that contains the report to be rendered and select it.

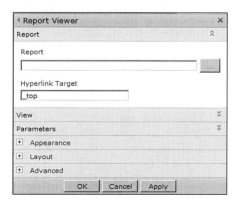

FIGURE 5.5   Web part properties.

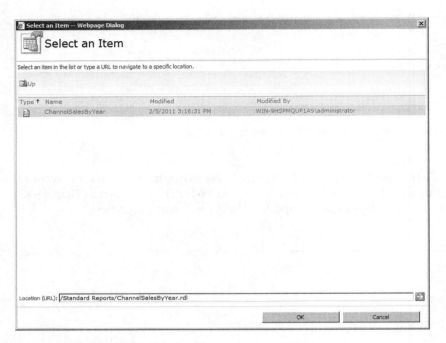

FIGURE 5.6   Select report.

The report to be rendered must be in the form /folder/reportname.rdl (for example, /Standard Reports/ChannelSalesByYear.rdl). The Report Server URL is specified in the configuration of the Reporting Services add-in for SharePoint Integrated mode (covered in Chapter 3), so it is not required here. The page being edited belongs to a particular SharePoint site, so an absolute URL is not required either; just the folder name (that contains the report) relative to the site root and the actual report name are required.

> **TIP**
>
> You can upload a report (i.e. a .RDL file) to a SharePoint document library by using the built-in Upload Document button found on the Documents tab in the library. Navigate to a document library, click the Upload Document button, and select the RDL file to upload.

At this point, the minimum configuration of the Report Viewer web part is complete. The report selected displays sales data by channel and year. The year is a parameter. The web part displays a form to allow the user to enter values for any parameters defined in the report. Figure 5.7 shows the rendered report.

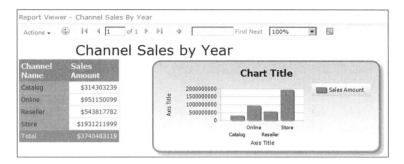

FIGURE 5.7   Channel Sales by Year report rendered in Report Viewer web part.

SharePoint Integrated Mode Web Part Properties

All web parts have many properties that can be set to configure various aspects of their functionality. The Report Viewer web part properties are shown in Figure 5.8. The Report property identifies the report to be rendered. The Hyperlink Target determines how to render any linked content in the report. The valid values are _blank, which loads the content in a new browser window; _self, which opens the content in the current frame; and _top, which uses the current window.

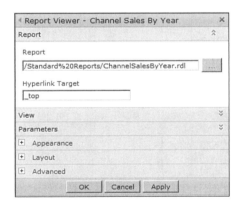

FIGURE 5.8   Report properties.

The View group has several check boxes that toggle the visibility of items on the toolbar, as shown in Figure 5.9.

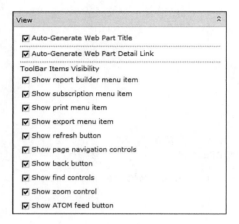

FIGURE 5.9   View properties.

Several of the toolbar visibility items are included in the Actions drop-down menu, as shown in Figure 5.10. Moving from the Actions menu to the right is the refresh command, page navigation commands (first, previous, go to page number, next, and last), go back to parent report, search text box, find next command, zoom, and ATOM Feed. The ATOM Feed button is new with SQL Server Reporting Services 2008 R2, providing the capability to extract the data in the report as an ATOM data feed. One use of the ATOM data feed is to import the data into a PowerPivot worksheet in Excel 2010.

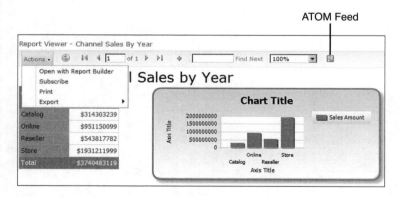

FIGURE 5.10   Report Viewer toolbar.

The Parameters group provides for loading the parameters defined in the report. Click the **Load Parameters** button, as shown in Figure 5.11. Loading the parameters is required to connect a filter web part to the Report Viewer web part, as discussed in the next section.

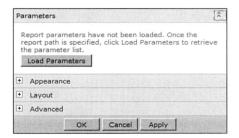

FIGURE 5.11   Parameters properties.

The parameters defined in the report are added to the form, as shown in Figure 5.12, providing a choice between using the defaults as defined in the report or specifying a value.

The remaining web part properties are common to all web parts, so they are not discussed here.

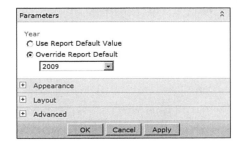

FIGURE 5.12   Parameters loaded.

SharePoint Integrated Mode Web Part Connections

Web parts support connections where the value of one web part (for example, a filter web part) can be assigned to a parameter of another web part. In the case of the Report Viewer web part, if there are parameters defined in the report, the parameter values can be specified in a filter web part and passed to the report instead of having the Report Viewer web part render a parameter entry form.

A number of filter web parts are included with SharePoint 2010 Server, as shown in Figure 5.13.

NOTE

The filter web parts are not included in SharePoint 2010 Foundation; they are only available in SharePoint 2010 Server.

FIGURE 5.13   Filter web parts.

The following is a list of the filter web parts and a brief description:

▶ Choice Filter is a drop-down list of available selections; the list is entered in the web part properties form.

▶ Current User Filter provides properties of the current user.

▶ Date Filter provides for the entry of a date; a calendar icon is available to pop up a calendar.

▶ Filter Actions adds a button that is to be clicked when all filter web part values have been entered; this allows for transferring the values of all filter web parts at one time.

▶ Page Field Filter provides information about the current page.

▶ Query String (URL) Filter provides access to items in the query string.

▶ SharePoint List Filter populates a list of values from the contents of a SharePoint list.

▶ *SQL Server Analysis Services* (SSAS) Filter populates a list of values from an SSAS cube.

▶ Text Filter allows entry of a text value.

Figure 5.14 shows a web part page that has a Text Filter and a Filter Actions web part and the Report Viewer web part. Note the warning message underneath the Text Filter stating that it is not connected. The message goes away after the web part gets connected to the Report Viewer web part.

FIGURE 5.14   Web part page with filter web parts.

Follow these steps to connect the Text Filter web part to the Report Viewer web part:

1. Edit the properties for the Report Viewer web part and expand the Parameters group, as shown in Figure 5.15.

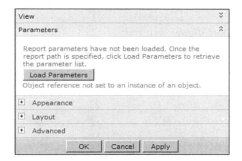

FIGURE 5.15   Report parameters.

2. Click the **Load Parameters** button to retrieve the parameters defined in the report. The parameters defined in the report are displayed in the web part properties, as shown in Figure 5.16.

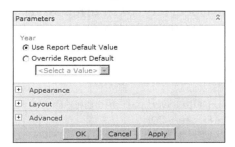

FIGURE 5.16   Report parameters loaded.

3. Click **OK** on the web part properties form to save these changes.

4. Move the mouse over the title bar of the Text Filter, click the glyph, select **Connections** from the drop-down menu, **Send Filter Values To**, and **Report Viewer – ChannelSalesByYear**, as shown in Figure 5.17.

5. The Configure Connection dialog is displayed, as shown in Figure 5.18. This connects the filter web part to a parameter defined in the report. Select the report parameter from the drop-down and click **Finish**.

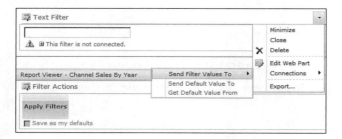

FIGURE 5.17   Connecting the filter web part to the Report Viewer web part.

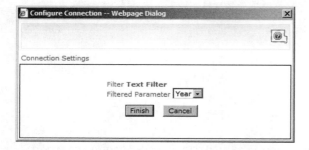

FIGURE 5.18   Configure connection.

If the preceding dialog does not display, check for a prompt in the browser that is asking whether to allow pop-ups. To display the dialog, enable pop-ups (at least temporarily).

The web part connections are now complete, and the page is ready to accept parameters and render the report, as shown in Figure 5.19. Note that the Text Filter no longer shows the warning message that the filter is not connected, as shown earlier in Figure 5.14.

Enter the year parameter value for the report in the Text Filter web part and click the **Apply Filters** button to render the report, as shown in Figure 5.20.

Text Filter

Sending values to:
Report Viewer - Channel Sales By Year

Filter Actions

Apply Filters

☐ Save as my defaults

FIGURE 5.19   Web part page with connections.

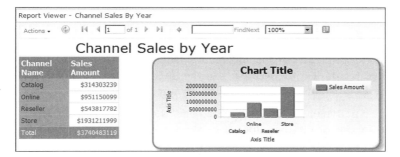

FIGURE 5.20   Report rendered with web part connection.

Configuring the Native Mode Web Parts

Reporting Services includes SharePoint web parts that work with a Report Server running in native mode. There are two web parts:

▶ Report Explorer displays the list of reports in a folder (similar to what you see in the Report Manager, which is the web application used to work with Reporting Services running in native mode).

▶ Report Viewer renders a report. It can either render a report selected in the Report Explorer web part or simply render the report specified in its web part properties.

The native mode web parts are not installed automatically; there is a manual step required to install them. The default location of the web parts varies based on the version of SQL Server. (For example, on a 64-bit install of SQL Server 2008 R2, the web parts are located in the file rswebparts.cab in the folder C:\Program Files (x86)\Microsoft SQL Server\100\Tools\Reporting Services\SharePoint.) To install the web parts, open the

SharePoint 2010 Management Shell (in the Microsoft SharePoint 2010 Products program group) and run the following command (verify the location of the rswebparts.cab file):

```
Install-SPWebPartPack "C:\Program Files (x86)\Microsoft SQL
 Server\100\Tools\Reporting Services\SharePoint\rswebparts.cab" –GlobalInstall
```

> **TIP**
>
> A user must be a member of the SharePoint_Shell_Access role on the SharePoint con-
> figuration database in order to execute PowerShell scripts. In addition the user must be
> a member of the WSS_ADMIN_WPG local group on the server where SharePoint is
> installed. Farm administrators automatically have these required permissions.

The -GlobalInstall parameter puts the *dynamic link library* (DLL) in the *Global Assembly Cache* (GAC); this is required to connect the web parts to the filter web parts, which provide for entering and setting parameter values required by a report.

Follow these steps to add the native mode web parts to a page (the steps for setting up the web parts for native mode are practically the same as the steps covered earlier for the SharePoint Integrated mode web part):

1. Create a new page or navigate to an existing page (refer to details in the preceding section).

2. Click the **Insert** tab under Editing Tools and then click **Web Part** on the toolbar ribbon.

3. Select **Miscellaneous** from the Categories list, and the two available web parts are visible in the Web Parts list, as shown in Figure 5.21.

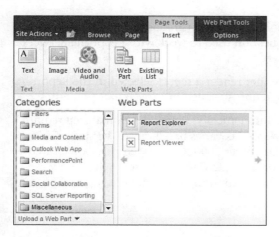

FIGURE 5.21   Selecting web parts for native mode.

4. Add the Report Explorer web part to the page.

5. Add the Report Viewer web part to the page.

6. The page displays the added web parts as shown in Figure 5.22.

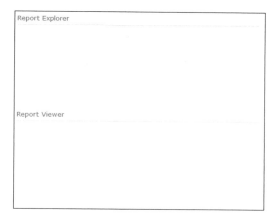

FIGURE 5.22   Native mode web parts added to page.

7. Move the mouse into the Report Explorer web part title area and then click the glyph to display the context menu; click **Edit Web Part**.

8. Fill in the Configuration properties, as shown in Figure 5.23.

9. Click **OK** when done.

FIGURE 5.23   Configuring the Report Explorer web part.

> **TIP**
>
> The Report Manager URL is the URL that opens the Report Manager web application
> that is used with a native mode installation of Reporting Services; (for example
> http://servername/reports). The Start Path identifies the folder in the Report Server
> that contains the list of reports to be displayed.

The Report Explorer web part display is refreshed and now shows the list of reports in the
specified Report Manager folder, as shown in Figure 5.24.

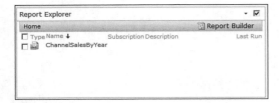

FIGURE 5.24   Report Explorer web part.

To configure the Report Viewer follow these steps:

1. Move the mouse into the web part title area.

2. Click the glyph to display the context menu.

3. Click **Connections**, **Get Report From**, then **Report Explorer**, as shown in Figure 5.25.

   The Connections option in the context menu in Figure 5.25 is obscured; the Report
   Explorer menu option overlays it. The Report Viewer web part now renders the
   report that is selected in the Report Explorer web part.

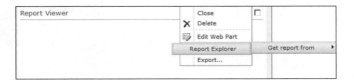

FIGURE 5.25   Connecting Report Viewer to Report Explorer.

4. Click the **ChannelSalesByYear** report in the Report Explorer web part to render the
   report, as shown in Figure 5.26.

The Report Viewer web part can also be configured to render a specific report. Fill in the
Report Manager URL (for example, http://server/reports) and report path, as shown in
Figure 5.27. Note that the buttons adjacent to the text boxes pop-up a window that
accepts only text; they do not provide any help in navigating to the Report Manager URL
or the report.

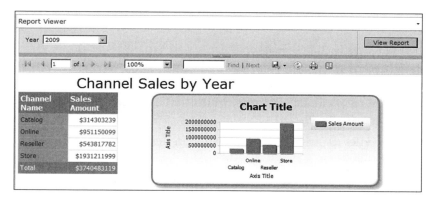

FIGURE 5.26   Channel Sales by Year Native report rendered in web part.

FIGURE 5.27   Specifying a report in the Report Viewer web part.

Summary

The Report Viewer web parts provide the capability for rendering Reporting Services reports on a SharePoint page. There are separate web parts for reports deployed to a Report Server running in SharePoint Integrated mode versus reports deployed to a Report Server running in native mode. The SharePoint Integrated mode web part is installed with the Reporting Services add-in for SharePoint installation; the native mode web parts are packaged with SQL Server and can be installed with the `Install-SPWebPartPack` PowerShell command. The web parts contain a number of properties that can be specified to fine-tune how a report is rendered.

Best Practices

The following are best practices from this chapter:

▸ If possible, run Reporting Services in SharePoint Integrated mode; the Report Viewer web part included with the Reporting Services add-in for SharePoint is much newer than the native mode web parts, which have remained unchanged for quite some time.

▸ There are many properties available for customization in the report web parts. Take advantage of this flexibility.

▸ SharePoint 2010 Server includes a nice collection of filter web parts out of the box. Use the filter web parts to accept report parameters and connect them to the SharePoint Integrated mode Report Viewer web part instead of relying on the parameter form that the Report Viewer web part renders by default.

PART III

PerformancePoint Services

IN THIS PART

PerformancePoint Services Configuration

PerformancePoint Services, one of the new features in SharePoint Server 2010 Enterprise, makes possible the development of dashboards. Dashboards can contain interactive charts, scorecards, and reports that enable users to gain deeper insights into data, which is the goal of any *business intelligence* (BI) application.

The previous version of PerformancePoint was a combination of the Microsoft Office Business Scorecard Manager and ProClarity, which Microsoft purchased in April 2006. Initially, separate licensing was required for PerformancePoint Server, which was a major roadblock for the software to gain traction in Microsoft BI projects. In April 2009, Microsoft changed the licensing requirements to allow the software to be installed for those companies that have a *client access license* (CAL) for SharePoint Enterprise, which opened the door for acceptance of the software in terms of licensing costs but still relied on a separate configuration and servers before PerformancePoint could be brought into the environment.

In the new release of SharePoint Server 2010 Enterprise, PerformancePoint Services has been integrated without the need for additional licensing or software. In addition, configuring PerformancePoint Services is now relatively simple after SharePoint Server has been set up and configured.

Adding PerformancePoint Services

By default, PerformancePoint Services is included when a web application is created. However, if the application is set up via a custom selection of services and PerformancePoint

Services is not included in the initial creation, follow the steps listed here in SharePoint 2010 Central Administration to add the service:

1. Click the **Application Management** link from the Central Administration home page, and then click **Configure Service Application Associations**.

2. For the web application being modified, in the Application Proxy Group column, click the custom link.

3. Figure 6.1 displays the Configure Service Application Associations menu. Click the **PerformancePoint Application** check box and click **OK**.

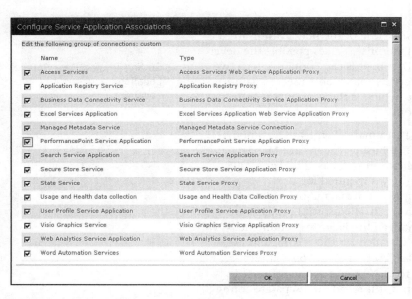

FIGURE 6.1   Configure Service Application Associations menu.

Setting up the Secure Store Service

By default, the Business Intelligence Center creation results in a menu on the main page of the site collection that contains Monitor Key Performance, Build and Share Reports, and Create Dashboards options. Each menu item has a Start Using PerformancePoint Services link. If you click the link, Dashboard Designer is presented to allow development within PerformancePoint. If you are using a data source connection, and if the network has not been set up for a Kerberos delegation on a per-user identity basis, PerformancePoint Services requires an unattended service account. The unattended service account is set up in the PerformancePoint settings, but can be set up only if the Secure Store Service is set up for the web application. If either the unattended service account is not set up or the Secure Store Service was not set up initially for PerformancePoint Services, the application presents a message (when Dashboard Designer is connecting to the data source) stating that PerformancePoint Services has not been configured correctly.

The Secure Store Service is set up within a web application to map encrypted user and group credentials to the credentials of the external data sources. The Secure Store Service requires an initial pass phrase, which is used for the encryption process. To set up the Secure Store Service, complete the following steps:

1. Click the **Application Management** link on the Central Administration home page and then click **Manage Service Applications**.

2. In the list of service applications for the web application, click the **Secure Store Service** link.

   On the Secure Store Application Secure Store Service menu, a Generate New Key button is available for encrypting the credentials, as shown in Figure 6.2.

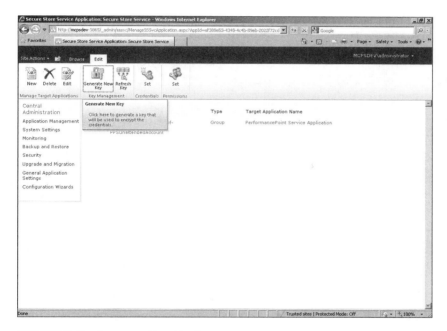

FIGURE 6.2   Generate New Key button.

3. When a Generate New Key menu appears, supply and confirm the pass phrase to encrypt the credentials.

Applying PerformancePoint Service Application Settings

PerformancePoint Services has a list of configurations available to customize the length of a query timeout, the number of items in a filtered list, and other options. However, the main setting is the setting of the secure store and unattended service account. The secure store and unattended service account authenticate the user to the data sources during the runtime of the PerformancePoint content. The settings are set within the SharePoint 2010 Central Administration as follows:

1. Click the **Application Management** link on the Central Administration home page, and then click **Manage Service Applications**.

2. In the list of service applications for the web application, click the **PerformancePoint Service Application** link.

3. Click the **PerformancePoint Service Application Settings** link.

4. Supply the Secure Store Service application name and the unattended service account, as shown in Figure 6.3.

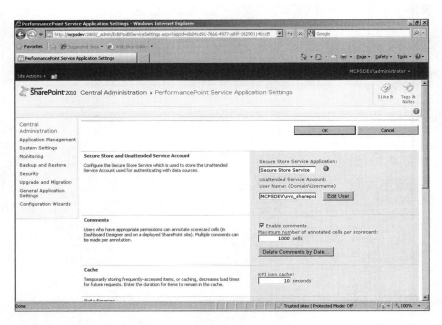

FIGURE 6.3   PerformancePoint Service Application settings.

Other settings available include the following:

▶ **Comments:** Allows authenticated users to annotate scorecard cells. You can enable this feature and set the maximum annotated cells per scorecard. By default, this setting is enabled and the maximum number set to 1,000 cells.

▶ **Cache:** Defines the storage time for frequently accessed items. The default is 10 seconds.

▶ **Data Sources:** You can set the query timeout in the case that no response is received from the data source. The default is 300 seconds

▶ **Filters:** Dashboards enables you to select values out of a filter to see specific data associated within the dashboard from the selection. The Filters setting limits how long the filter remains active for a user before resetting itself and how many items will appear in the filter list. The active filter default is set for 90 days and 5,000 items for the filtered list.

▶ **Select Measure Control:** Sets the maximum number of members to be selected for a dashboard Select Measure control. The default is 1,000 measures.

▶ **Show Details:** Limits the number of rows returned when Show Details is selected. The initial retrieval limit default is 1,000 rows, and the maximum retrieval limit is 10,000 rows.

▶ **Decomposition Tree:** Defines the maximum number of items returned for a level within a tree to be displayed via the Decomposition Tree control. The default maximum number is 250.

Enabling Non-Business Intelligence Center Sites with PerformancePoint Services

When you are creating a site for a SharePoint web application, you can create a site without using the Business Intelligence Center template and still want to incorporate PerformancePoint Services.

NOTE

Creating a site using the Business Intelligence Center template enables PerformancePoint Services by default.

To turn on the PerformancePoint application for these sites, the site collection and the site itself must be enabled to use PerformancePoint. To provide PerformancePoint Services to a non-Business Intelligence Center site, follow these steps:

1. Navigate to the site to add PerformancePoint Services and click **Site Actions, Site Settings**.

2. On the Site Settings page, under Site Collection Administration, click **Site Collection Features**.

3. Click the **Activate** button for the PerformancePoint Services Site Collection Features. After you click Activate, an Active status displays.

4. Click the **Activate** button for the SharePoint Server Publishing Infrastructure. After clicking Activate, an Active status displays.

   Figure 6.4 shows what the collection features look like when both the PerformancePoint Services Site Collections Features and the SharePoint Server Publishing Infrastructure settings have been activated.

FIGURE 6.4   Site collection features.

5. After the site collection has the features enabled to host PerformancePoint Services, the site can then set up PerformancePoint Services. Within the site, click **Site Actions, Site Settings**.

6. From the Site Actions menu, choose **Manage Site Features**.

7. Click the **Activate** button for the PerformancePoint Services Site Features. After you click Activate, an Active status displays.

8. After the features have been enabled within the site, PerformancePoint development cannot be started until a data connection library has been created. The data connection library can be created by clicking DataConnections Library for PerformancePoint in the Libraries section or by creating a new data connection library and then modifying the library to add the PerformancePoint data source content type.

The following steps explain how to create the library using the DataConnections Library for PerformancePoint option:

1. On the home page of the site, click the **Libraries** link.

2. In the upper left of the page, click the **Create** button.

3. Scroll to the DataConnections Library for PerformancePoint icon and supply a name for the library, as shown in Figure 6.5

4. After the library has been created, click the **Library Tools\Documents** tab and select **New Document, PerformancePoint Data Source**. The Dashboard Designer then launches and presents the Select a Data Source Template screen.

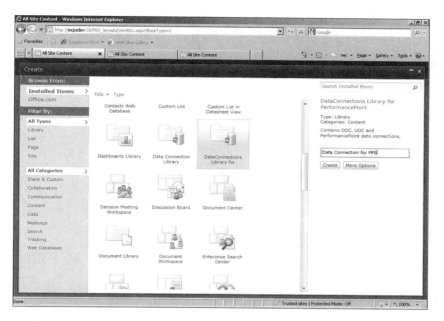

FIGURE 6.5   DataConnections Library for PerformancePoint option.

The following steps explain how to create the library using the data connection library:

1. From the home page of the site, click the **Libraries** link.

2. In the upper left of the page, click the **Create** button.

3. Scroll to the Data Connection Library icon and supply a name for the library, as shown in Figure 6.6.

4. After the library has been created, click the **Library Tools\Library** tab and click the **Library Settings** icon on the ribbon.

5. From the Content Types menu, choose the **Add from Existing Site Content Types**.

6. On the Add Content Types page, select the **PerformancePoint Data Source from the Available Site Content Types** list and click the **Add** button to move the content type to the Content Types to Add list. Then click **OK**.

7. Navigate back to the data connection library, click the **Library Tools\Documents** tab, and then select **New Document, PerformancePoint Data Source**. Dashboard Designer then launches and presents the Select a Data Source Template screen.

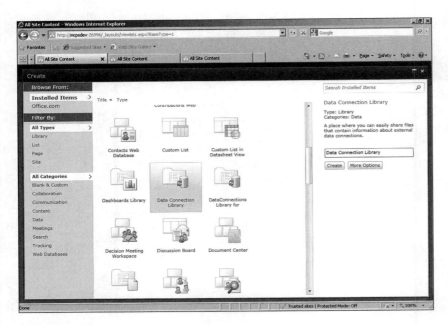

FIGURE 6.6   Data Connection Library.

Setting Trusted Data Source Locations and Trusted Content Locations

By default, all areas within the site collection are set as trusted, meaning there are no limits to where PerformancePoint content can use a data source for a report or where the PerformancePoint content can be saved. However, an administrator might want to restrict libraries and sites to prevent users from having access to data sources and content libraries. With this configuration requirement in mind, PerformancePoint Services enables an administrator to configure a trusted location within SharePoint 2010 Central Administration.

To set up a trusted data source location, complete the following steps:

1. Click the Application Management link from the Central Administration home page, and then click Manage service applications.

2. From the list of service applications for the web application, click the **PerformancePoint Service Application** link.

3. Click the **Trusted Data Source Locations** link.

4. By default, the **All SharePoint Locations** option is selected. Click the **Only Specific Locations** option, and then click **Apply**.

5. Click the **Add Trusted Data Source Location** link.

6. Supply the full site address on the Edit Trusted Data Source Location screen, as shown in Figure 6.7, and then click **OK**.

7. Repeat steps 4 and 5 for each data source location to grant access.

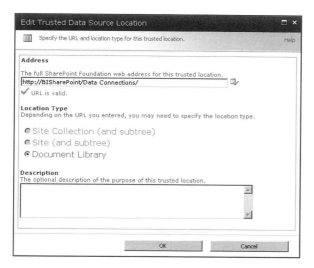

FIGURE 6.7   Edit Trusted Data Source Location screen.

To set up a trusted content location, complete the following steps:

1. Click the **Application Management** link on the Central Administration home page and then click **Manage Service Applications**.

2. From the list of service applications for the web application, click the **PerformancePoint Service Application** link.

3. Click the **Trusted Content Locations** link.

4. By default, the option All SharePoint Locations is selected. Click the **Only Specific Locations** option, and then click **Apply**.

5. Click the **Add Trusted Content Location** link.

6. Supply the full site address within the Edit Trusted Content Location screen, as shown in Figure 6.8, and then click **OK**.

7. Repeat steps 5 and 6 for each content location to grant access.

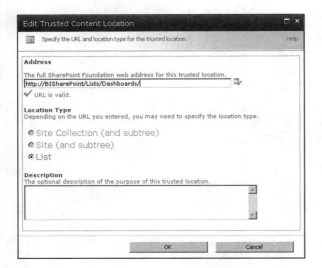

FIGURE 6.8   Edit Trusted Content Location screen.

Summary

PerformancePoint Services is a new feature in SharePoint 2010 Enterprise that allows for the creation of interactive dashboards that can display high-level analytics and the ability to drill further into the numbers for a more detailed analysis. However, although PerformancePoint Services is installed by default and available for SharePoint web applications, further configuration is needed before development can begin.

This chapter walked through the processes of configuring a web application to allow PerformancePoint Services, setting up authentication to communicate with the data sources, setting up trusted areas to store the content and data sources, and enabling a SharePoint site to build PerformancePoint content.

Best Practices

▶ Before setting up the unattended service account, ensure that you have set up the Secure Store Service within SharePoint.

▶ The unattended service account should follow service account guidelines and permit the account to access network resources needed for the application.

▶ By default, all areas within a SharePoint collection are trusted for data sources and PerformancePoint content. Administrators should limit which sites and libraries are available to ensure not exposing any sensitive data to nonprivileged users within the community.

CHAPTER 7

PerformancePoint Services Development

PerformancePoint Services is a highly visual, interactive, analytical component of Microsoft's *business intelligence* (BI) stack. Its main purpose is to surface data from established data sources to allow insight into how a company is performing using different metrics that are deemed valuable for the targeted audience. Through the use of dashboard development, managers and analysts can analyze trends, performance indicators, and analytical reports all in one page and then have the option to drill into a specific area of the data to ask and answer questions about company performance.

With PerformancePoint Services embedded into SharePoint 2010 Enterprise, all development is done from within a SharePoint site using Dashboard Designer. In addition, new items have been added to the toolset (for example, the Decomposition Tree and KPI Details report) as has improved functionality to existing objects such as scorecards, analytic charts, and analytic reports. With the latest release of PerformancePoint Services, the toolset can easily be seen as a robust analytical tool that is a must-have for any company in any industry.

This chapter details the development of the different PerformancePoint Services content using Dashboard Designer.

Using Dashboard Designer

Developing PerformancePoint Services content is all done from Dashboard Designer, which is installed as a component of SharePoint 2010 Enterprise. From Dashboard

Designer, data connections are established, content is developed, and the content is then saved to a SharePoint list (and in the case of dashboards, they are then deployed to a SharePoint library). In addition, content that has been developed and saved to the SharePoint web application can be reused for new development.

To open Dashboard Designer, you just navigate from a menu off of a Business Intelligence Center site or create a new item in a PerformancePoint content list. To bring up Dashboard Designer from a Business Intelligence Center site, complete the following steps:

1. Put the cursor over the Monitor Key Performance, Build and Share Reports, or Create Dashboards menu on the Business Intelligence Center default home page, and then click the **Start Using PerformancePoint Services** link.

2. On the PerformancePoint Services Samples page, click the **Run Dashboard Designer** button.

3. For the initial run, Dashboard Designer needs to install, and a prompt appears asking to install the program. Click the **Install** button.

After the installation completes, Dashboard Designer starts up, as shown in Figure 7.1.

To redirect to Dashboard Designer from a PerformancePoint content list, complete the following steps:

1. Navigate to the Business Intelligence Center site and click the PerformancePoint Content menu on the left.

2. Click the **List Tools\Items** menu.

3. Click the **New Item** button on the menu or click the **Add New Item** link on the list.

A Dashboard Designer Redirect screen appears with a message stating Loading Dashboard Designer and Dashboard Designer then starts up, as shown in Figure 7.1.

Dashboard Designer is broken down via objects that have been created and saved in the SharePoint web application or objects that are local development, which is considered the workspace. Dashboard Designer is made up of three menus and two categories. The menus (Home, Edit, and Create) manipulate the item within the category (data connections or PerformancePoint content), in the workspace. After the workspace content has been developed, saving the item publishes the item to the SharePoint site in a PerformancePoint Services content-enabled list, which is then available for reuse in multiple dashboards.

PerformancePoint content can be organized via created display folders from within Dashboard Designer. After the item is saved to a SharePoint list, the items are organized by content type within the SharePoint list itself. For all Dashboard Designer objects, the managing of the item's Display Folder is done in the Properties tab of the item. In the Properties tab, there is a textbox where you can type in the name of the display folder, which if it does not exist will create a new folder. You can also click on the Browse button next to the textbox and then select an existing folder or click the Create button to create the new folder. After creating or selecting the display folder, the name of the folder will appear in the Display Folder textbox. In addition, the folder will also appear in the menu on the left under either the Data Connections or PerformancePoint Content category, depending on the item being updated.

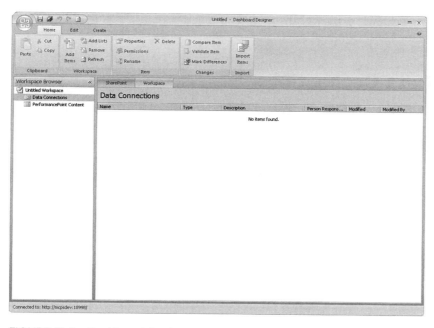

FIGURE 7.1 Dashboard Designer main screen.

For the Data Connections category, the following items are available to be selected and used for a PerformancePoint content object:

▸ **Analysis Services:** Connects to a SQL Server Analysis Services cube

▸ **Excel Services:** Connects to an Excel Services file in SharePoint

▸ **Import from Excel Workbook:** Connects to a local Excel file that has static numeric data

▸ **SQL Server Table:** Connects to a SQL Server database table

For the PerformancePoint Content category, the following objects are available to be developed:

▸ **KPI:** Creates a *key performance indicator* to be used on a scorecard

▸ **Filter:** Creates an object that will limit data in other objects within a SharePoint page

▸ **Report:** Creates a graphical or columnar representation of the data

▸ **Dashboard:** Creates a SharePoint page that displays a single or multiple PerformancePoint content objects and can combine those content objects with other SharePoint objects, such as an Excel Services file or Reporting Services report

▸ **Indicator:** Creates a series of object icons to be used in KPIs

▸ **Scorecard:** Creates a form for displaying KPIs

The remainder of the chapter explains how to develop the different PerformancePoint Services content using Dashboard Designer.

Creating Data Connections

For all PerformancePoint content, a data connection is required to be used for the content to perform. PerformancePoint Services has many different types of data connections available to use, and certain content objects can use only a specific data connection object. You can create a data connection by right-clicking **Data Connections** and selecting **New Data Source** or clicking the **Dashboard Designer Create** menu on the ribbon and clicking the **Data Source** button.

When the Select a Data Source Template screen appears, you have your choice of which data connection type to create. The following sections explain how to create each data connection type.

Analysis Services Data Connection

An Analysis Services Data Connection provides access to a *SQL Server Analysis Services* (SSAS) cube for consumption in a dashboard. An SSAS cube is made up of many measures and dimensions which allow for quick analytical processing of data via different aggregations and drill downs. The cube is developed via *SQL Server Business Intelligence Studio* (BIDS) and processed onto a server that is running SSAS. To create an Analysis Services data connection to an existing SSAS cube, complete the following steps:

1. Click the **Analysis Services** template.
2. Click the **Editor** tab; the default selection is the Use Standard Connection. To directly supply the connection string, skip steps 3–5.
3. Supply the server name.
4. Select the database on the supplied server.
5. Supply the SSAS cube role that the connection is going to impersonate. This is optional and can be left blank.
6. If supplying the connection string manually, click the **Use the Following Connection** option and supply the connection string.
7. Select the cube.
8. In the Authentication menu

   ▶ Leave the unattended service account; the default uses the Secure Store\Unattended Service Account configuration as set up in the Central Administration.

   ▶ Clicking the Unattended Service Account and Add Authenticate User Name in Connection String option results in the same configuration being used but adds an extra custom property for the username

▶ Clicking the Per-User Identity requires a Kerberos setup of SharePoint and SSAS to authenticate the user and retrieve only privileged data.

9. Click the **Properties** tab.

10. Supply the name of the data connection object.

11. Enter a display folder name, example *Data Sources*, for organizing the Dashboard Designer workspace file.

12. Fill in the description of the connection (optional).

13. Add any custom properties to pass to the SSAS cube by clicking the **New Property** button, selecting the type, and supplying the value.

14. Click the **Time** tab to associate the time dimension within the cube to the Analysis Services data source.

15. Select the time dimension member from the time dimension in the cube.

16. Select the beginning of the year for the selected time dimension. If a calendar year, this value is the 1/1/2010 value, for example. If using a fiscal year, this value represents the first day of the fiscal year.

17. Pick the hierarchy level that the data represents.

18. In the reference date, enter a date that represents the selected date.

19. From the Time Member Associations menu, select the time aggregation for each member of the time hierarchy available.

Figure 7.2 shows an example of the completed Time tab.

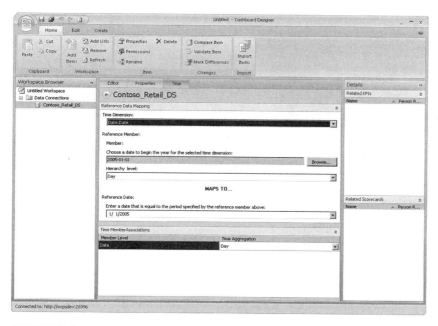

FIGURE 7.2   Analysis Services Time tab.

20. After finishing adding the properties of the connection, click the **Editor** tab, and then click **Test Data Source**.

21. Click the **Save** button.

Figure 7.3 shows a completed Analysis Services connection.

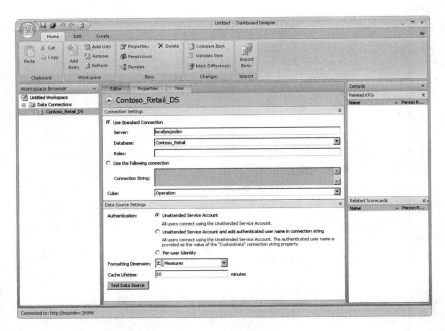

FIGURE 7.3   Analysis Services data connection.

Excel Services Data Connection

An Excel Services Data Connection provides an Excel workbook as a data source for building PerformancePoint Services content items. The Excel workbook is managed by SharePoint and is available to other authorized users on the SharePoint site where the Excel workbook is hosted. To create an Excel Services data connection for connecting to an existing Excel Services file, complete the following steps.

1. Click the **Excel Services** template.

2. Supply the SharePoint site to connect.

3. Select the library within the SharePoint site containing the Excel Services file.

4. Select the Excel workbook from the document library.

5. Either fill in the item name or, if available, select the item name from the drop-down.

> **NOTE**
>
> The item name is going to map to a named range or table within the Excel Services file. If you are connecting to an Excel 2007 workbook, type in the item name; it will not appear in the Item Name drop-down.

6. Click the Properties tab.
7. Supply a name of the data source.
8. Enter a display folder name, example *Data Sources*, for organizing the Dashboard Designer workspace file.
9. Fill in a description of the data source (optional).
10. Click the **Time** tab.
11. If applicable, supply the time dimensional data.
12. Click the **View** tab to see the data from the Excel file.
13. Click the **Editor** tab.
14. Click the **Test Data Source** button.
15. Click the **Save** button.

Figure 7.4 shows a completed Excel Services connection.

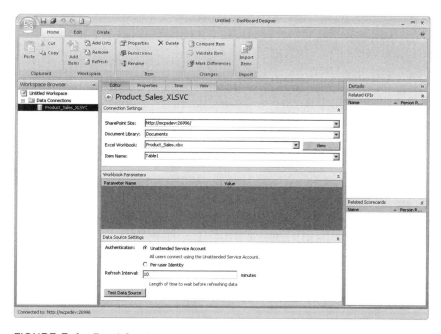

FIGURE 7.4   Excel Services data connection.

Import from Excel Workbook Data Connection

The Import from Excel Workbook data connection allows for loading of a local Excel into PerformancePoint to then be used by a PerformancePoint Services content item. The Import from Excel Workbook connection differs from the Excel Services data connection in that the imported Excel file is not managed by SharePoint, changes to the local file are not sent back to the connection after the import succeeds, and PerformancePoint stores the imported data. To create an Import from Excel Workbook data connection, complete the following steps:

1. Click the **Import from Excel Workbook** template.

2. Click the **Import** button, navigate to the local Excel workbook to import the data, and then click **Open**.

> **NOTE**
>
> After the workbook is imported, a local copy is created within Dashboard Designer and can be modified only from the Edit tab of the data source. The original workbook can change its data, and the data modification will have no effect on the imported data.

3. On the Edit Data in Excel pop-up screen, uncheck the default **Headers in First Row** check box or leave checked and click **Accept Changes**.

4. On the View tab, review the fields and make any modifications in the Properties menu for each column:

   ▸ Add a column name.

   ▸ Add a unique column name.

   ▸ Select a column type to state whether a column is a dimension, fact, key, time dimension, or to ignore the column.

   ▸ If the column type is fact, select the aggregation method.

   ▸ If the column is a dimension or time dimension, select the column that is of the type key that represents the key for the column.

5. Click the Properties tab.

6. Supply a name of the data source.

7. Enter a display folder name, example *Data Sources*, for organizing the Dashboard Designer workspace file.

8. Fill in a description of the data source (optional).

9. Click the **Save** button.

Figure 7.5 shows a completed Import from Excel Workbook connection.

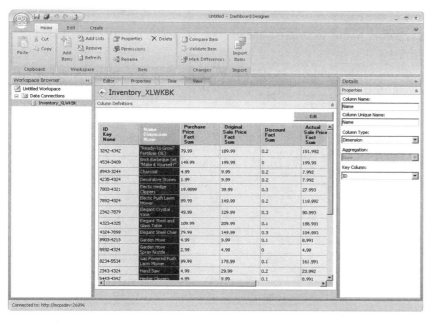

FIGURE 7.5   Import from Excel Workbook data connection.

SharePoint List Data Connection

The SharePoint List data connection allows content that exists in a SharePoint List to be manipulated via a PerformancePoint content item. The data itself is seen as a Tabular reference so Analytical reports cannot use the data source. However, the data is available for KPIs and other types of reports. To create a SharePoint List data connection, complete the following steps:

1. Click the **SharePoint List** template.
2. Supply the SharePoint site to connect.
3. Select the SharePoint site list.
4. Select the SharePoint list from the list collection.
5. Click the **View** tab and update the property for each column.
6. Click the **Preview Data** button to review the list data.
7. Click the **Editor** tab and click the **Test Data Source** button.
6. Click the **Properties** tab.

7. Supply a name of the data source.

8. Enter a display folder name, example *Data Sources*, for organizing the Dashboard Designer workspace file.

9. Fill in a description of the data source (optional).

10. Click the **Save** button.

Figure 7.6 shows a completed SharePoint list connection.

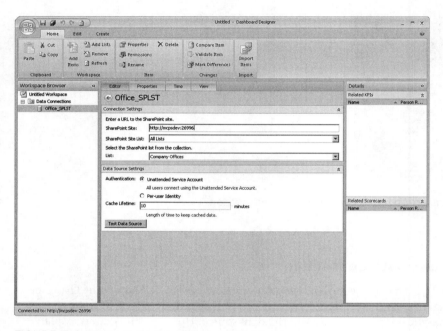

FIGURE 7.6   SharePoint list data connection.

SQL Server Table Data Connection

A SQL Server Table data connection enables a SQL Server table or view to be consumed by a PerformancePoint content item. To create a SQL Server Table data connection, complete the following steps:

1. Click the **SQL Server Table** template.

2. If using the Use Standard Connection option, supply the server name and click the database on the Database drop-down.

3. If using the Use the Following Connection option, supply the connection string.

4. Select the table from the Table drop-down.

5. Click the **Properties** tab.

6. Supply a name of the data source.

7. Enter a display folder name, example *Data Sources*, for organizing the Dashboard Designer workspace file.

8. Fill in a description of the data source (optional).

9. Click the **View** tab and update the property for each column.

10. Click the **Preview Data** button to test the data.

11. Click the **Editor** tab and keep the **Unattended Service Account** option selected or click the **Per-User Identity** button if a Kerberos configuration is in place.

12. Click the **Test Data Source** button.

13. Click the **Save** button.

Figure 7.7 shows a completed SQL Server table connection.

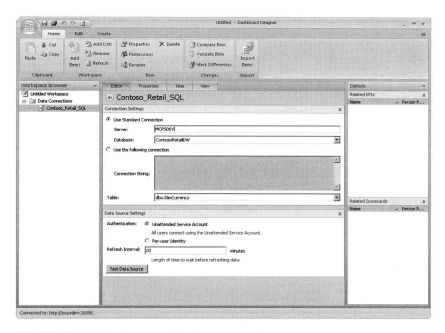

FIGURE 7.7   SQL Server table data connection.

Building Key Performance Indicators

Key performance indicators (KPIs) are graphical representations of the "health of a company" tracking metric. KPIs are designed individually for each metric and contain properties for how the graph should represent the metric based on a comparison of an actual value to a target value. In Dashboard Designer, two types of KPIs can be created: Blank KPI and Objective. After the KPI has been developed, the KPI is placed onto a scorecard for display in a dashboard.

Blank KPI

A Blank KPI is for comparing an actual measurement to a target value for determining the indicator of the measurement. To create a Blank KPI, complete the following steps:

1. In the PerformancePoint Content category, either click the **Create** menu and click the **KPI** button or right-click the **PerformancePoint Content** menu and select **New\KPI**.

2. On the Select a KPI Template screen, click **Blank KPI** and click **OK**.

3. For the Actual row, the Compare To column is left blank. The Target row's Compare To column defaults to the name of the Actual row.

4. Click the **Default** link in the Number Format for both the Actual and Target row and supply the property values on the Format Numbers screen.

5. In the Data Mappings column for the Actual and Target row, click the original **1 (Fixed Values)** link. The default of 1 for a Fixed Value data mapping is displayed. To hard code a different value of what the row should represent, change the value to the appropriate value and click OK and skip to step 12. For KPIs that tie the row item to data source values, click the **Change Source** button.

6. On the Select a Data Source screen, click the data connection to use either within the workspace or on the SharePoint site. In addition, a calculated metric can be used as the source.

   Calculated metrics are new to PerformancePoint Services. Clicking the Calculated Metric tab brings up templates for commonly used metrics such as gross profit margin and customer retention rate. Within the metric, a data source is chosen for the source of the fields that are being used in the calculation.

7. Select a measure that represents the Actual and Target value from the data source for the KPI. If there are any filters to be placed on the KPI via a dimensional value, click the **New Dimension Filter** button.

8. Click the dimension to filter by on the Select Dimension screen.

9. Click the **Default All Members** link and select the dimension values to filter and then click **OK**.

10. If adding a Time Intelligence filter, click the **New Time Intelligence Filter** button.

> **NOTE**
>
> The data source must set up Time Intelligence for this filter option to be configured correctly.

11. Supply the time formula. The formula is set via the following syntax:

    ```
    [(]<Period>[<Offset>[)]][.<Function>[<Offset>]]]
    ```

    Examples:

    Previous Day: day-1

Last 10 days including today: day:day-9

Parallel year: (year-1).day

12. Click the **Preview** button for validation of the formula. Figure 7.8 shows a sample time formula.

FIGURE 7.8   Time Formula Editor example.

13. Click the **OK** button.

14. Select the aggregation method in the Aggregate Members By drop-down.

15. To supply an MDX tuple formula, click the **Use MDX Tuple Formula** check box and add the MDX statement.

16. Click the **OK** button.

17. For the Target row, click the Indicators column and click the **Set Scoring Pattern and Indicator** button on the Thresholds screen.

18. On the Select Scoring Pattern screen, click the **Scoring Pattern** from the three types:

   ▶ **Increasing Is Better:** The higher the number is from the worst score (0 for sales, for example), the better.

   ▶ **Decreasing Is Better:** The lower away the number is from the worst score (1 million returns, for example), the better.

   ▶ **Closer to Target Is Better:** The closer to the target number (daily machine uptime hours, for example), the better.

19. Select the banding method from the three types:

   ▶ **Band by Normalized Value of Actual/Target:** Depending on the scoring pattern, the ratio of distance from the actual to the worst divided by distance from the target to the worst. If decreasing is better, subtract the ratio from 1.

▶ **Band by Numeric Value of Actual:** Using the actual value to determine the bands.

▶ **Band by Stated Score:** Using a stated score, such as a variance, to determine the banding.

20. Click **Next**.

21. Select the indicator and click **Next**.

The third screen will vary based on the banding method:

▶ If the banding method is Band by Normalized Value of Actual/Target, enter the worst score and click **Finish**.

▶ If the banding method is Band by numeric value of Actual, enough information is present; click **Finish**.

▶ If the banding method is Band by Stated Score, click the **Specify Data Mapping** button, enter a fixed value for the stated score, or click the **Change Source** button and select the data source, click **OK**, and then select the measure that will be used as the stated score.

22. Based on the scoring pattern and banding method, fill out the Best\Worst\Thresholds for the KPI.

23. In the Calculation column for the Actual and Target row, click the **Default Value** link.

24. For a KPI developed using an Analysis Services data source, select the **Data Value** calculation and click **OK**. The Data Value calculation allows the Decomposition Tree to be enabled when the KPI is used in a scorecard.

25. New to PerformancePoint Services is the ability to add multiple actuals and targets to the KPI and relate the new row back to other existing target and actual values. To add a new actual or target, click the **New Actual** or **New Target** button and develop the row as needed.

26. Enter a display folder name, example *KPIs*, for organizing the Dashboard Designer workspace file.

27. Click the **Save** button.

Figure 7.9 shows a completed KPI.

Objective

An *Objective* is for rolling up multiple KPIs for an overall combined score. Objectives can roll up to a higher objective level as well. Making use of objects allows for clean interface of management of lower level KPIs and provides the user with a quick view of how a subject is performing. Follow these steps to create an objective:

1. In the PerformancePoint Content category, either click the **Create** menu and click the **KPI** button or right-click the **PerformancePoint Content** menu and select **New\KPI**.

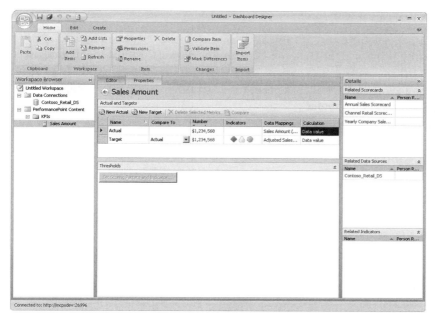

FIGURE 7.9   Key performance indicator.

2. On the Select a KPI Template screen, click **Objective** and click **OK**.

3. Click the **Properties** tab and supply a name for the objective.

4. Enter a display folder name, example *KPIs*, for organizing the Dashboard Designer workspace file.

5. Because the purpose of the Objective is to roll up child KPIs for a combined score, click the **Save** button. The objective will be a used as a header KPI in scorecard development, and the calculation method will default to a No value.

Developing Scorecards

A scorecard, in its simplest form, is the container for displaying KPIs within a dashboard. However, when developed properly, scorecards group like KPIs into multiple categories to display a bigger picture of the overall status of an entity.

In PerformancePoint Services, new features have been added to allow for drilling into the data via KPI Details reports and viewing Decomposition Trees, flexible layout options, and the inclusion of dynamic hierarchies in the display.

Follow these steps to create a scorecard:

1. In the PerformancePoint Content category, either click the **Create** menu and click the **Scorecard** button or right-click the **PerformancePoint Content** menu and select **New\Scorecard**.

2. On the Select a Scorecard Template screen, there are three categories of templates: Microsoft, Standard, and Tabular.

   ▶ The Microsoft category creates a scorecard from an Analysis Services data source. Selecting the Analysis Services scorecard allows for interaction with the Decomposition Tree.

   ▶ The Standard category allows for selecting either a blank scorecard or a fixed values scorecard:

      ▶ A Blank Scorecard template presents a screen where KPIs and Dimensions are dragged and dropped into the scorecard.

      ▶ A Fixed Values Scorecard template is a list of fixed value KPIs.

   ▶ The Tabular category allows for selecting from an Excel Services, Excel workbook, SharePoint list, or a SQL Server table:

      ▶ Excel Services template creates a scorecard from an Excel Services data source. The KPIs are then developed based on the data within the Excel Services file.

      ▶ Excel Workbook template creates a scorecard from an Excel workbook data source. The KPIs are then developed based on the data within the Excel workbook that has been stored within PerformancePoint Services at the time of import.

      ▶ SharePoint List template creates a scorecard from a SharePoint list data source. The KPIs are then developed based on the data within the SharePoint list.

      ▶ SQL Server Table template creates a scorecard from a SQL Server table data source. The KPIs are then developed based on the data within the SQL Server table.

   Click the **Microsoft** category, the **Analysis Services** template, and then click **OK**.

3. Click the **Analysis Services** data source to use for the scorecard, and then click **Next**.

4. On the Select a KPI Source screen, two options display:

   ▶ Create KPIs from SQL Server Analysis Services Measures

   ▶ Import SQL Server Analysis Services KPIs

   If KPIs have been developed within the Analysis Services cube, click the **Import SQL Server Analysis Services KPIs**, and then click **Next**. If creating a new KPI from measures within the cube, keep the default option selected and click **Next**. To import previously built workspace or SharePoint site KPIs, either option allows the next screen to import the KPIs.

NOTE

It is recommended that KPIs have either been developed within the cube or previously developed in Dashboard Designer before you create the scorecard.

5. If the Create KPIs from SQL Server Analysis Services measures option was selected, click **Add KPIs** for each measure to create the new KPI against. If the Import SQL Server Analysis Services KPIs was selected, check each cube KPI to import.

6. Click the **Select KPI** button to import KPIs from the workspace or SharePoint site.

7. Select each KPI and click **OK**. After all KPIs are created\imported and selected, click the **Next** button.

8. On the Add Measure Filters screen, to allow for dashboard filters to limit the data, check the **Add Measure Filters** check box.

9. Click **Select Dimension in the Member Filters** and select the dimension for the filter.

10. Click the **Select Members** button for the actual measure filter, check the members to filter the scorecard, and then click **OK**.

11. Click the **Select Members** button for the target measure filter, check the members to filter the scorecard, and then click **OK**.

12. To add Time Intelligence, enter a time formula in both the actual and target measure filters.

13. Click **Next**.

14. Check the **Add Column Members** check box for scorecards that will present a column header.

15. Click the **Select Dimension** button, select the dimension for the column header. In PerformancePoint Services, a hierarchy can be selected to allow user interaction with the scorecard.

16. Click the **Select Members** button, select the members for the column headers, and click **OK**.

17. Click **Next**.

18. On the Locations screen, select the SharePoint list where the created KPIs will be stored.

19. Click **Finish**.

The wizard completes and displays the original creation of the scorecard with all KPIs created and selected at the same level, as shown in Figure 7.10.

20. For those KPIs that have been created as objectives, move the KPIs in an organized header location. Select the objective KPI and click the up or down arrows on the Edit menu to the desired location.

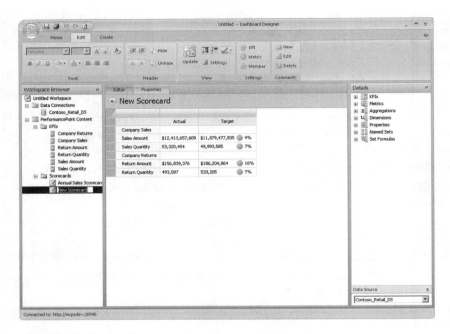

FIGURE 7.10   Wizard scorecard.

21. For those KPIs that are considered child KPIs of the objective KPIs, click the up or down arrows on the Edit menu to the desired location underneath the objective and click the **Indent** button to associate the child KPI to the objective KPI.

22. After the scorecard has been adjusted, click the **Update** button on the Edit menu to display the KPI data.

23. Click the **Properties** tab and supply a name for the scorecard.

24. Enter a display folder name, example *Scorecards*, for organizing the Dashboard Designer workspace file.

25. Click the **Save** button.

Figure 7.11 shows a completed formatted scorecard.

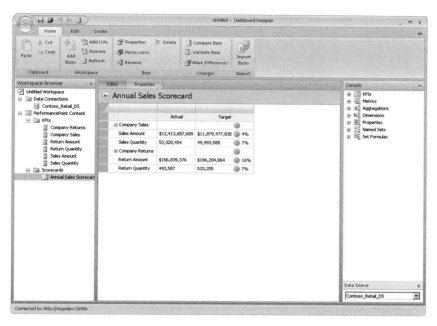

FIGURE 7.11 Formatted scorecard.

Creating Reports

Essential to every organization is the ability to view different metrics and activity to help analysts understand the who, where, what, how, and why an event happened, which can then lead to a business decision to help further growth, stop negative actions, or maintain a profitable situation. Within PerformancePoint Services, several different types of reports can be created to provide users the corporate story for making these business decisions.

Based on the report type, users can build custom views of the report, filter the report, and drill into different slices of the data. In addition, PerformancePoint Services enables users to connect to external websites, view Excel Services workbooks, and display other company reports from other reporting servers that use SQL Server Reporting Services or ProClarity Analytics Server.

The following report types are available in PerformancePoint Services:

- **Analytic Chart:** Connects to a SQL Server Analysis Server data source to create bar charts, pie charts, and line charts. The Analytic Chart report allows for drilling into the chart to gain deeper insight into the data.

- **Analytic Grid:** Connects to a SQL Server Analysis Server data source to create reports that display the data in a rows-and-columns grid.

- ▶ **Strategy Map:** Connects a scorecard for interaction with a Microsoft Office Visio 2007 or later file.

- ▶ **KPI Details:** Displays detailed information about a KPI.

- ▶ **Reporting Services:** References a report stored on a SQL Server Report Server.

- ▶ **Excel Services:** Displays a new view of an Excel Services workbook.

- ▶ **ProClarity Analytics Server Page:** References an existing ProClarity Analytics Server page.

- ▶ **Web Page:** References an existing web page.

Analytic Chart

For enhanced user interaction and the display of graphical reports, the Analytic Chart report is the report of choice most common in PerformancePoint Services dashboards. The Analytic Chart allows for user interaction to drill into the data that makes up the chart information from within the SSAS cube. The Analytic Chart also exposes custom drill through actions that have been defined in the SSAS cube. To create an Analytic Chart report, complete the following steps:

1. In the PerformancePoint Content category, either click the **Create** menu and click the **Analytic Chart** button or right-click the **PerformancePoint Content** menu and select **New\Report**. In either case, the Select a Report Template screen displays. Click **Analytic Chart**, and then click **OK**.

2. On the Create Analytic Chart Report screen, click the Analysis Services data source to use for the report and click **Finish**.

   You can supply custom MDX for the report on the Query tab.

> **NOTE**
>
> Adding custom MDX into the query disables the ability for the report to use the Decomposition Tree feature.

3. On the Design tab, drag the measures and dimensions needed for the report into the Series and Bottom axis.

4. If any filtering is planned against the report for a dimension value that is not going to have an axis to display data, drag that dimension into the Background.

> **NOTE**
>
> To display dimension values in the Series and Bottom Axis and not have the measure name appear in the legend, move the measure to the Background.

5. The default chart is a bar chart. Click the **Edit** menu and click **Report Type** to change the type.

6. The default is not to show the information bar. Click **Settings** on the Edit menu and check the **Show Information Bar** check box to display it.

7. To filter out empty items from the Series and Bottom axis, click the **Filter** button on the Edit menu and click the **Filter Empty Series** and **Filter Empty Axis** items.

8. Click the **Properties** tab and supply a name.

9. Enter a display folder name, example *Reports*, for organizing the Dashboard Designer workspace file.

10. Click the **Save** button.

Figure 7.12 shows a completed Analytic Chart report.

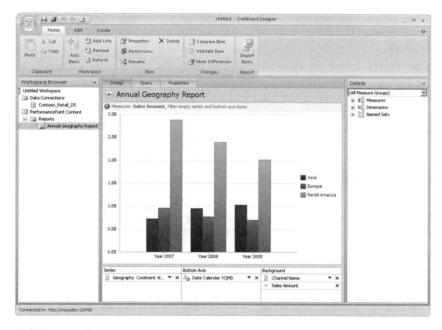

FIGURE 7.12   Analytic Chart report.

Analytic Grid

In step with the Analytic Chart report is the Analytic Grid report, in the terms of interchangeability for users by just changing the report type. Instead of displaying the data in a chart format though, the Analytic Grid displays that data in rows in columns. The measurements contained within the chart are then available for drilling as if right-clicking within an Analytic Chart. Follow these steps to create an Analytic Grid report:

1. In the PerformancePoint Content category, either click the **Create** menu and click the **Analytic Grid** button or right-click the **PerformancePoint Content** menu and select **New\Report**. In either case, the Select a Report Template screen displays. Click **Analytic Grid**, and then click **OK**.

2. On the Create Analytic Chart Report screen, click the Analysis Services data source to use for the report and click **Finish**.

   You can supply custom MDX for the report on the Query tab.

> **NOTE**
>
> Adding custom MDX into the Query will disable the ability for the report to use the Decomposition Tree feature.

3. On the Design tab, drag the measures and dimensions needed for the report into the rows and columns.

4. If a report is being developed for a Dashboard that has known dimension filters but the grid being developed does not want to display that filtered dimension value, drag the dimension being used in the filter to the Background section of the report. By adding the dimension to the background in the report, the Dashboard filter can then link to the report and pass the filter's value to the report for limiting the data in the grid.

> **NOTE**
>
> To measure values in the grid and not have the measure appear in a column or row header, move the measure to the Background. However, dragging multiple measures into the grid automatically moves the measures to the column axis.

5. The default is not to show the information bar. Click **Settings** on the Edit menu and check the **Show Information Bar** check box to display it.

6. To filter out empty items from the rows and columns, click the **Filter** button on the Edit menu and click the **Filter Empty Rows** and **Filter Empty Columns** items.

7. Click the **Properties** tab and supply a name.

8. Enter a display folder name, example *Reports*, for organizing the Dashboard Designer workspace file.

9. Click the **Save** button.

Figure 7.13 shows a completed Analytic Grid report.

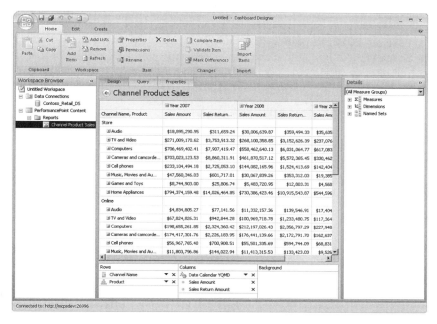

FIGURE 7.13   Analytic Grid report.

Strategy Map

A Strategy Map report is a Visio diagram that organizes company goals graphically via a flowchart of steps that overall represent the organization's strategy. In combination with a scorecard, the strategy map objects connect to KPIs to display how the strategy is performing. Follow these steps to create a Strategy Map report:

1. In the PerformancePoint Content category, either click the **Create** menu and click the **Other Reports** button or right-click the **PerformancePoint Content** menu and select **New\Report**. In either case, the Select a Report Template screen displays. Click **Strategy Map**, and then click **OK**.

2. On the Create a Strategy Map screen, select the scorecard to use as the data for the Visio diagram and click **Finish**.

3. Click the **Edit** menu and click **Edit Strategy Map**.

4. Click **Import Visio File** and navigate to the Visio diagram and click **Open**.

5. In the Visio diagram, click the shape to connect to a KPI and click the **Connect Shape** button.

6. On the Connect Shape screen, click the KPI and click the **Connect** button and then click **Close**.

7. Repeat steps 5 and 6 for each shape in the Visio diagram to tie to a KPI.

HINT

If using Visio Professional 2010, you can switch between the Strategy Map Editor and the Connect Shape without having to close the window. You can then repeat steps 5 and 6 for all KPIs by clicking the Connect button and then moving to the next KPI to be mapped.

8. After connecting all shapes, click **Apply**.

9. Click the **Properties** tab and supply a name for the strategy map.

10. Enter a display folder name, example *Reports*, for organizing the Dashboard Designer workspace file.

11. Click the **Save** button.

Figure 7.14 shows a completed Strategy Map report.

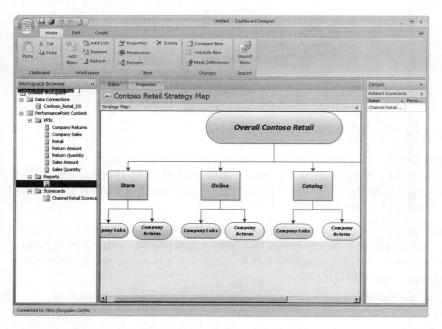

FIGURE 7.14   Strategy Map report.

KPI Details

New to PerformancePoint Services is the ability to create a KPI Details report. The KPI Details report allows the drilling of information about the KPI from a scorecard. Follow these steps to create a KPI Details report:

1. In the PerformancePoint Content category, either click the **Create** menu and click the **KPI Details** button or right-click the **PerformancePoint Content** menu and

select **New\Report**. In either case, the Select a Report Template screen displays. Click **KPI Details** and then click **OK**.

2. On the Editor tab, check the KPI sections within the tab for displaying the details about a KPI in reference to the checked category. When a scorecard connects to the KPI Details report in a dashboard, each KPI on the scorecard is then available to be clicked. Clicking on the connected scorecard's KPI will display the checked KPI Details report category information within the KPI Details report.

3. Click the **Properties** tab and supply a name.

4. Enter a display folder name, example *Reports*, for organizing the Dashboard Designer workspace file.

5. Click the **Save** button.

Figure 7.15 shows a completed KPI Details report.

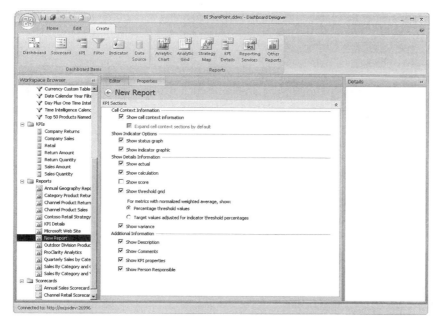

FIGURE 7.15   KPI Details report.

Reporting Services

Within the Microsoft BI stack, SQL Server Reporting Services is another complementary toolset that brings information to the user community to enhance informed decision making. Because Reporting Services reports could prove useful in combination with other PerformancePoint content items in a dashboard, the ability to view a specific report is created by connecting to the report itself on the Report Server. To link to a Reporting Services report, complete the following steps:

1. In the PerformancePoint Content category, either click the **Create** menu and click the **Reporting Services** button or right-click the **PerformancePoint Content** menu and select **New\Report**. In either case, the Select a Report Template screen displays. Click **Reporting Services** and then click **OK**.

2. On the Editor tab, supply the Report Server report settings.

   ▶ Select the server mode: SharePoint Integrated or Report Center.

   ▶ If SharePoint Integrated, supply the Report Server URL and the full path of the report RDL filed as stored in the SharePoint site.

> **NOTE**
>
> The Report Server URL is the path to the actual report server for the Integrated SharePoint site and is usually of the form *http://sharepointserver/reportserver*. In configuring a site for SharePoint integrated mode, the path supplied in setting up the Reporting Services server is the same information supplied in this step of the creating the report.

   ▶ If Report Center, supply the server name and click **Browse** to select the report.

   ▶ Check on or off the **Show Toolbar**, **Show Parameters**, and **Show DocMap** check boxes.

   ▶ Click the **Zoom** percent of the report.

   ▶ Click the **Format** for presentation of the report.

   ▶ Supply the **Report Parameter** values.

3. Click the **Properties** tab and supply a name.

4. Enter a display folder name, example *Reports*, for organizing the Dashboard Designer workspace file.

5. Click the **Save** button.

Excel Services

Excel workbooks being maintained by SharePoint within Excel Services allow for the sharing of workbook data amongst a business group. Accessing these Excel Services workbooks and displaying other PerformancePoint content items within a singular dashboard enables users to gain even better insight and analytics. To display an Excel Services Workbook report, complete the following steps:

1. In the PerformancePoint Content category, either click the **Create** menu and click the **Other Reports** button or right-click the **PerformancePoint Content** menu and select **New\Report**. In either case, the Select a Report Template screen click is presented. Click **Excel Services** and click **OK**.

2. Supply the SharePoint site containing the Excel Services workbook.

3. Select the document library.

4. Select the Excel workbook and click **View** to display the workbook.

5. Select an item name of the table or named range to narrow the view of the data from the workbook.

6. Click the **Properties** tab and supply a name.

7. Enter a display folder name, example *Reports*, for organizing the Dashboard Designer workspace file.

8. Click the **Save** button.

ProClarity Analytics Server Page

Before PerformancePoint Services, there was ProClarity and Microsoft Office Business Scorecard Manager. Microsoft has discontinued support for Microsoft Office Business Scorecard Manager because the application was rarely implemented. However, not all companies have removed the ProClarity instance altogether and therefore still contain valuable information to be relayed back to the user community. PerformancePoint Services allows for the inclusion of this information by linking to the ProClarity Analytics Server. Follow these steps to link to a ProClarity Analytics Server page:

1. In the PerformancePoint Content category, either click the **Create** menu and click the **Other Reports** button or right-click the **PerformancePoint Content** menu and select **New\Report**. In either case, the Select a Report Template screen click is presented. Click **ProClarity Analytics Server Page** and click **OK**.

2. In the Server URL field, supply the ProClarity server URL.

3. Click the **Browse** button.

4. Leave the **Use Windows Credentials** check box checked or uncheck it and supply the credentials to connect to the server.

5. Select the page and click **OK**.

6. In the configuration options, select the option to turn off a feature of user interaction (optional):

   ▶ ad; (Disable Decomposition Tree)

   ▶ dd; (Disable Drill to Detail)

   ▶ ad;dd; (Disable Decomposition Tree and Drill to Detail)

   ▶ st; (All Interaction Disabled)

7. Click the **Properties** tab and supply the name for the report.

8. Enter a display folder name, example *Reports*, for organizing the Dashboard Designer workspace file.

9. Click the **Save** button.

Web Page

Outside web pages are useful in providing external information to further enhance the dashboard story being told. PerformancePoint Services provides this capability. The following steps outline how to link to a web page, which is then stored as a report within PerformancePoint Services content:

1. In the PerformancePoint Content category, either click the **Create** menu and click the **Other Reports** button or right-click the PerformancePoint Content menu and select **New\Report**. In either case, the Select a Report Template screen click is presented. Click **Web Page** and click **OK**.

2. In the URL text box, supply the URL.

3. Click the **Properties** tab and supply the name for the report.

4. Enter a display folder name, example *Reports*, for organizing the Dashboard Designer workspace file.

5. Click the **Save** button.

Filtering Data

Filters within PerformancePoint Services enable users to limit data to one or more PerformancePoint Service content items within a dashboard, provided those content items have been set up to use the filter. In the SQL Server Reporting Services world, you can consider the filter the same as applying a parameter for the report; but for PerformancePoint Services, the filter can alter the data for multiple objects simultaneously.

The following filter types are available in PerformancePoint Services:

- ▶ **Custom Table:** Uses a table of information from a SQL Server, Excel workbook, Excel Services, or SharePoint list data source as its filter values

- ▶ **MDX Query:** Connects to a SQL Server Analysis Server data source and uses custom MDX to supply the filter values

- ▶ **Member Selection:** Connects to any data source that has dimension fields defined to use as the filter values

- ▶ **Named Set:** Connects to a SQL Server Analysis Server data source containing named sets, which are then used as the filter values

- ▶ **Time Intelligence:** Uses a data source that has time intelligence set up and creates a formula to be used as the filter values

- ▶ **Time Intelligence Connection Formula:** Uses a data source that has time intelligence set up and uses a calendar control to be used as the filter values

To create a filter, in the PerformancePoint Content category either click the **Create** menu and click the **Filter** button or right-click the **PerformancePoint Content** menu and select **New\Filter**. When the Filter Template screen appears, click the type of filter to build. Repeat this step for creating any type of filter to be used in a dashboard.

Custom Table

A Custom Table filter allows for retrieving data values from a tabular data source as an item to limit other PerformancePoint Services content in a dashboard. To create a Custom Table filter, follow these steps:

1. On the Select a Filter Template screen, select the **Custom Table** filter and click **OK**.
2. Select a data source and click **Next**.
3. On the Preview Table screen, review the data and click **Next**.
4. On the Choose Key Columns screen
    ▶ Select a key for the filter.
    ▶ Select a parent key for the key item. The parent key is used to generate a filter tree.
    ▶ Select the display value.
    ▶ Select the **Is Default** column.
5. Click **Next**.
6. Select a display method for the filter values:
    ▶ **List:** Displays all items as one list, and only one item can be selected
    ▶ **Tree:** Displays the filter values in a tree structure, but only one item can be selected
    ▶ **Multi-Select Tree:** Displays the filter values in a tree structure, but allows for multiple selections to be used as the filter value
7. Click **Finish**.
8. Click the **Properties** tab and supply a name.
9. Enter a display folder name, example *Filters,* for organizing the Dashboard Designer workspace file.
10. Click the **Save** button.

MDX Query

An MDX Query filter is an MDX Set statement against an SSAS data source for retrieving dimensional members on the dashboard. One major advantage for creating an MDX Query filter is that you can limit specific dimension values based upon a condition without having to update the SSAS cube. To create an MDX Query filter, follow these steps:

1. On the Select a Filter Template screen, select the **MDX Query** filter and click **OK**.
2. Select a data source and click **Next**.
3. Enter the MDX set definition that is to be used as the filter values and click **Next**.
4. Select a display method for the filter values.
5. Click **Finish**.
6. Click the **Properties** tab and supply a name.

7. Enter a display folder name, example *Filters,* for organizing the Dashboard Designer workspace file.

8. Click the **Save** button.

Member Selection

A Member Selection filter makes dimension members available from an SSAS data source to drill into PerformancePoint content items on a dashboard. When defining the filter, you select the dimension, the specific members of the dimension and the default member for the filter. To create a member selection filter, follow these steps:

1. On the Select a Filter Template screen, select the **Member Selection** filter and click **OK**.

2. Select a data source and click **Next**.

3. Click the **Select Dimension** button.

4. On the Select Dimension screen, select the **Dimension** field and click **OK**.

5. Click the **Select Members** button.

6. On the Select Members screen, check the members for the filter. To set the member to use as the default, right-click the member and select **Set as Default Selection**.

7. Click **OK**.

   The default member selected on the Select Members screen should appear in the Default Member Selection text box.

8. Click **Next**.

9. Select a display method for the filter values.

10. Click **Finish**.

11. Click the **Properties** tab and supply a name.

12. Enter a display folder name, example *Filters,* for organizing the Dashboard Designer workspace file.

13. Click the **Save** button.

Named Set

A Named Set filter makes available an SSAS Named Set that has been defined within the SSAS cube. A named set is a calculated member that creates a limited list of dimension members based upon a condition of the data. An example of a named set would be a Top 10 Salesperson set that is determined by Total Sales. To create a Named Set filter, follow these steps:

1. On the Select a Filter Template screen, select the **Named Set** filter and click **OK**.

2. Select a data source and click **Next**.

3. Select the named set from the cube and click **Next**.

4. Select a display method for the filter values.

5. Click **Finish**.

6. Click the **Properties** tab and supply a name.

7. Enter a display folder name, example *Filters,* for organizing the Dashboard Designer workspace file.

8. Click the **Save** button.

Time Intelligence

The Time Intelligence filter allows you to enter a Time Intelligence formula expression as the filter to be passed to a PerformancePoint content item in a dashboard. Examples of a Time Intelligence formula are day:day-9 (for range of last ten days) and yeartodate. To create a Time Intelligence filter, complete these steps:

1. On the Select a Filter Template screen, select the **Time Intelligence** filter and click **OK**.
2. Click the **Add Data Source** button.
3. Select a data source and click **OK**.
4. Click **Next**.
5. Add a time formula expression into the Formula text box and supply a name for the formula.
6. Click the **Preview** button to validate the formula.
7. Repeat steps 5 and 6 for each formula to add for the filter.
8. Click **Next**.
9. Select a display method for the filter values.
10. Click **Finish**.
11. Click the **Properties** tab and supply a name.
12. Enter a display folder name, example *Filters,* for organizing the Dashboard Designer workspace file.
13. Click the **Save** button.

Time Intelligence Connection

The Time Intelligence Connection filter presents the user with a calendar to pick a date from and evaluates the Time Intelligence expression against the chosen date. To create a Time Intelligence Connection Formula filter, complete the following steps:

1. On the Select a Filter Template screen, select the **Time Intelligence Connection Formula** filter and click **OK**.
2. Click the **Add Data Source** button.
3. Select a data source and click **OK**.
4. Click **Next**.

   The Time Intelligence Calendar Tool will be highlighted.
5. Click **Finish**.
6. Click the **Properties** tab and supply a name.

7. Enter a display folder name, example *Filters,* for organizing the Dashboard Designer workspace file.

8. Click the **Save** button.

Constructing Dashboards

The dashboard is the user interface that connects all the PerformancePoint content into a singular analytic tool for user consumption. The dashboard is made up of filters, reports, and scorecards, which are displayed in zones as the dashboard organization.

To create a dashboard, in the PerformancePoint Content category either click the **Create** menu and click the **Dashboard** button or right-click the **PerformancePoint Content** menu and select **New\Dashboard**. When the Dashboard Page Template screen appears, click the originating page layout template to use. However, after selecting a template, the dashboard can have zones added, split, or deleted by right-clicking in a zone and performing an action. The list of options is displayed in Figure 7.16.

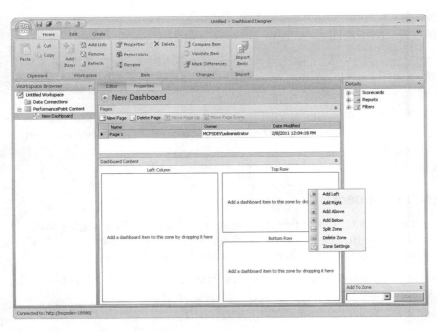

FIGURE 7.16   Dashboard zone manipulation.

The main building of a dashboard is done by dragging content from the Details section into a dashboard zone. After you design the dashboard layout and fill the zones with content items, the following actions are performed in the Editor tab to finish the interactive section of the dashboard development:

▶ Connecting filters to dashboard content objects

▶ Linking a KPI Details report to a scorecard

▶ Creating a multiple pages within the dashboard

▶ Deploying the dashboard to SharePoint

When you've completed the Editor tab, click on the Properties tab and update the name of the dashboard, add the display folder, example *Dashboards*, for organizing the Dashboard Designer workspace. Select the Document Library that the dashboard will deploy to in the SharePoint site and select a SharePoint site's master page for formatting the dashboard itself to conform to the rest of the SharePoint site pages.

Connecting Filters to Dashboard Content Objects

Connecting filters to dashboard content items is performed by setting up the content's connection to the value from the filter. The following steps illustrate how to set up a filter connection:

1. For each PerformancePoint content item that is going to have its data affected by the filter, on the right side of the item in the zone there is a drop-down arrow. Click the arrow and select **Create Connection**. The menu is shown in Figure 7.17.

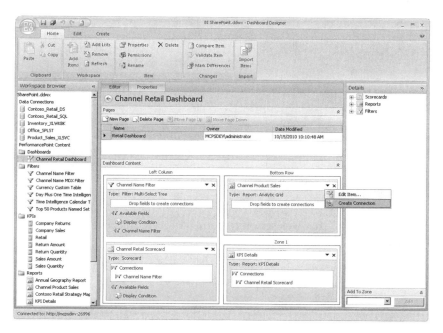

FIGURE 7.17   Create Connection menu.

HINT

Connecting a filter to a PPS content item in a zone can be achieved by hovering over the filter to display the filter's list of properties, such as Member Unique Name, and then dragging that property onto the PPS content item's **Drop fields to create connections** section (or if a connection already exists, this section is named **Connections**).

2. On the Connection screen, select the filter in the Get Values From drop-down, as shown in Figure 7.18.

FIGURE 7.18   Filter connection.

3. Click the **Values** tab and select the data item from the content that will have the data filtered and the source value from the filter to use as the supplied value. If using an Analysis Services data source as the filtered item, the connection will usually be done on the member unique name, as shown in Figure 7.19.

4. Click **OK**.

After connecting, the content item that was set up to connect to the filter will have the filter listed in its **Connections**.

FIGURE 7.19   Filter value mapping.

Linking KPI Details Report to a Scorecard

Similar to setting up a filter on dashboard, a KPI Details report receives its information from a KPI that is stored on a scorecard, of which the scorecard can be set up with a filter to limit the KPIs available. To set up the link for a KPI Details report from a scorecard, complete the following steps:

1. Click the arrow in the upper-right corner for the KPI Details report and select **Create Connection**.
2. On the **Items** tab of the Connection screen, select the scorecard that will be supplying the KPI.
3. Click the **Values** tab, and the Connect To drop-down will have the cell selected.
4. In the Source value, select **Cell: Context**, as shown in Figure 7.20.
5. Click **OK**.

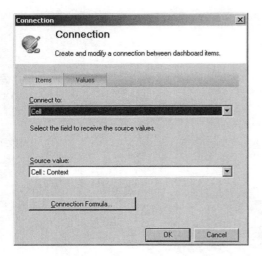

FIGURE 7.20   Filter value mapping.

After connecting, the KPI Details report that was set up to connect to the scorecard has the scorecard listed in its connections.

Creating Multiple Pages in a Dashboard

Dashboard Designer enables you to create multiple pages within the dashboard content. Each page is its own entity, and the connections can share data from other content items on the same page. Follow these steps to add pages to a dashboard:

1. Build the first page as you would any other dashboard: Lay out the dashboard, drag content items, and link connections for filters and KPIs.

2. In the Pages section, supply a name.

3. To add another page, click the **New Page** button and supply a name for the new page.

4. Design the new page as you would for the first page.

5. After all pages have been developed, click the **Properties** tab for the dashboard content item.

6. Supply a name for the dashboard. This is the name that will display in the SharePoint library.

7. In the Deployment properties, select the document library to deploy the dashboard.

8. Click the **Include Page List for Navigation** check box. The property ensures that when the dashboard is deployed each page has a link to bring up the dashboard content developed on the page. Figure 7.21 displays a sample dashboard Properties page.

9. Click the **Save** button.

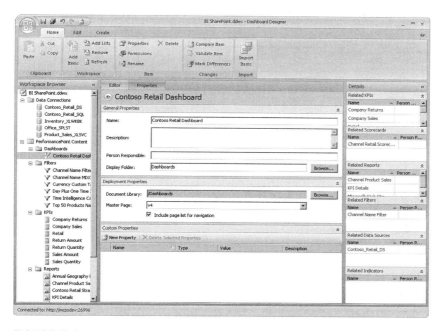

FIGURE 7.21   Dashboard Properties page.

Deploying the Dashboard to SharePoint

After developing the dashboard, the last step is to deploy the dashboard to SharePoint for users to interact with the dashboard. Within Dashboard Designer, there are two ways to accomplish this task:

▶ Right-click the dashboard from within the content and select **Deploy to SharePoint**, as shown in Figure 7.22.

▶ Click the Dashboard Designer **Home** icon and select **Deploy**, as shown in Figure 7.23.

After you deploy the dashboard, the dashboard displays within the Dashboard library.

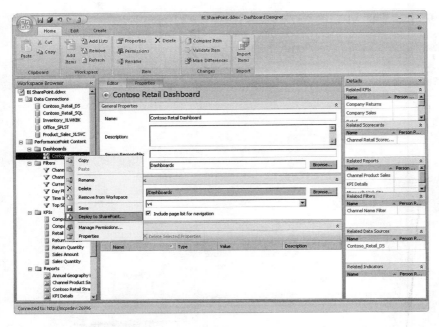

FIGURE 7.22   Deploy to SharePoint menu.

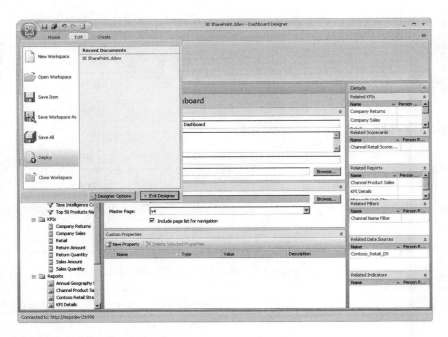

FIGURE 7.23   Main deploy.

User Interaction with the Decomposition Tree

PerformancePoint Services has made the Decomposition Tree available as another method of drilling into the details to break down other objects that that make up the rolled-up dashboard value being displayed. The Decomposition Tree is not a development option. Instead, it is a menu item made available when drilling from a scorecard KPI or interacting with an analytic chart and grid.

To allow the enabling of the Decomposition Tree for a KPI, the KPI's calculation method must be set to Data Value, which is explained in the "Building Key Performance Indicators" section of this chapter. For the analytic chart or grid, the report's query should have been created using the Design tab and not have supplied custom MDX for the report.

Viewing the Decomposition Tree from a KPI, right-click the KPI value to drill into and select **Decomposition Tree**, as shown in Figure 7.24.

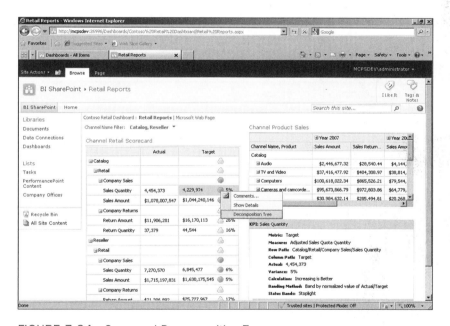

FIGURE 7.24   Scorecard Decomposition Tree menu.

Viewing the Decomposition Tree from an analytic chart or grid, right-click the value to drill into and select **Decomposition Tree**, as shown in Figure 7.25.

After you select the Decomposition Tree from the menu, a new window appears that allows for user interaction with the Decomposition Tree. Clicking a tree item displays a menu that allows you to expand the tree to another dimension or view the properties of the selected tree item. If the tree item is part of a hierarchy, an Expand button is available to the left of the tree item, to drill into the next level of the hierarchy. Figure 7.26 shows an example Decomposition Tree.

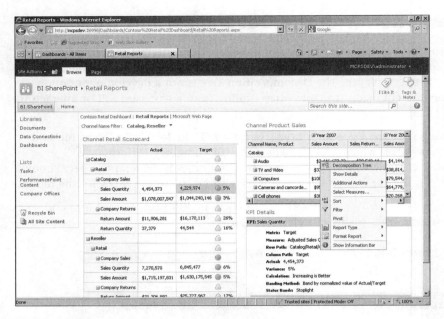

FIGURE 7.25   Analytic Decomposition Tree menu.

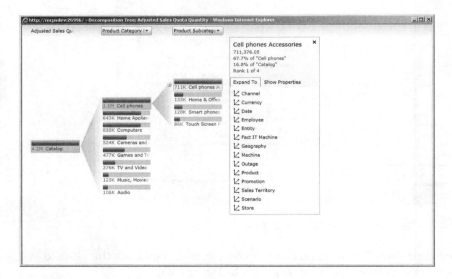

FIGURE 7.26   Decomposition Tree drilling.

Summary

PerformancePoint Services integration with SharePoint has made the technology readily available to the analysts and management team who want to manipulate information without having to contact a report developer every time a new scenario is considered. Developers familiar with developing for PerformancePoint 2007 will have little issue getting up to speed to create dashboards for PerformancePoint Services. Those less familiar with the toolset will feel confident with the ease of using Dashboard Designer in building PPS content items and dashboards. PerformancePoint Services for SharePoint 2010 is a powerful business intelligence tool for delivering information to the analytical community, which enhances their ability to make well informed business decisions.

This chapter walked through the process of developing each piece of PerformancePoint content: KPIs, scorecards, report, filters, and dashboards. In addition, the chapter explained how to develop the content to enable other features and thus further enhance the user experience, such as setting up the content for allowing the Decomposition Tree to display. In later chapters, a complete end-to-end solution shows how PerformancePoint Services fits into the overall BI stack and how the components from this chapter are used to build the complete solution.

Best Practices

The following are best practices from this chapter:

- ► Within Dashboard Designer, organize PerformancePoint content by creating display folders and saving the objects within the folder.

- ► Setting up the Data Source for Time Intelligence expands the functionality of other PerformancePoint Services content for creating custom time formulas.

- ► Develop KPIs before creating scorecards, instead of creating the KPI during the scorecard development. KPIs have a vast number of properties that have to be configured, which will either enable or disable other user interaction, such as enabling the Decomposition Tree and creating a KPI Details report.

- ► Try not to use custom MDX for the Analytic Grids and Charts reports. Using the Design tab and dragging source items into the report will allow for the Decomposition Tree to be visible when viewing the report in a dashboard.

- ► If building a Strategy Map report, use a Visio diagram that has simple objects and not multilayered diagrams. The diagram objects will be connecting to scorecard elements via a mapping, which cannot be created in a multilayered Visio diagram.

- ► Organizing the layout of a dashboard is just as important as the content that will be displayed within the dashboard. If the content does not appear user friendly or workable, the user will not want to use the content, which defeats the purpose of bringing the information to the user in the first place.

PerformancePoint Services Security

PerformancePoint Services integration into SharePoint 2010 Enterprise has simplified security setup and maintenance by having the security maintained within SharePoint for development, deployment, and accessing the dashboards. From a data source perspective, the delegation has been changed from connecting on a server level to connecting on a per-data-source connection.

This chapter explains the data source delegation options, SharePoint permissions needed for deploying and using dashboards, and how groups are created within a SharePoint site.

Data Source Delegation

Data sources individually contain the method for connection when a PerformancePoint Services content item is retrieving its data. In the security model, PerformancePoint Services ensures that the data sources are not queried against from untrusted query objects and instead use content that is stored in a trusted location. The options for connecting are as follows:

- ► **Unattended Service Account:** Single shared access account to use for any connection that is not connecting on a per-user basis.

- ► **Per-user Identity:** The user account is used as the login account to the data source.

- ► **Custom Data:** Used for SQL Server Analysis Services data sources only and adds the current user as a custom property to the data connection.

The unattended service account requires setting up a secure store and the service account itself, which is configured in SharePoint Central Administration. The configuration steps are covered in Chapter 6, "PerformancePoint Services Configuration."

To set up a data source connection to use a per-user identity connection, you must set up Kerberos delegation within the network. With regard to Kerberos configuration, the following Microsoft white paper illustrates the steps to be done by a domain administrator to the SharePoint farm and other servers and service accounts that PerformancePoint Services will be using for connecting: http://go.microsoft.com/fwlink/?LinkID=196600.

> **NOTE**
>
> External data sources must exist in the same domain as the SharePoint farm. However, you can make external data sources outside of the domain in per-user scenarios. To do so, refer to "Planning Considerations for Services That Access External Data Sources" at http://technet.microsoft.com/en-us/library/cc560988.
> aspx#ConsiderationsForAccessingExternalData.

When an *SQL Server Analysis Services* (SSAS) data source is being used, an extra option is available for use as an authentication method: Unattended Service Account and Add Authenticated User Name in Connection String. When this option is set, the authenticated user is passed as part of the Custom Data property of the PropertyList in the session.

Figure 8.1 shows the result of enabling the Unattended Service Account and Add Authenticated User Name in Connection String option and clicking Test Data Source.

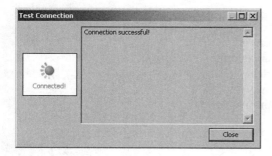

FIGURE 8.1   Additional SSAS authentication option.

To view the connection information being passed from PerformancePoint Services to the SSAS server, create a SQL Profiler trace to view the event.

> **NOTE**
>
> In order to create a trace in SQL Server Profiler against the SSAS server, you must be a member of the Analysis Services server role.

The following steps create a trace to view the Authenticated User information:

1. Launch SQL Server Profiler (Start\Programs\Microsoft SQL Server 2008\Performance Tools\SQL Server Profiler).
2. Click File\New Trace, a Connect to Server window appears.
3. Select Analysis Services as the Server Type and type in the name of the SSAS server in the Server name textbox and then click the Connect button.
4. A Trace Properties window appears with two tabs: General and Events Selection. Click on the Events Selection tab.
5. Expand the Security Audit event and check the Audit Login event.
6. Expand the Session Events event and check the Session Initialize event.
7. After selecting the events, the Trace Properties window will look like Figure 8.2.
8. Click the Run button to start the trace.

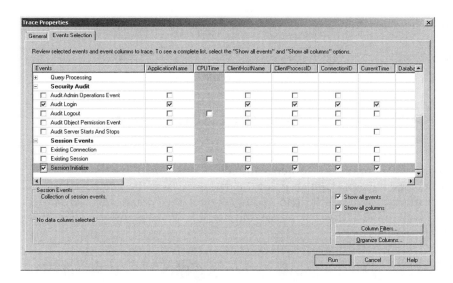

FIGURE 8.2   SQL Server Profiler trace property selection.

In the SQL Profiler trace, two events are captured when the Test Data Source button is clicked. An Audit Login event occurs, which displays information about the unattended service account that was configured for PerformancePoint Services. In addition, a Session Initialize event occurs that has the same connection information as the unattended service account. However, as displayed in Figure 8.3, the Property List XML contains the Custom Data property with the authenticated user information.

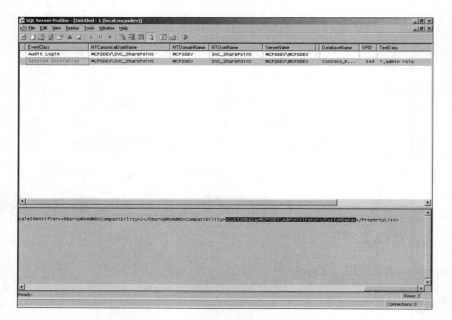

FIGURE 8.3   SQL Profiler trace containing the Custom Data property.

PerformancePoint Services and SharePoint Permissions

In PerformancePoint 2007, dashboard contents and items were stored in a separate Monitoring SQL Server database, at which point the dashboard was then deployed to a SharePoint site for interaction. In PerformancePoint Services, the content items are stored within SharePoint content SQL Server databases and use SharePoint permissions for saving the content into the database.

> **NOTE**
>
> A PerformancePoint Services database, by default named *PerformancePoint Service Application_GUID* (the GUID is auto generated), is created on the SharePoint database server. However, the database is used for saving Scorecard comments and annotations, not the PerformancePoint content items.

For a typical dashboard, building Performance Point Services content is done as follows:

1. Launch Dashboard Designer.
2. Create a data source and save it to a SharePoint library.
3. Create the PerformancePoint Services content and save it to a SharePoint list.
4. Create a dashboard that uses the PerformancePoint Services content and deploy the dashboard to a dashboard library.
5. View the dashboard and interact to perform analytics.

To execute any of these steps, you must have the requisite permissions set up within SharePoint for your Windows account, as shown in Table 8.1.

TABLE 8.1   PerformancePoint Tasks to SharePoint Permission

User Task	Permissions Required
Launch Dashboard Designer	None, being an authorized user in the SharePoint 2010 site
Create data source and save it to a SharePoint library	Contributor
Create the PerformancePoint Services content and save it to a SharePoint list	Contributor
Create and deploy dashboards	Designer
View dashboards	Read
Manage user permissions	Full Control (site) or Site Collection Administrator

*_Source: http://technet.microsoft.com/en-us/library/ee748591.aspx_

8

When you are using the Business Intelligence Center, SharePoint groups are initially created that contain the proper rights for creating and deploying dashboards. However, an administrator might want to create new groups within the site to structure the security differently than the default group set. To create new SharePoint site groups and assign users to the group, follow these steps:

1. Click **Site Actions** and select **Site Permissions**.
2. Click the **Create Group** button on the SharePoint site ribbon.
3. On the Create Group page, supply a group name and select the permissions for the group as needed according to Table 8.1. Figure 8.4 displays the group permissions available.

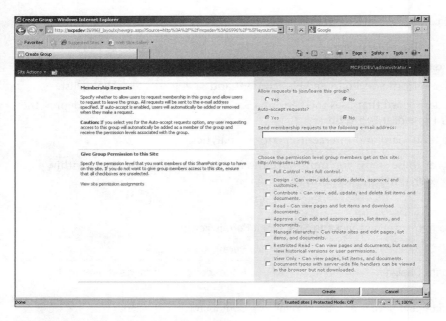

FIGURE 8.4   Creating a SharePoint group.

4. Click the **Create** button after setting the permissions for the group.

5. Click the **New\Add Users** button on the newly created group page to assign users to the group.

6. Supply the user accounts to the Grant Permissions screen, as shown in Figure 8.5.

7. Click **OK**.

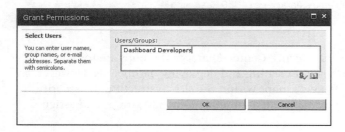

FIGURE 8.5   Assigning a user account.

Summary

PerformancePoint Services has updated the architecture to remove a single method for data source authentication and allows for data source connections to be configured on a per-item basis. In addition, the saving of the content and deploying to SharePoint has now been brought into the SharePoint security model. By having SharePoint manage the security, PerformancePoint Services has simplified the overall administration of the application.

This chapter explained the different data source delegation methods, the mapping of Dashboard Designer tasks to SharePoint group permissions, and how to create the groups needed for the development and consumption of PerformancePoint Services content.

Best Practices

▶ When setting up Kerberos delegation, ensure that all servers reside in the same domain to be used for per-user identity data source connections.

▶ SharePoint group permissions are used for creating and storing Dashboard Designer content. Administrators should follow the same methodology established on other sites in the farm with regard to how users are granted appropriate access.

▶ To ensure that authentication methods are being used as expected with SQL Server Analysis Services data sources, capture Audit Login and Session Initialize events using the SQL Profiler in a trace that has these events selected.

8

PART IV
PowerPivot

CHAPTER 9

PowerPivot for Excel

One of the more exciting recent additions to the Microsoft business intelligence (BI) suite is a technology known as PowerPivot. I use the word *technology* because PowerPivot is not a new product so to speak, but rather it is a new capability for very powerful data analysis, and it impacts Excel, SharePoint, and SQL Server. PowerPivot is available as a standalone add-in to Excel, and is also available as a SharePoint service. This chapter explores PowerPivot for Excel.

Overview of PowerPivot

Business users, and in particular business analysts, need to be able to process data to do their job. Much of that data processing responsibility goes through the IT department, but for a number of reasons, business users also need to be able to access and analyze data on their own. As a result, Microsoft Excel has become an indispensable tool for business.

However, although Excel is a powerful data tool, standard Excel has some limitations when it comes to large datasets. Also, when you want to combine different datasets in Excel, it's possible, but difficult and not very efficient. Wouldn't it be great to have a tool that could process literally millions of rows of data, do so extremely quickly, enable you to create relationships between different sets of data, and do all this in a familiar user interface? Well, *that* is PowerPivot!

So, how does PowerPivot do all this? By leveraging some of the technology from Microsoft Analysis Services. In fact, the engine behind PowerPivot is an in-memory, column-based data store known as the VertiPaq data engine, and it actually creates memory-resident analytic cubes. This is what enables the ultra-high performance of PowerPivot. Millions of rows of data can be grouped, sorted, analyzed, and so on within seconds. What's more, the VertiPaq engine allows for relationships to be created between different tables in much the same way that relationships are created between database tables. This makes it easy to combine disparate datasets to perform some powerful analysis, all from the desktop, all within the familiar Excel interface.

Additionally, to distribute and manage these PowerPivot applications, Microsoft provides the PowerPivot service in SharePoint 2010, which is discussed in the next chapter.

Installing PowerPivot

PowerPivot for Excel is available as a free download from Microsoft and is installed as an add-in to Excel 2010. Excel 2010 is required to experience the complete capabilities of PowerPivot and to create or modify a PowerPivot workbook. You can use Excel 2007 or Excel 2010 without the PowerPivot add-in to view PowerPivot workbooks, but the workbook will be static and read-only.

PowerPivot is available in both 32-bit (x86) and 64-bit (x64/amd64) versions. You need the version that matches the bit level of Microsoft Excel 2010 that is installed (x86 or x64). If you are unsure as to whether you have 32-bit or 64-bit Excel 2010, you can find out by doing the following:

1. Launch Excel 2010.
2. From the File menu, select **Help**.
3. In the information listed in the right portion of the screen, under About Microsoft Excel, you will see the version number along with the bit level in parentheses.

32-BIT OR 64-BIT?

Deciding on the 32-bit versus 64-bit version of Excel requires consideration. The 32-bit version of Excel is considered to be the most flexible for backward compatibility with third-party add-ins. However, if you use the 32-bit version of Excel, you are limited to a maximum in-memory workspace of 2GB. The 64-bit version supports working with up to 4GB of data in memory, but might not support legacy third-party add-ins. You must decide what is best for your specific situation and the types of analysis you might be performing.

To install PowerPivot for Excel, perform the following steps:

1. Go to Microsoft.com and enter **download powerpivot for Excel** in the search box. Follow the results until you are able to download either the 32-bit or 64-bit MSI files.
2. Download the version of PowerPivot you will use and click **Run** when prompted.

3. Accept the license agreement, and then click **Next**.

4. Enter your name, and then click **Next**.

5. Click **Install**.

6. After the installation is complete, click **Finish**.

The first time you launch Excel after installing the PowerPivot add-in, a dialog box will open asking if you want to install this customization. Click **Install** to complete the installation.

Using PowerPivot

The best way to think about how to use Excel with PowerPivot is to realize that there are really two steps that everyone takes when working with any kind of data. The first step is to get the data and prepare it (that is, import, clean, create calculations, and so on). The second step is to present that data (that is, create a pivot table, create a chart, and so forth). With that in mind, PowerPivot introduces the PowerPivot window as the design surface for getting and preparing the data, while the standard Excel worksheet is the design surface for presenting pivot tables and charts based on the data.

After installing the PowerPivot add-in to Excel, you will see a new tab menu named PowerPivot. Select that tab and you will notice that the first icon on the toolbar is for the PowerPivot window. This will open the PowerPivot window and still leave the Excel worksheet as is. You can move back and forth between the two separate design surfaces.

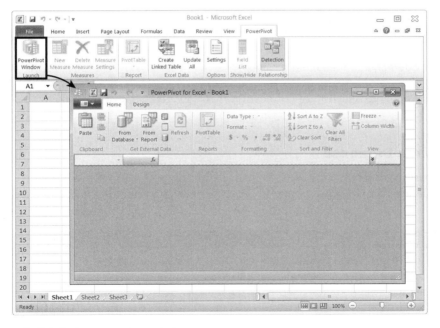

FIGURE 9.1   PowerPivot window.

To illustrate how PowerPivot can be used, let's assume the following scenario:

You are a marketing analyst for Contoso and are wondering whether the company should modify its marketing strategy based on income level. To explore this, you decide to see if a correlation exists between the average size of a sale and average income level. To perform this analysis, you have Product Sales data available from the company database. You also have gathered median income data, which is publicly available. (Note: For simplicity in this demonstration, the median income data is at a state level.)

Getting the Data

1. Open Excel 2010.
2. Display the PowerPivot tab, and then open the PowerPivot window.
3. In the Get External Data section of the toolbar, select **From Other Sources**, as shown in Figure 9.2, (Note: Depending on screen resolution, the text may not display.)

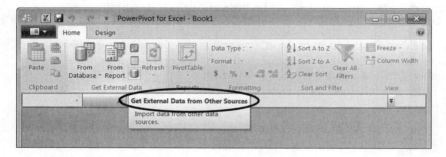

FIGURE 9.2   Get external data from other sources.

PowerPivot provides a large selection of connection managers right out of the box, as shown in Figure 9.3.

Importing from a Database

PowerPivot can easily connect to corporate databases and import data from them. The following example uses the Contoso sample BI database available from Microsoft's website.

INSTALLING THE CONTOSO DATABASE

To follow along with the example provided, you will need to install the Contoso database. Download the file named ContosoBIdemoBAK.exe from www.microsoft.com, double-click to extract the files, and then restore the database in SQL Server.

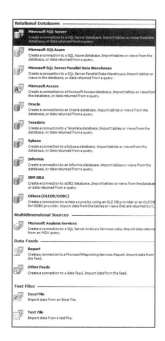

FIGURE 9.3   Data sources.

1. The Contoso database is a SQL Server database, so select **Microsoft SQL Server** from the list.

2. After establishing a connection to the database, the Import Wizard prompts whether you want to select tables from a list or write a SQL query that will specify the data to import. Choose **Select from a List of Tables**.

3. The Import Wizard presents a list of all the tables in the database. For this analysis, you are concerned only with sales in the United States. So, check the **DimGeography** check box and then click the **Preview & Filter** button (see Figure 9.4).

   A preview of the data in the Geography dimension is displayed. In addition, PowerPivot makes it easy to refine the data that will be imported, both at a column level and a data value level. Scroll to the right, locate the RegionCountryName column, and click the drop-down to the right of the column name. Clear all countries except United States as shown in Figure 9.5 and click **OK**.

   The ETLLoadID, LoadDate, and UpdateDate columns are fields that don't provide analytic value. Clear the check box in front of these fields so that they aren't imported. Click **OK** to apply the filters to the DimGeography table.

5. Back on the Select Tables and Views dialog, notice that DimGeography now lists Applied Filters in the Filter Details column. This makes it easy to see which dimensions have filtering in place. You can also click the Preview and Filter button again to further modify the filtering options if necessary.

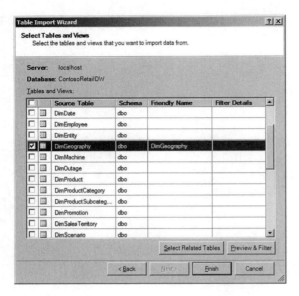

FIGURE 9.4   Table Import Wizard.

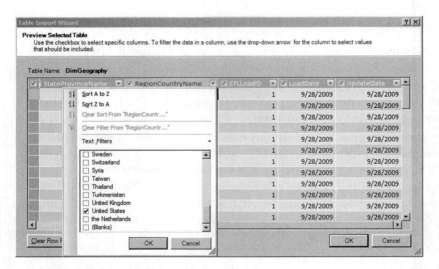

FIGURE 9.5   Filtering prior to import.

6. Select the check box next to the following tables to include them in the data model:

   ▶ DimDate

   ▶ DimProduct

   ▶ DimProductCategory

> ► DimProductSubCategory

> ► DimStore

> ► FactSales

Then click **Finish**.

The data import begins and a status box displays the status of each of the tables, as shown in Figure 9.6. Notice that PowerPivot can work with large datasets; more than three million records were imported from the fact table, and done quickly!

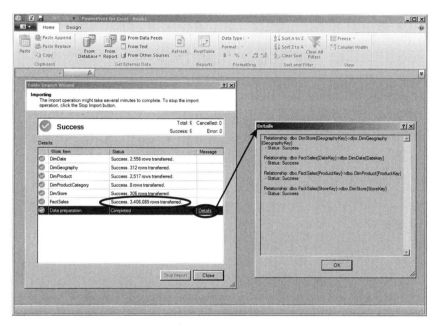

FIGURE 9.6   Import results.

The final step in the import process is data preparation, and this is where PowerPivot builds the necessary relationships to tie the tables together (see Figure 9.6). How does it know how to do this? Well, if the data source is a relational database, PowerPivot analyzes the schema of the source database and looks for foreign key relationships in the schema. If the relationships area not in the source data, PowerPivot provides ways to create them, as discussed later.

Importing from a Flat File

1. As stated in the scenario, you want to compare the Contoso sales data with average income data that you received from a third party. This data lists the average annual income by state and is in a CSV file. To import this text file into PowerPivot, select **From Text** from the Home tab of the PowerPivot window toolbar.

2. Enter a friendly name for this connection and the file path and name for the file (or browse and locate the file). At this point, you will see data in the preview window.

3. Select whether the first row contains the column headers, select the columns that are to be imported into PowerPivot, and clear the check box for columns that should not be imported (see Figure 9.7). When done, click **Finish**. The new data appears in PowerPivot as another table.

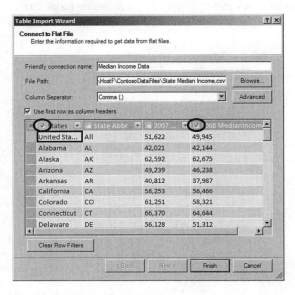

FIGURE 9.7   Flat file import.

TABLES OR WORKSHEETS?

When working in PowerPivot, the data that is imported is listed by tabs along the bottom of the screen, similarly to how Excel lists worksheets. However, under the hood, PowerPivot handles this data more like database tables than like worksheets, which is one reason why it is able to manage much more data and do it so quickly. The difference might seem subtle, but it is important to keep in mind. For example, in a worksheet, you can modify an individual cell without affecting the cells around it. In PowerPivot, you don't change individual cells; you make changes at the column level, and when you change something on a particular column, it affects all rows in the table.

Preparing the Data

Now that the data has been imported, we need to do some additional work to get it ready for use.

Creating Relationships Between the Tables

A relationship needs to be created between the imported Income data and the Sales data. Because this is Median Income by State, we relate it to the DimGeography table joined on the state name:

1. Click the **Design** tab above the toolbar. This is where we can modify the data that has been imported into PowerPivot.

   Select **Manage Relationships** (as shown in Figure 9.8), and a dialog box appears displaying the existing relationships. Click the **Create** button to launch the Create Relationship dialog.

FIGURE 9.8   Manage relationships.

2. Select **State Median Income** for the Table, and **States** for the Column. Then select **DimGeography** for the Related Lookup Table and the **StateProvinceName** for the Related Lookup Column as shown in Figure 9.9.

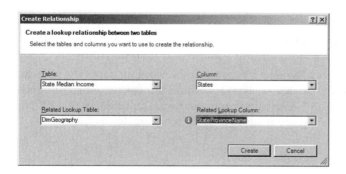

FIGURE 9.9   Create a relationship.

3. You will notice that PowerPivot immediately puts an information bullet next to the Related Lookup column. This is because relationships need to be defined in a one-to-many direction, and currently this is defined in the reverse direction. However, PowerPivot automatically corrects this issue when the Create button is clicked. Click the **Create** button to create this relationship. The new relationship is now listed along with the others in the Manage Relationships dialog.

Adding Calculated Fields

We could use the Median Income values as they are, but it is more useful from an analysis standpoint to have these grouped into income categories. PowerPivot includes a rich expression language known as DAX, short for *Data Analysis Expressions*, which are similar to Excel functions and can be used to add calculated fields to the data model. To provide income groupings, we use a series of IF statements.

1. Select the **State Median Income** tab to select that table.
2. Click the **Add** button on the toolbar as shown in Figure 9.10.

FIGURE 9.10   Adding a calculated column.

3. Enter the following DAX expression into the Function box (fx):

   ```
   =IF([2008 MedianIncome] < 40000, "< 40k",
    IF([2008 MedianIncome] < 45000, "40-45k"
    IF([2008 MedianIncome] < 50000, "45-50k",
      IF([2008 MedianIncome] < 55000, "50-55k", "55k +"))))
   ```

4. After you enter the expression, a new column named CalculatedColumn1 is added to the table. Right-click the column name and rename it to **IncomeGroup**.

   You might notice that the expression doesn't appear to be working correctly, because all rows are shown with a value of '55k+'. That is because our calculated column is a numeric calculation, but the [2008 MedianIncome] field was imported as a text field. By default, PowerPivot imports flat file fields as strings, but provides the ability to change the data type for any field.

5. Select the column heading for the 2008 MedianIncome.

6. Select the **Home** tab on the toolbar and select **Data Type** in the Formatting portion of the toolbar. From the drop-down list of options, select **Whole Number** as shown in Figure 9.11.

   The Calculated IncomeGroup automatically recalculates and now looks as expected.

7. To have this table match the naming convention of the others, right-click the tab for the table and change the name from State Median Income to **DimIncomeLevel**.

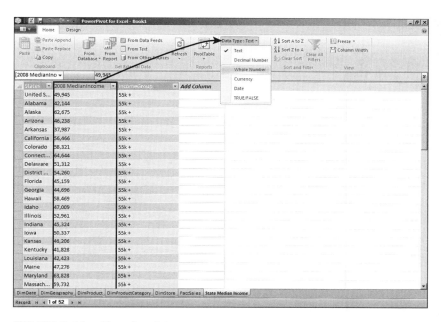

FIGURE 9.11   Changing data types.

Hiding Unwanted Fields

During the import process, PowerPivot provides the opportunity to select which fields will be imported. This is useful for eliminating fields that have no use for analysis, such as the ETL tracking fields.

However, some fields, such as Primary Key fields, are necessary for the table relationships and need to be imported, but ideally these shouldn't be exposed to the end users. PowerPivot provides an opportunity to hide those fields and any other unnecessary fields, as well:

1. From the PowerPivot window, select the **FactSales** table.
2. Select the **Design** toolbar, and then select **Hide and Unhide** from the toolbar.
3. PowerPivot provides the option to hide or show each field in the PowerPivot window as well as in any PivotTables or PivotCharts that would be created (see Figure 9.12). In general, hide internal-only fields from both PowerPivot and PivotTables, and display Key fields in PowerPivot window for design purposes but hide them from PivotTables so that they are not exposed to end users.
4. Move through each of the tables and hide/unhide columns as necessary.
5. At this point, the data has been imported and prepared. Save the file.

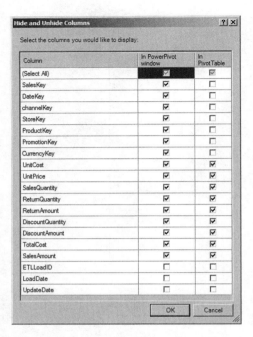

FIGURE 9.12   Hiding and unhiding columns.

Presenting the Data

As mentioned earlier, the PowerPivot window can be thought of as a data design surface, with the original Excel worksheet then as the presentation design surface. PowerPivot provides several layout options for creating PivotTables, PivotCharts, or combinations of the two:

1. From the PowerPivot window, select **PivotTable** from the toolbar and **PivotTable** from the drop-down list as shown in Figure 9.13.

2. Select **New Worksheet**. If you are familiar with creating PivotTables, this process will be familiar; however some significant differences exist, including the following (see Figure 9.14):

   ▶ The field list on the right side of the screen is not the standard PivotTable field list. This is actually a PowerPivot field list.

   ▶ All the tables are listed the same way. There is no distinction in PowerPivot between fact tables and dimension tables as there is when using Excel against an Analysis Services OLAP cube.

   ▶ PowerPivot introduces the idea of slicers, which provide enhanced options for filtering and interacting with the data.

3. Expand DimIncomeLevel and drag IncomeGroup to the Row Labels pane.

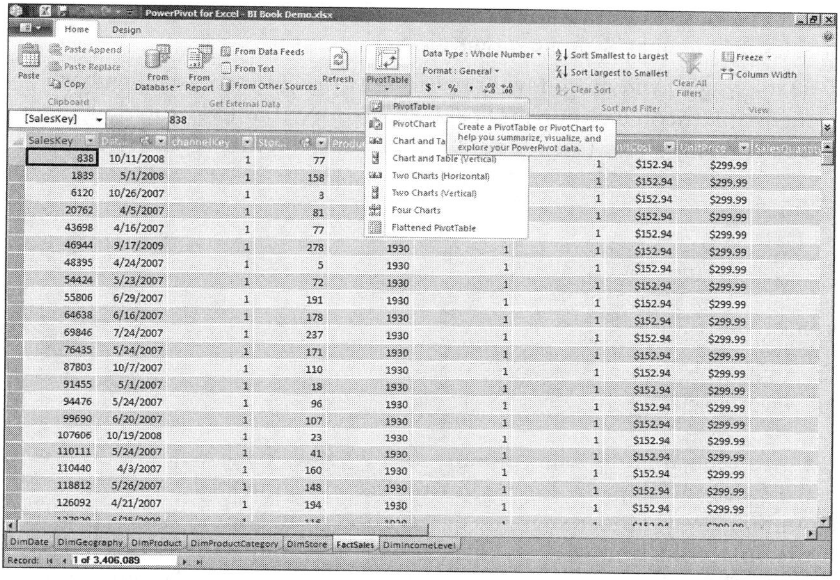

FIGURE 9.13   Creating a PivotTable from the PowerPivot window.

FIGURE 9.14   PowerPivot field list.

4. Expand FactSales and drag SalesAmount to the Values pane. You now have a basic PivotTable of Sales by IncomeGroup as shown in Figure 9.15.

   From the PivotTable, select the drop-down next to Row Labels and clear the check mark next to the blank Income Group and click **OK**. Notice that the drop-down icon has now changed from an arrow to a funnel to indicate that a filter is in effect.

Row Labels ▾	Sum of SalesAmount
40-45k	$ 46,289,982
45-50k	$ 1,197,347,744
50-55k	$ 782,369,147
55k +	$ 5,010,649,585
	$ 5,377,001,151
Grand Total	$ 12,413,657,609

FIGURE 9.15   Initial PivotTable.

5. Expand FactSales, and again drag SalesAmount to the Values pane. SalesAmount will now be reflected twice in the pane. Right-click the second SumOfSalesAmount entry, select Summarize By, and change the aggregation from Sum to Average. Now there is both the Total Sales and Average Sales by income group in the PivotTable. Highlight the cells under Sum of Sales Amount and Average of Sales Amount and format as currency.

6. Expand DimDate and drag CalendarYear to the Slicers Vertical pane. A slicer pane is now added to the worksheet. Slicers provide an intuitive way for users to filter the results; a slicer shows values that have data in black text and values that don't have data in gray text. At first glance, it might seem as though the values in the slicer are not ordered, but they are. However, the values with data come first, followed by the values without data.

7. Expand DimProductCategory and drag ProductCategoryName to the Slicers Vertical pane (see Figure 9.16). Click through the various product categories and notice that the average sale amount is definitely higher for the higher income levels.

We now have a tool for analyzing sales by income level or any of the other attributes in our data model.

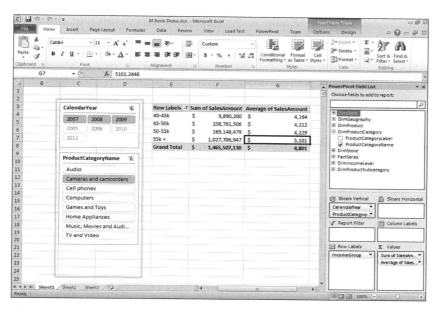

FIGURE 9.16   PivotTable with slicers.

Summary

PowerPivot is one of the more exciting additions to the Microsoft BI suite. It is a tool that enables users to process literally millions of rows of data extremely quickly, allows creation of relationships between different sets of data, and leverages the familiar user interface of Microsoft Excel.

In this chapter, we used PowerPivot to combine more than three million records of sales data with third-party Median Income data, and produced a flexible and user-friendly analysis tool to analyze average sales by income level.

Best Practices

The following are best practices from this chapter:

▶ Filter off fields that will not have any analytic value during import (ETL fields, for example).

▶ Include fields that *might* have analytic value during import, and then hide them if they are not immediately necessary, because it is easy to just un-hide them if the need arises.

▶ When trying to lighten the data volume, do not bother filtering small dimension tables; they likely have only a few hundred records. Instead, try to identify ways to filter the fact data if possible. For example, if the analysis will only be for 2008-2009, but the data source provides data from 2005 forward, filter off the fact data prior to 2008 to significantly minimize the data volume that PowerPivot needs to manage.

▶ PowerPivot is great for a variety of end-user situations, but if Parent/Child dimensions, Role-Playing dimensions, or drill-down hierarchies are required, Analysis Services is the better option. In these cases, PowerPivot might be useful for business analysts as a rapid prototyping tool that could aid in the design of a full-fledged Analysis Services cube.

CHAPTER 10

PowerPivot for SharePoint

The preceding chapter discussed how PowerPivot for Excel is a powerful tool for end users to create analytic applications. However, without some management of these applications, they are unlikely to become reliable enterprise tools that benefit the organization. This kind of application management is one of the primary benefits of SharePoint, and this chapter explores PowerPivot for SharePoint.

Overview of PowerPivot for SharePoint

IT departments have their hands full maintaining mission-critical enterprise applications and developing new enterprise applications to meet the needs of the business. As a result, business users often end up developing their own departmental applications for data analysis. Although these applications often prove quite useful, they do not receive the management benefit that IT can provide, such as keeping the applications accessible, current, and organized.

This situation represents a significant risk to an organization. Often, the business user who created the application moves on to a different department or leaves the company, and then these departmental tools either die or IT has to scramble to become familiar with an application that they had no part in developing.

The ideal scenario is to have a tool that enables business users to create a variety of analytic applications themselves and then those applications can be placed in an environment where IT can manage the distribution and data requirements. This will also enable IT to monitor the usage of these applications to plan future resources and development. This scenario illustrates the benefit of PowerPivot for SharePoint.

Installing PowerPivot for SharePoint

The process of installing PowerPivot for SharePoint is obviously impacted by the kind of SharePoint environment that is intended to host the service. The simplest installation is a single-server SharePoint installation, but this is really only practical for evaluation environments or very small production environments. A typical PowerPivot for SharePoint installation is to a multiserver SharePoint farm. However, because of the tight integration of PowerPivot with several SharePoint services, this installation path involves several complex steps.

As a result, the smoothest approach to installing PowerPivot for SharePoint is to make this part of an initial farm install. Of course, that is not a requirement, and Microsoft has developed excellent installation guides for installing PowerPivot for SharePoint on existing farms, but installation to an existing multiserver SharePoint farm is the most complex installation path. For this reason, this section does not attempt to address all the different configurations in detail, but instead addresses single server installation and multiserver installation from a high level, intending to provide sufficient information to guide the installation process.

Hardware and Software Requirements

Server sizing and capacity planning depend on numerous factors, but the biggest variable for PowerPivot servers is memory. Because PowerPivot for SharePoint is a SQL 2008 R2/SharePoint 2010 feature, the minimum system requirements are essentially the same as for those two applications. In addition, because PowerPivot uses an in-memory data analysis engine, the application server that will host PowerPivot for SharePoint should have enough additional memory to accommodate the expected concurrent file use. For example, to support 20 different PowerPivot applications, each 1GB in size, an additional 20GB of memory is needed on the server (even if more than 20 users will be accessing these applications).

Microsoft's recommended standard configuration for a PowerPivot server includes the following:

- ► 64-bit Quad-core processor running at a minimum of 3GHz
- ► 32GB to 64GB of RAM
- ► 80GB to 100GB of storage (because PowerPivot caches data files on disk)
- ► Windows Server 2008 SP2 or Windows Server 2008 R2 (64-bit)
- ► SharePoint 2010 with Excel Services and Secure Store Service
- ► SQL Server 2008 R2 Enterprise

New Single-Server Install

The following steps are for a single server installation of SharePoint and PowerPivot:

1. Prepare domain accounts for the SharePoint Service accounts and the SQL Service accounts.

DOMAIN ACCOUNT

A domain account is *required* for PowerPivot. If this is a standalone server used for evaluation, it must be a domain controller. The installation rule checkers will warn about this being a domain controller, but those warnings can be ignored because there is no way to bypass the domain account requirement for PowerPivot. Running on a Domain controller is only recommended for evaluation purposes and is *not* recommended for a production installation as it presents security risks.

---

2. Launch the SharePoint 2010 Prerequisite Installer to ensure all prerequisites are installed, and then reboot.

3. Launch SharePoint 2010 setup in Administrator mode and choose the Complete installation.

4. Do *not* configure the server yet! When prompted to configure the server, click **Cancel**. The PowerPivot for SharePoint installation configures the new SharePoint 2010 farm.

5. Launch the SQL Server 2008 R2 setup in Administrator mode and select the **New Installation or Add Features to an Existing Installation** option.

6. After the setup files are installed, select **New Installation or Add Shared Features** for installation type, as shown in Figure 10.1.

7. After entering the product key and accepting the licensing terms, you are prompted to select a setup role. Select **SQL Server PowerPivot for SharePoint**, **New Server**, as shown in Figure 10.2.

8. Proceed through the next few screens. The installer tests the installation rules, prompts for SharePoint farm configuration, and creates a new instance of the SQL Server Engine and the Analysis Services Engine. When prompted for the service accounts, enter the service accounts created earlier.

9. Be sure to add the current user on both the Database Engine Configuration screen and the Analysis Services Configuration screen so that the administrator is set up for those services.

10. Click through the remaining confirmation screens and initiate the install process. This process could take up to 30 minutes.

11. After successful installation, click **Close**.

You should now be able to verify the successful installation by browsing to http://<*machinename*> (with *machine name* being the name of the server). The Welcome page of the SharePoint 2010 site should load, and you should see an entry for the PowerPivot Gallery on the left-side navigation, as shown in Figure 10.3.

10

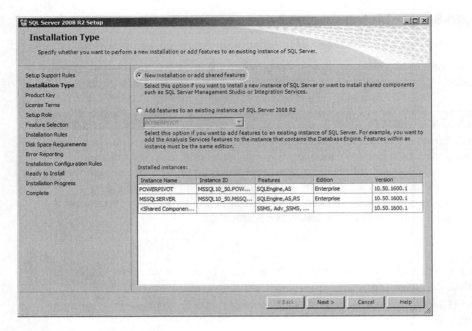

FIGURE 10.1   Installation type.

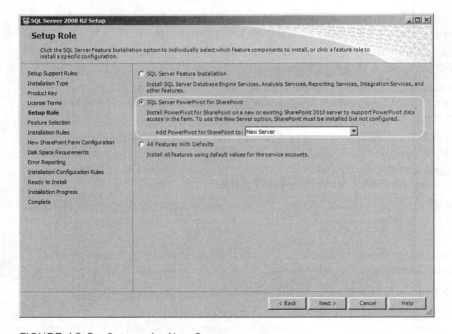

FIGURE 10.2   Setup role: New Server.

FIGURE 10.3   SharePoint home page with PowerPivot Gallery.

You have now completed a successful single-server installation of PowerPivot for SharePoint.

Multiserver Farm Install

In the steps for performing a single-server install, SharePoint was first installed but not configured, and the PowerPivot Installation Wizard handled the configuration of SharePoint. When installing PowerPivot in a multiserver farm, the SharePoint farm needs to be set up and configured first, and then the PowerPivot application servers can be added. Note that PowerPivot needs to be installed using a Farm Administrator account, otherwise SQL Server setup will not pass the pre-requisites tests. The following steps assume that this is a new farm install. Detailed instructions on SharePoint installation are beyond the scope of this chapter, but a summary of the steps involved is provided for guidance. If the farm already exists, you may skip ahead to the section on preparing the application servers.

INSTALLATION TIP

Getting the installation environment set up correctly can sometimes be a challenge. It is a good idea to first perform a single-server installation to a *virtual machine* (VM) to become acquainted with the installation process and to get all the services configured properly. Using a VM will also enable you to undo any changes more easily if you desire to configure things differently.

1. If not already done, prepare domain accounts for the SharePoint Service accounts and the SQL Service accounts following standard best practices for SharePoint farm design.

2. Prepare the database server.

   ▶ Install SQL Server 2008 R2 on the database server.

3. Prepare the *web front-end servers* (WFEs) and create the farm.

   ▶ Install SharePoint on the *first* WFE using the Complete Installation option. At the end of the installation process, check the box to **Run the SharePoint Products and Technologies Configuration Wizard**. This will enable you to create the new farm. Step-by-step instructions for this process are beyond the scope of this chapter, but be sure to enable the following services:

      ▶ Excel Services

      ▶ Secure Store Service

      ▶ Usage and Health data collection (see the "Monitoring PowerPivot" section later in this chapter for more information)

   ▶ Install SharePoint on any additional WFEs and run the Configuration Wizard to join to the farm and specify the database server and passphrase that were established earlier.

4. Prepare the application servers.

   ▶ Install SharePoint on the application servers, run the Configuration Wizard and join to the farm, and specify the database server and passphrase that were established earlier.

5. At this point, the SharePoint farm is installed and configured. The next step is to install PowerPivot on the application server.

   ▶ On the application server, launch the SQL Server 2008 R2 setup from the installation media. Select **Installation**, **New Installation or add features to an existing installation**.

   ▶ Proceed through the next few screens, and on the Setup Role screen, select **SQL Server PowerPivot for SharePoint**, and choose **Existing Farm** from the drop-down list, as shown in Figure 10.4.

   ▶ Proceed through the next few screens, and on the Server Configuration screen, specify the Analysis Services service account. Also be sure to add the current user to the Analysis Services Engine screen so that the SharePoint Farm Admin has access to Analysis Services.

   ▶ Proceed through the remaining screens to complete the installation. After it's complete, launch SharePoint Central Administration and navigate to **System Settings**, **Manage Servers in this Farm**, and you can confirm that the SQL Server PowerPivot System Service is running on the application server.

6. Deploy and configure PowerPivot on the SharePoint farm.

   ▶ From Central Administration, navigate to **System Settings**, **Manage Farm Solutions**.

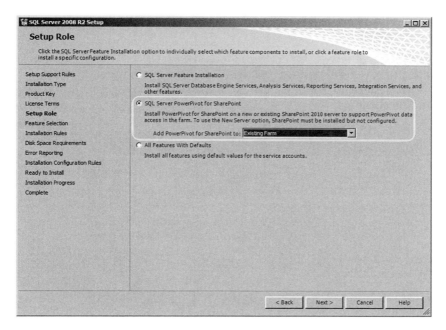

FIGURE 10.4   Setup role: Existing Farm.

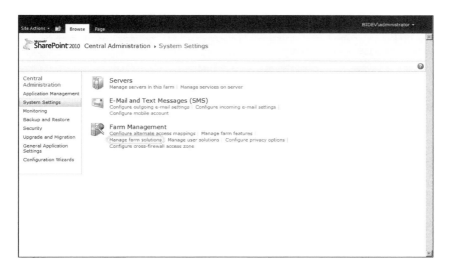

FIGURE 10.5   Manage farm solutions.

From here, you should see two solutions: powerpivotfarm.wsp and powerpivotwebapp.wsp. The powerpivotwebapp.wsp is probably already deployed to Central Administration (notice the port number), but still needs to be deployed to the default web application. Click the **Deploy Solution** link and specify when you want the deployment to occur. Be sure to select the default web application from the Deploy To drop-down.

> ▶ Next, a PowerPivot service application is required for the WFEs to communicate with the PowerPivot services via the PowerPivot System Service proxy. From Central Administration, navigate to **Application Management**, **Manage Service Applications**.

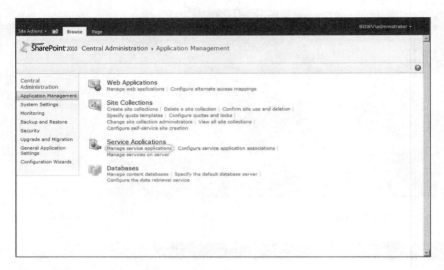

FIGURE 10.6   Manage service applications.

7. Select **New** from the menu bar and choose **SQL Server PowerPivot Service Application**.

FIGURE 10.7   New PowerPivot service application.

A configuration screen will appear allowing specification of application pool and proxy settings. Generally, it is considered more secure to have application services running under separate application pool IDs. However, the PowerPivot service application and the PowerPivot System Service require Farm account rights to access the Secure Store Service database. For this reason, it is recommended to change the following two settings:

▶ Application Pool: Select **Use Existing Application Pool** and select **SharePoint Web Services System**.

▶ Check the box at the bottom of the page to add the proxy to the Default Proxy group.

8. Lastly, the PowerPivot feature needs to be activated. Launch the default website from a WFE and select **Site Actions**, **Site Settings**. Under Site Collection Administration, select **Site Collection Features**. Scroll down to the PowerPivot Feature Integration for Site Collections entry and click the **Activate** button, as shown in Figure 10.8.

FIGURE 10.8   PowerPivot feature activation.

9. Stop Excel Calculation Services on the WFE.

Because the SharePoint instance on the WFE was installed as a Complete installation, *Excel Calculation Services* (ECS) are installed and running. However, if the instance of ECS on the WFE tries to connect to PowerPivot, it will fail because the Analysis Services OLE DB driver is not installed on the WFE. Because this farm is architected for PowerPivot work to be handled by the application server, ECS should only be running on the application server and should therefore be stopped on the WFEs:

▶ From Central Administration, navigate to **System Settings**, **Manage Services on Server**.

10

> ▸ From the drop-down, make sure that the server selected is the WFE.

> ▸ Scroll down to Excel Calculation Services and click **Stop**.

10. Creating the PowerPivot Gallery.

    For setup on an existing SharePoint farm, navigate to **More Options** in the **Site Actions** menu, find **PowerPivot Gallery** in the Libraries column, and create a new library.

PowerPivot is now installed, configured, and active on the SharePoint Farm.

IS KERBEROS REQUIRED??

When accessing data on a multiserver SharePoint Farm, users have to be authenticated from the WFE, to the other servers. This is often referred to as the *double-hop* situation (although with PowerPivot it would be more than a double-hop). The way this was handled in MOSS 2007 was to configure Kerberos delegation, which was often very frustrating to get working correctly. With SharePoint 2010, Microsoft has introduced the Windows Identity Foundation, which provides a claims authentication mechanism. As a result, Kerberos is *not* required for PowerPivot to work in a multiserver environment in SharePoint 2010.

Using PowerPivot for SharePoint

PowerPivot applications are created using Excel 2010 with the PowerPivot add-in, as covered in the preceding chapter. After a PowerPivot application is created, it should be uploaded to the SharePoint PowerPivot Gallery to be shared across the organization.

PowerPivot Gallery

When documents are loaded into a typical SharePoint library, they are presented in a simple list. This works fine, but wouldn't it be great if the documents were able to be previewed in a library visually, like how photos are presented with thumbnail previews? Well, that is precisely what the PowerPivot Gallery provides for PowerPivot applications. Although this might seem like simple eye-candy, this has significant benefits for usability and user adoption. It's much easier for users to remember an application visually than simply by the filename. Also, the ability to visually review the applications in the gallery makes them more engaging, which can lead to increased user adoption.

SILVERLIGHT AND THE GALLERY

The PowerPivot Gallery uses Silverlight for the various presentations. As a result, Silverlight needs to be installed to use the gallery. In addition, Silverlight is a 32-bit-only application, so the 32-bit version of Internet Explorer is required, as well.

The PowerPivot Gallery offers three different presentations: Gallery view, Carousel view, and Theater view. These are selectable from the Library ribbon, as shown in Figure 10.9.

FIGURE 10.9   PowerPivot Gallery view selection.

▶ **Gallery view:** The Gallery view is the most basic of the views and lists a preview of the file along with a smaller thumbnail view of each sheet in the file. As you hover over each thumbnail, the primary view changes to show that sheet. Clicking the primary view or the thumbnail launches the PowerPivot viewer and loads the file full screen for interactivity.

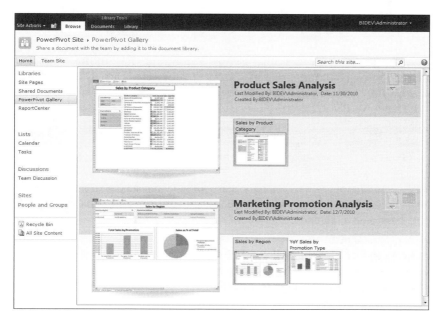

FIGURE 10.10   PowerPivot Gallery view.

10

▶ **Carousel view:** The Carousel view replaces the vertical scrolling with a rotating presentation, with only a single PowerPivot file sheet shown at any one time. Clicking the center sheet launches the sheet in the PowerPivot viewer.

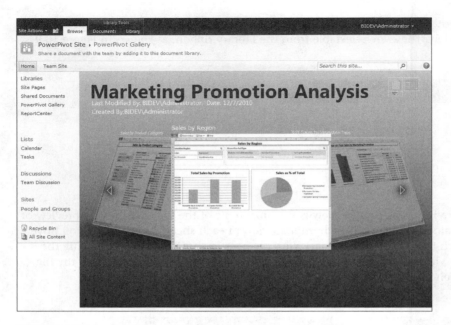

FIGURE 10.11   PowerPivot Carousel view.

▶ **Theater view:** The Theater view is similar to how you would view photos, with the selected sheet nearly full screen in size and a series of thumbnails across the bottom of the screen with the ability to scroll right to left. Clicking the center sheet launches the sheet in the PowerPivot viewer.

POWERPIVOT APPLICATIONS = THE NEW BRIEFING BOOKS?

Microsoft acquired ProClarity a number of years ago and has been incorporating the ProClarity technologies into the *business intelligence* (BI) stack, primarily through PerformancePoint Server. One of the nice features that ProClarity provided was the notion of a "briefing book." Analytic views would be collected into a briefing book, and these books would be stored in libraries.

One of the benefits of this briefing book approach was that the analytic views could be presented in a specific sequence (an analytic path, if you will) to help the user see the complete business picture. In the process of migrating away from ProClarity, one option for reproducing this briefing book concept is to create an Excel file with the sheets organized in the sequence required. Excel Services provides this capability already, but the PowerPivot Galley makes it possible to preview the sheets in the browser, without even opening the file, which is pretty cool and can have a powerful effect from a usability and user-adoption standpoint. When the user wants to perform analysis, he or she can simply open the file and navigate through the sequence of sheets.

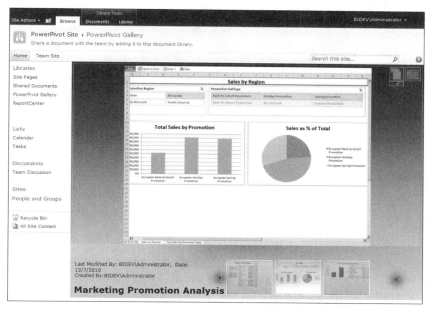

FIGURE 10.12   PowerPivot Theater view.

Data Refresh and Snapshots

If the PowerPivot Gallery just provided static thumbnail views, that would be useful, but the gallery is actually more intelligent than that and can refresh the data in the PowerPivot workbooks to keep them current.

When viewing the workbooks in the gallery, you will notice two faint icons in the upper-right corner for each workbook. The icon on the right, which looks like a calendar, is the Manage Data Refresh function. Clicking this icon launches a page where a data refresh schedule can be created. Currently, the highest frequency that can be set for data refresh is daily. This can be useful for applications where the data is loaded nightly, because the PowerPivot applications could then be set to refresh each morning.

When a PowerPivot workbook gets refreshed, PowerPivot needs to take a new "snapshot" of each sheet for visual presentation in the gallery. The PowerPivotGallery component initiates this snapshot process automatically, but if a user attempts to look at the gallery before the snapshot has been updated, PowerPivot places an hourglass icon on the outdated views as a visual indicator that these views are not yet current. (see Figure 10.13). Keep in mind that this hourglass is simply an indicator that the visual snapshot has not been updated. If the user were to open the workbook, the data in the workbook would be current.

10

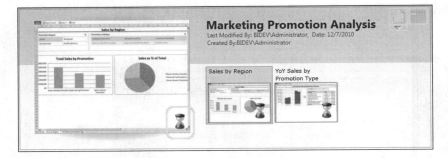

FIGURE 10.13   Out-of-date snapshot images.

Publishing Workbooks

Publishing PowerPivot workbooks to SharePoint can be done by either the Upload function from within the SharePoint PowerPivot Gallery, the Save As option from within Excel, or the Save and Send option for publishing from within Excel. Although all of these methods produce the same result (that is, getting the file into SharePoint), the mechanisms and options used are different.

▶ The Upload option is initiated from within the SharePoint PowerPivot Gallery. The Upload function is a synchronous transfer and is the fastest option but also results in more bandwidth usage than the Excel save options.

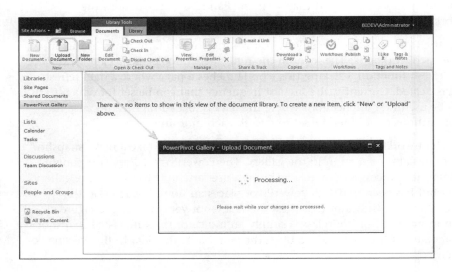

FIGURE 10.14   Upload initiated from SharePoint.

▶ The Save As option is initiated from within Excel by selecting **Save As** and browsing to the PowerPivot Gallery in SharePoint as the destination. This option uses an asynchronous transfer, which enables the bandwidth demand to be more balanced, but takes more time than the Upload option.

▶ The Save and Send option is similar to the Save As option but enables the user to specify publishing options, including selecting which sheets of the workbook to expose in the browser and setting parameter values that may be used in the worksheet.

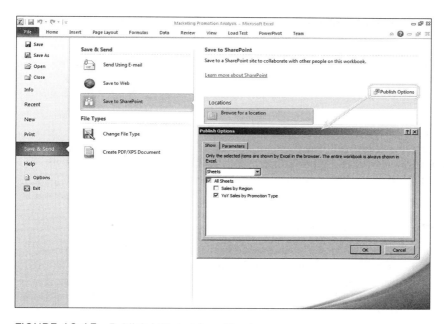

FIGURE 10.15   Publish initiated from Excel.

Although there is no way to force a particular PowerPivot publishing method, each organization should consider whether there is a preferred method and recommend this to their users.

Controlling Data Exposure and Spreadmarts

Although the uploading of PowerPivot workbooks is beneficial to an organization, allowing these workbooks to be downloaded can be very detrimental. Because these PowerPivot applications contain significant data and may also contain business rules, allowing them to be downloaded can be risky. In addition, downloading these applications usually results in multiple copies of various versions of the application, which is a very unmanageable scenario. This scenario has been thought of as a datamart of spreadsheets, or a spreadmart. This can be controlled by preventing users from downloading these applications.

To prevent users from downloading the workbooks into Excel, Excel Services provides a SharePoint group named "Viewers." Users placed into the "Viewers" group can still fully interact with the workbook, including changing the slicer values, but they are prevented from downloading the Excel file.

Monitoring PowerPivot

One of the biggest advantages of a tool like PowerPivot is the ability to give end users the freedom to build the analytic applications that they find useful for managing the business. However, one of the biggest concerns for SharePoint administrators is being able to manage the effect that these applications will have on the rest of the SharePoint environment and to plan for future resources.

To meet this need, PowerPivot for SharePoint includes some very useful tools for monitoring which files are being used and how they are performing. The SharePoint Usage and Health Data Collection service is used to collect this information, and the PowerPivot Management Dashboard is used to monitor this information.

Enabling Usage and Health Data Collection

The Usage and Health Data Collection service is new to SharePoint 2010. This service collects and logs SharePoint health indicators and usage metrics for analysis and reporting purposes. During the multiserver farm install process, there was a statement about making sure the Usage and Health Data Collection service was enabled. To do this, follow these steps:

1. Go to Central Administration and navigate to **Monitoring, Configure Usage and Health Data Collection**.

2. Confirm that the **Enable Usage Data Collection** box is checked, and then check the boxes for PowerPivot data collection, namely the following:

   ▶ **PowerPivot Connections**

   ▶ **PowerPivot Load Data Usage**

   ▶ **PowerPivot Unload Data Usage**

   ▶ **PowerPivot Query Usage**

3. Confirm that the **Enable Health Data Collection** box is checked.

Using the PowerPivot Management Dashboard

To launch the dashboard, go to Central Administration and navigate to **General Application Settings, PowerPivot Management Dashboard.**

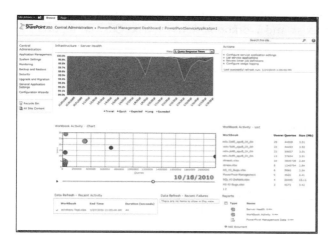

FIGURE 10.16   PowerPivot management dashboard.

The dashboard is divided into the following sections:

▶ **Infrastructure - Server Health:** Provides graphical trend charts for the following statistics:

Query Response Times

Average Instance CPU

Average Instance Memory

Activity

Performance

▶ **Actions:** Links to PowerPivot-related settings within SharePoint.

▶ **Workbook Activity:** This is a chart of the number of queries by the number of users over time, but it is more than just a static chart. It enables you to "play" the chart and watch how the usage occurs over the time span presented. This is useful for tracking peak activity and determining when additional resources might be necessary.

▶ **Data Refresh:** The automatic data refresh capability of PowerPivot is one of its most useful features. As such, it's extremely important to know whether those refreshes succeed or fail, and if they fail, why. The Data Refresh section contains a list of

10

recent activity, which can be drilled down to see all history for a particular data file. The Data Refresh section also contains a list of recent failures for troubleshooting.

▶ **Reports:** The Server Health and Workbook Activity sections are actually displays from a PowerPivot application, which is connected to an Analysis Services cube named *ITOps Sandbox*. The Excel files that provide that information are listed in the Reports section as Server Health.xlsx and Workbook Activity.xlsx. Custom reports can also be created against this cube.

Summary

While PowerPivot enables end users to create powerful analytic applications, the PowerPivot features of SharePoint enable IT to keep the applications accessible, current, and organized.

In this chapter, we explored how PowerPivot for SharePoint is installed, how the PowerPivot Gallery can be used to access and refresh these applications, and how the PowerPivot Management Dashboard can be used to keep things running smoothly.

Best Practices

The following are best practices while working with PowerPivot for SharePoint:

▶ **Don't skimp on memory:** Because PowerPivot for SharePoint loads the workbooks into the server's memory, the application server hosting PowerPivot services should have plenty of memory. The recommended amount of memory for an enterprise PowerPivot server is 32GB to 64GB. This will vary from organization to organization, but the determining factor is the number and size of concurrent workbooks that will be used.

▶ **Review and set file size limits:** Because PowerPivot applications include the actual data, the files can be larger than what is commonly stored in SharePoint. By default, SharePoint limits the size of uploaded files to 50MB and Excel Services limits the size of a workbook to 10MB. These limits should be reviewed and adjusted as necessary to meet the requirements for the environment.

▶ **In a multiserver SharePoint farm, turn off Excel Calculation Services on the WFEs:** If the instance of ECS on the WFE tries to connect to the PowerPivot application service, it will fail because the Analysis Services OLE DB driver is not installed on the WFE.

▶ **Turn off the Excel Web Access warning:** Because PowerPivot applications require Excel Services to query external data, users will frequently be prompted with the SharePoint Excel Web Access external data warning. In the Excel Services Application settings, the Warn on Refresh check box should be cleared.

PART V

Visio Services

Configuring Visio Graphics Service

Visio Graphics Service is a new feature in SharePoint Server 2010 Enterprise Edition. It allows publishing of data-driven web drawings from Microsoft Visio 2010 Professional or Premium. It enables users to view web drawings in the browser without installing Visio on their local machines. Users can connect their diagrams to one or more data sources, including Microsoft Excel, SQL Server, and SharePoint Foundation Services lists. The Visio Graphics Service enables users to create visually compelling, interactive dashboards by combining Visio diagrams, real-time data, and different applications in SharePoint Server 2010. Users can also schedule a job to refresh the linked data at specific time intervals.

Adding the Visio Graphics Service

By default, Visio Graphics Service is included when a web application is created. However, if the application is set up via a custom selection of services and Visio Graphics Service is not included in the initial creation, follow these steps in SharePoint 2010 Central Administration to add the service using Farm Configuration Wizard:

1. Click the **Configuration Wizards** link on the Central Administration page and then click the **Launch the Farm Configuration Wizard** link.

2. Click the **Start the Wizard** link and then check the Visio Graphics Service check box.

NOTE

If the Visio Graphics Service check box is already checked and disabled, it means Visio Graphics Service was installed previously. You can click Cancel and come out of the Farm Configuration Wizard. You can ignore steps 3 and 4.

3. After checking the Visio Graphics Service check box, click the **Next** button. The wizard then asks you to configure a new site. You can click the **Skip** button to avoid creating a new site.

4. Click the **Finish** button to complete the Farm Configuration Wizard. Doing so brings you back to the Central Administration page.

5. Click the **Manage Service Applications** link on the Central Administration home page. This will bring you to the Service Applications page as shown in Figure 11.1. Confirm that Visio Graphics Application Service is already started on Service Applications page.

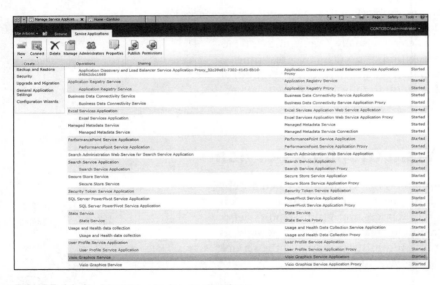

FIGURE 11.1   Manage service applications.

NOTE

It is not required to use the Farm Configuration Wizard only to add Visio Graphics Service to your SharePoint farm but it surely makes your job easy. You can add the Visio Graphics Service using a manual approach also. You can also use the Windows PowerShell command prompt to create Visio Graphics Service application. Detailed steps for adding Visio Graphics Service to your site are shared by Microsoft Technet website at http://technet.microsoft.com/en-us/library/ee524059.aspx.

Configuring Visio Graphics Service Global Settings

Visio Graphics Service has some global configuration settings that optimize performance, caching, and security. You can configure these settings from the SharePoint 2010 Central Administration page as follows:

1. Click the **Manage Web Applications** link on the Central Administration home page and then click **Manage Service Applications**.

2. In the list of service applications, click the **Visio Graphics Service** link.

3. Click the **Global Settings** link; it will bring you to the Visio Graphics Service Settings page as shown in the Figure 11.2 to configure following:

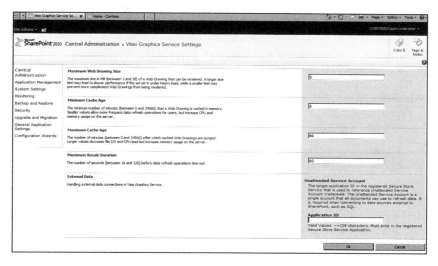

FIGURE 11.2   Visio Graphics Service settings.

▶ **Maximum Web Drawing Size:** You can change the maximum size of a web drawing that Visio Graphics Service will render using this global setting. By default, the maximum web drawing size is 5MB.

▶ **Minimum Cache Age:** Caching enables multiple users to view the same diagram without forcing the server to render it every time. If a diagram changes, it is automatically removed from the cache. The default minimum cache age is 5 minutes. Value ranges from 0 to 34560 minutes.

▶ **Maximum Cache Age:** Defines the maximum storage time for frequently accessed items. The default maximum cache age is 60 minutes. I/O and CPU

load decreases for larger Cache Age value but it increases memory usage on the
server.

▶ **Maximum Recalc Duration:** Defines the maximum time Visio Graphics
Service data refresh operation takes before it times out. By default, it takes 60
seconds before it times out.

▶ **External Data:** Defines the unattended service account used by Visio
Graphics Service to connect to external data sources such as SQL.

NOTE

If you are not sure which application ID to use for the unattended service account,
leave the application ID value blank for now. Chapter 13, "Visio Graphics Service
Security," shares more details about the unattended service account. Review Chapter
13 first before configuring the External Data global setting.

Configuring a Visio Graphics Service Global Settings Parameters by Using Windows PowerShell

One can also use Windows PowerShell command prompt to add Visio Graphics Service
application to their SharePoint farm. Steps shared below provide you more details on how
to use Windows PowerShell command prompt.

NOTE

Before moving forward with Windows PowerShell command prompt, verify that your user
id is the member of SharePoint_Shell_Access role. To learn more about PowerShell, go
to http://technet.microsoft.com/en-us/library/ee662539.aspx.

1. Click on the Start menu on your desktop.

2. Select All Programs from the Start menu and then Click on the Microsoft
   SharePoint 2010 Products folder.

3. Click on the SharePoint 2010 Management Shell to start the PowerShell
   command prompt.

4. Type the following syntax to manage the performance parameters in the Visio
   Graphics Service application, and then press ENTER:

```
Set-SPVisioPerformance -MaxDiagramCacheAge <Minutes> -MaxDiagramSize <SizeMB>-
MaxRecalcDuration<Seconds>-MinDiagramCacheAge<Minutes>-
VisioServiceApplication<VisioServiceApp>
```

5. Type the following syntax to manage the data configuration parameters in the
   Visio Graphics Service application, and then press ENTER:

```
Set-SPVisioExternalData -VisioServiceApplication <VisioServiceApp> -
UnattendedServiceAccountApplicationID <ApplicationID>
```

Visio Graphics Service Trusted Data Providers

Visio Graphics Service maintains a list of trusted data providers. If a user publishes a web drawing that is connected to a data source that is not trusted, Visio Graphics Service does not attempt to connect to it.

By default, data providers shared in Table 11.1 are trusted by Visio Graphics Service application. You can easily add or remove a provider from the SharePoint 2010 Central Administration page as by using following steps:

1. Click the **Manage Web Applications** link on the Central Administration home page and then click **Manage Service Applications**.

2. From the list of service applications, click the **Visio Graphics Service** link.

3. Click the **Trusted Data Providers** link. The system will take you to Visio Graphics Service Trusted Data Providers page as shown in Figure 11.3, where you can add, edit, or remove data providers.

TABLE 11.1   Trusted Data Providers

Provider	Provider ID	Provider Type
Microsoft SQL Server OLE DB Driver (MDAC)	SQLOLEDB	OLEDB
Microsoft SQL Server OLE DB Driver (MDAC SQL Server 2000)	SQLOLEDB.1	OLEDB
Microsoft SQL Server ODBC Driver (MDAC)	SQL Server	ODBC
Microsoft SQL Server ODBC DSN Driver (MDAC)	SQL Server	ODBC with DSN
Microsoft SQL Server OLE DB DSN Driver for ODBC	SQLOLEDB.1	ODBC with DSN
Microsoft SQL Server OLE DB Driver (SNAC)	SQLNCLI	OLEDB
Microsoft SQL Server OLE DB Driver (SNAC SQL Server 2005)	SQLNCLI.1	OLEDB
Microsoft SQL Server ODBC Driver (SNAC)	SQL Native Client	ODBC
Microsoft SQL Server ODBC DSN Driver (SNAC)	SQL Native Client	ODBC with DSN
Oracle Provider for OLE DB	OraOLEDB.Oracle.1	OLEDB

TABLE 11.1   Trusted Data Providers   continued

Provider	Provider ID	Provider Type
Oracle ODBC Driver for Oracle 9.2	Oracle in OraHome92	ODBC
Oracle ODBC DSN Driver for Oracle 9.2	Oracle in OraHome92	ODBC with DSN
IBM OLE DB Provider for DB2	IBMDADB2	OLEDB
IBM DB2 ODBC Driver	IBM DB2 ODBC DRIVER	ODBC
IBM DB2 ODBC DSN Driver	IBM DB2 ODBC DRIVER	ODBC with DSN
Microsoft SQL ODBC Driver	MSDASQL.1	ODBC
Microsoft SQL ODBC DSN Driver	MSDASQL.1	ODBC with DSN
Microsoft SharePoint List	WSSList	SharePoint List
Excel Web Services	Microsoft.Office.Visio.Server.EcsDataHandler, Microsoft.Office.Visio.Server, Version=14.0.0.0, Culture=neutral, PublicKeyToken=71e9bce111e9429c	Custom Data Provider

TIP

Most of the time, you do not need to make any changes with default data providers. You will be using the add/edit/remove feature mainly when you use custom data providers for your web drawings. Review Chapter 12, "Visio Graphics Service Development," to learn more about custom data providers.

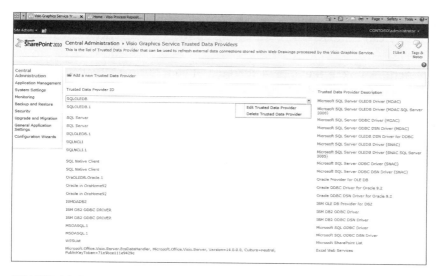

FIGURE 11.3   Trusted data providers.

TIP

You can also add, edit or delete trusted data providers using Windows PowerShell command prompt. Detailed steps are shared at following technet URL, http://technet. microsoft.com/en-us/library/ee524056.aspx.

Visio Process Repository Site Template

Visio Process Repository is a new SharePoint site template that contains a library for documentation and process diagrams. The Process Diagrams document library comes prepopulated with several templates that can be used to create new process diagrams. Because the Visio Process Repository is built on top of SharePoint 2010, users can also take advantage of other SharePoint features. For instance, you can configure workflows, set up automatic email notifications on document change, and view the revision history for a given document.

NOTE

It is not necessary to use the Visio Process Repository site template to store your Visio web drawings. Published Visio drawings (.vdw files) can be stored in any SharePoint document library to be opened in a browser.

In just a few clicks, a SharePoint administrator can create a Visio Process Repository. Visio Process Repository can be added to your existing Business Intelligence Center site as follows:

1. Click the **Site Actions** link in the upper-left corner of your Business Intelligence Center site, and then click the **More Options** link.

2. Select **Visio Process Repository** from the Items list as shown in Figure 11.4 and click the **More Options** button.

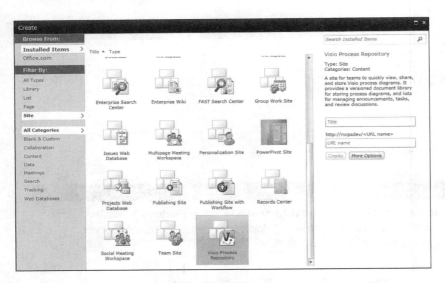

FIGURE 11.4   Creating a Visio Process Repository site.

3. Supply Title, Description, and Website Address text values of your choice. You can let the repository use the same permissions as the parent site for now. For Navigation Inheritance, select the **Yes** radio button to let the repository use the top link bar from the parent site.

4. Click the **Create** button to complete the process. Doing so creates a new link for Visio Process Repository on the top link bar as shown in Figure 11.5.

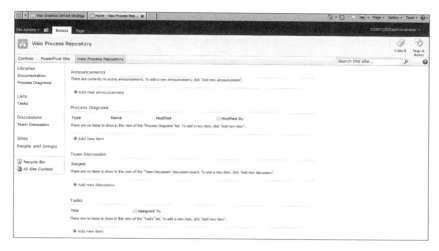

FIGURE 11.5   Visio Process Repository site.

Summary

Visio Graphics Service is a new feature in SharePoint 2010 Enterprise. It allows the sharing with others of data-driven Visio diagrams online in a browser. The Visio Process Repository site template comes out of the box in SharePoint 2010 and lets users effectively manage their Visio process diagrams.

This chapter walked through the process of configuring Visio Graphics Service for your existing Business Intelligence Center site and brought you to the point where you can start developing and publishing Visio diagrams. Review Chapter 12 to learn how to develop and publish data-driven Visio diagrams.

Best Practices

The following are best practices from this chapter:

▶ Before setting up the unattended service account, ensure that you have set up the Secure Store Service within SharePoint. Review Chapter 13 to learn more about unattended service account and Secure Store Service setup.

▶ By default, the maximum web drawing size is 5MB. You can increase or decrease the size based on your organization's storage policies. A larger size limit defined under Maximum Diagram Size global settings may slowdown system performance if the server is under heavy load, whereas a smaller value may prevent large drawings to display.

▶ Minimum and maximum cache age settings should be tuned based on how frequently data is refreshing and how often users are accessing web drawings.

Visio Graphics Service Development

To gain a full view of information that matters to your business requires both a high-level perspective and detailed data. Visio 2010 in integration with SharePoint 2010 lets you share your Visio drawings with your users in an effective manner. Users can see your real-time data through web drawings in their browsers without having Visio installed on their local machines. They can pan and zoom in the online diagram, follow hyperlinks embedded in shapes, and refresh the data manually or on a set schedule. They can interact with other SharePoint web parts to create visually compelling and interactive dashboards. Visio Graphics Service allows publishing diagrams directly from Visio Professional or Premium edition to a SharePoint document library.

Prerequisites

Developing Visio Graphics Service content is all done from Microsoft Visio 2010, which is installed as a separate component of Microsoft Office 2010. Data-driven Visio web drawings can be developed using either Microsoft Visio 2010 Professional or Premium. You can download a trial version of Visio 2010 Premium edition from http://technet.microsoft.com/en-us/evalcenter/ee390821.

> **NOTE**
>
> You can learn more about Microsoft Visio 2010 version differences at http://office.microsoft.com/en-us/visio/visio-edition-comparison-FX101838162.aspx.

This chapter requires that you have a basic understanding of how Visio drawings are created. We do not cover all available features of Visio 2010 Premium edition in this chapter. Our focus is mainly on how to create a data-driven Visio web drawing using data from Excel Services, SharePoint Foundation List, and SQL Server database.

In this chapter, we first develop a data-driven Visio web drawing using Visio 2010 Premium edition. We use multiple external data sources to pull data into the same drawing. The ContosoRetailDW database is used for all development work. After the Visio web drawing is created, we publish it online in our SharePoint 2010 document library. We review features available for browsing the drawing online. You also learn how to refresh the data embedded in the drawing manually and via automated schedule. Toward the end of this chapter, you learn how to make your drawing interactive by integrating it with other SharePoint 2010 web parts.

NOTE

You can download the ContosoRetailDW database from http://www.microsoft.com/downloads/en/details.aspx?FamilyID=868662DC-187A-4A85-B611-B7DF7DC909FC&displaylang=en.

Developing a Data-Driven Visio Web Drawing

To develop a data-driven Visio web drawing connected to an Excel workbook, first we need to confirm that workbook is hosted on a same SharePoint farm where we are planning to deploy our Visio web drawing. Also verify that Excel and Visio Graphics Services are running on the SharePoint farm. Once confirmed then set up a connection to that workbook using following steps:

1. Open Microsoft Visio 2010 Premium edition from the All Programs menu. A window similar to Figure 12.1 will pop up on your screen.

2. Create an empty drawing by selecting the **Blank Drawing** template from the File menu.

3. After a blank drawing has been created, click the **Data** tab on the top ribbon and then click **Link Data to Shapes**.

4. The Data Selector window will open as shown in Figure 12.2. Select the **Microsoft Excel Workbook** radio button, and then click **Next**.

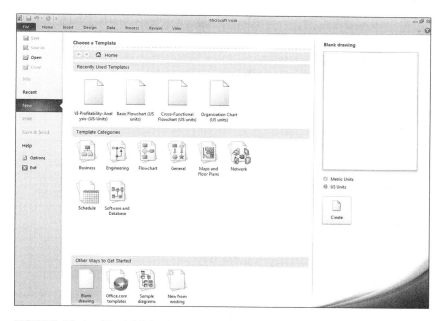

FIGURE 12.1   Blank Visio drawing.

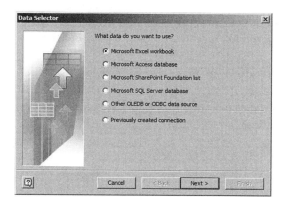

FIGURE 12.2   Data provider selection.

NOTE

For this section, we prepare an Excel data sheet manually and upload it to our SharePoint document library first. We use this Excel sheet as an external data source. I have executed the following SQL query against the ContosoRetailDW database to extract sales data by channel. You can either manually prepare this Excel sheet or use this book's resource material to access the ContosoSalesData Excel sheet.

```
SELECT       b.CalendarYear
           , a.ChannelKey
           , MAX(c.ChannelLabel) AS ChannelLabel
           , MAX(c.ChannelName) AS ChannelName
           , SUM(a.salesamount) AS SalesAmount
           , SUM(a.TotalCost) AS TotalCost
FROM         FactSales a
INNER JOIN   DimDate b ON a.Datekey = b.Datekey
INNER JOIN   DimChannel c ON a.ChannelKey = c.ChannelKey
GROUP BY     b.CalendarYear, a.ChannelKey
ORDER BY     b.CalendarYear, a.ChannelKey
```

5. You are now ask to provide the location of your Excel workbook as shown in Figure 12.3. Type the path where your Excel workbook is stored on SharePoint and then click **Next**.

6. Select the worksheet to use from the drop-down menu as shown in Figure 12.4 and then click **Next**.

7. Select the unique key identifier in your dataset as shown in figure 12.5 and then click **Next**. Click **Finish** in the next window.

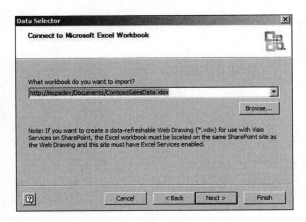

FIGURE 12.3   Excel workbook location.

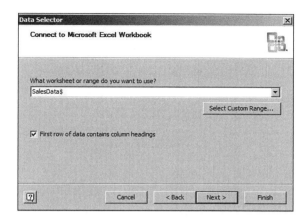

FIGURE 12.4   Excel worksheet selection.

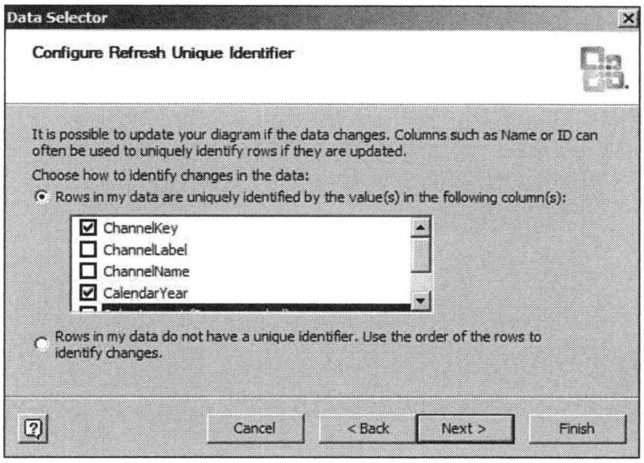

FIGURE 12.5   Unique identifier selection.

You should now see the data from Excel sheet at the bottom of your drawing as shown in Figure 12.6

We will now put some shapes and text boxes on our drawing, which we want to link with this external dataset. You can choose shapes of your own choice or retrieve the Visio drawing file (ContosoSalesByChannel.vdw) from this book's resource material. ContosoSalesByChannel.vdw file looks similar to Figure 12.7.

1. When the drawing is ready with shapes and text boxes, you can then link those shapes and text boxes to actual data rows available at the bottom of the drawing. To link shapes to the data, just drag data rows from the bottom of the drawing to the actual shape or text box on your drawing. You can link one row to one shape or a text box.

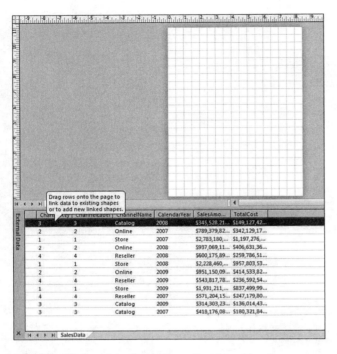

FIGURE 12.6   Linked data from Excel workbook.

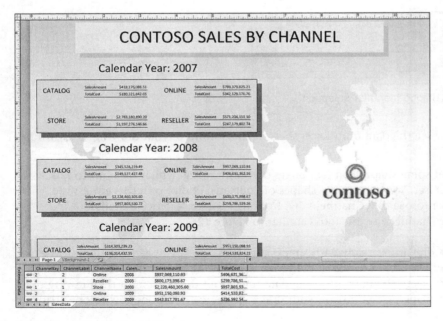

FIGURE 12.7   Visio web drawing.

2. After links have been established between shapes and text boxes and the data rows, you will notice a link icon appear beside the data row. You can now right-click the actual shape or text box and choose to edit the data graphic from the menu. Figure 12.8 shows how to edit the data graphics for textbox with caption "ONLINE". This textbox is linked to sales data from online channel.

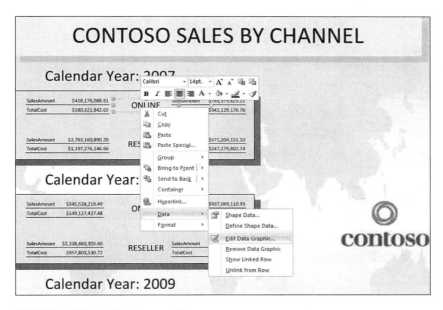

FIGURE 12.8   Edit data graphics.

3. You can double-click each data item and update its data graphic settings. You can display data as text, data bar, icon set; or you can present your data with different colors based on your defined business rules. In the Details section, you can also choose to format data differently. Figure 12.9 displays the Edit Item window which pops up when you double click on any data item.

4. We now have the Visio drawing, which has shapes and text boxes linked to Excel Services data. Our next step is to create another data source connection to the SQL Server database. The process to connect to a SQL data source is very similar to what we just did to connect to Excel Services data. Click the **Data** tab and then click the **Link Data to Shapes** button.

5. Select the **Microsoft SQL Server** database in the Data Selector window and then click **Next**.

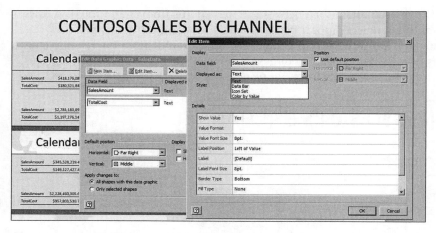

FIGURE 12.9   Edit data item.

6. Type the server name and provide the correct security credentials in the Data Connection Wizard window (Figure 12.10) and then click **Next**. You can use either SQL or Windows authentication. For user-level security, it is recommended to use Windows authentication.

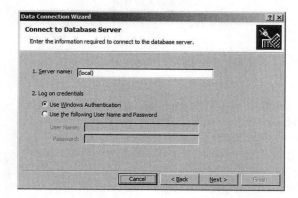

FIGURE 12.10   Data Connection Wizard.

7. Select the ContosoRetailDW database from the Database drop-down menu. Click **Next** after the V_Profit view has been selected as shown in Figure 12.11.

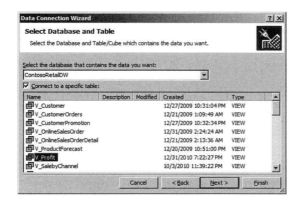

FIGURE 12.11   View Selection window.

NOTE

A view (V_Profit) has been created under the ContosoRetailDW database using the following SQL statement. This view calculates profit by calendar year. We will use this view as an additional data source for our Visio drawing. Create the view in your ContosoRetailDW database using following SQL statement:

```
Create View V_Profit

AS

SELECT TOP (100) PERCENT
  b.CalendarYear
, SUM(a.SalesAmount) - SUM(a.TotalCost) AS Profit

FROM          dbo.FactSales AS a

INNER JOIN    dbo.DimDate AS b ON a.DateKey = b.Datekey

GROUP BY      b.CalendarYear

ORDER BY      b.CalendarYear
```

8. Name the ODC file **V_Profit** and click **Finish**. To ensure that the connection file is always used when the data is updated, click the **Always attempt to use this file to refresh this data** check box (Figure 12.12). This check box ensures that updates to the connection file will always be used by all workbooks that use that connection file. Save this file in the same SharePoint document library where you will publish your Visio drawing.

9. Click **Next** in the Data Selector window, and in the next window make sure the path is the same as your SharePoint path for the ODC file. Next you have an option to pick columns and rows for your dataset as shown in Figure 12.13. We will choose all columns and all rows and click **Next** again.

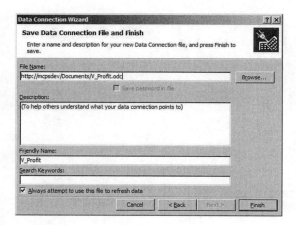

FIGURE 12.12   Save the data connection file.

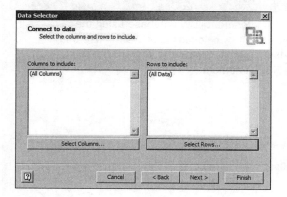

FIGURE 12.13   Data Connection Wizard.

10. Select **Calendar Year** as a unique identifier and click **Next**. Click **Finish** in the next window.

    You will notice another dataset at the bottom of your drawing (Figure 12.14). This dataset is using SQL Server as its external data source.

11. Create a **Total Profit** text box for each year as shown in Figure 12.15, and then link the data rows from our SQL Server dataset to these text boxes.

12. We will display this new data set as an icon set. To do that, right-click the text box connected to the V_Profit dataset, and select **Edit Data Graphic** from the **Data** menu. Double-click the **Profit** data item and then choose **Icon Set** from the Displayed As drop-down menu.

13. Select the **Traffic Lights** option under the Style menu and define rules for different light options as shown in Figure 12.16. Click **OK**.

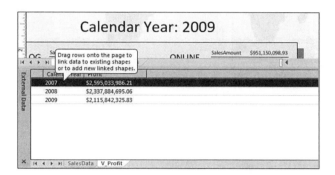

FIGURE 12.14   Linked data from SQL server database.

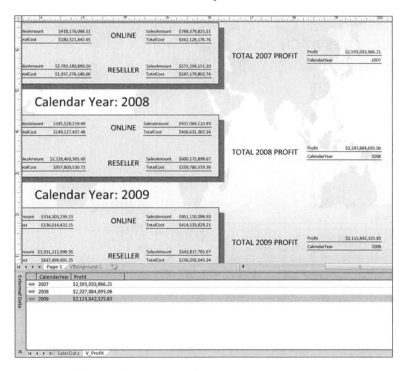

FIGURE 12.15   Linking data to the text box.

14. You will now see a colored traffic light appear in the upper-right corner of each text box (Figure 12.17). Adjust the formatting as you prefer. You can also add a legend to the same drawing by clicking **Insert Legend** on the top Data menu. At this point, you have successfully connected your drawing to the SQL Server database.

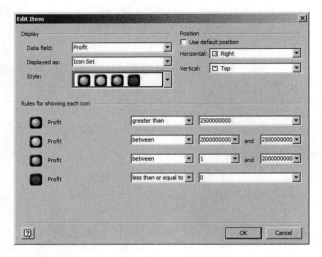

FIGURE 12.16   Traffic Light style option.

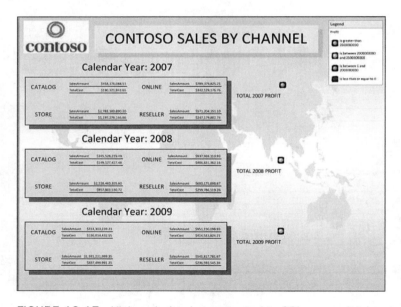

FIGURE 12.17   Visio web drawing connected to SQL server database.

We will now create a new connection to a SharePoint list to use it as an external data source on the same Visio drawing. We will use the same process as before:

1. Click the **Link Data to Shapes** tab. Then choose **Microsoft SharePoint Foundation List** from the Data Selector window and click **Next** again.

NOTE

A SharePoint Foundation List was manually created that displays the top three employee names as list items (Figure 12.18). These three employees have done the most business in the past three years. We will use the same list as an additional data source for our drawing. You can create one yourself before moving forward with this exercise. The list should have three columns: RecordKey, EmployeeName, and Total Profit.

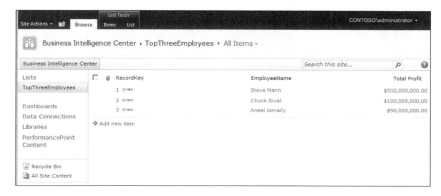

FIGURE 12.18   SharePoint list.

2. Provide the site address of your SharePoint site as shown in Figure 12.19 to the Data Selector window, and then click **Next**. Make sure both the Visio drawing and the SharePoint list are on the same SharePoint 2010 site.

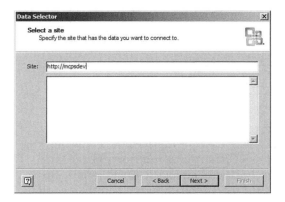

FIGURE 12.19   SharePoint 2010 site hosting custom list.

3. When you click **Next**, you are asked to choose a list from all available lists on that SharePoint site. The list you will select is used as an external data source for our Visio web drawing. We will choose the **TopThreeEmployees** list (Figure 12.20) and then click **Next**. Click **Finish** in the next window.

You will now see a new dataset at the bottom of your drawing, TopThreeEmployees (Figure 12.21).

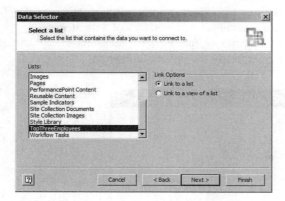

FIGURE 12.20 Custom list selection.

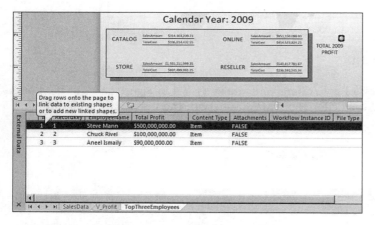

FIGURE 12.21 SharePoint Foundation List external data source.

4. You can again use the shapes and text boxes of your own choice to further develop this Visio drawing. After shapes and text boxes have been placed on a drawing, you can link them with the data rows of our new SharePoint Foundation List dataset. This time we will use data bars to display TopThreeEmployees Total Profit. Right-click the shape or text box you are using for this new data source and then choose **Edit Data Graphic** from the Data menu.

5. Double-click **Total Profit** and choose **Data Bar** from the Displayed As menu and select **Progress Bar** from the Style menu (Figure 12.22). Define the max value of a bar as **600000000** and click **OK**.

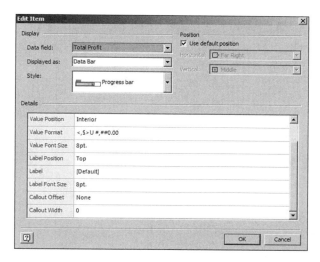

FIGURE 12.22   Progress bar style option.

You will now have TopThreeEmployees list data displayed as a progress bar on your Visio drawing (Figure 12.23).

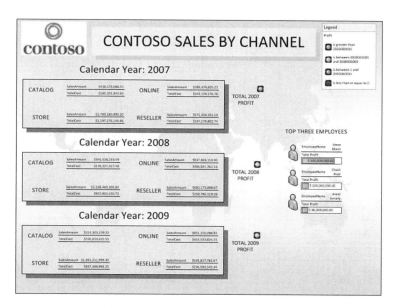

FIGURE 12.23   Visio web drawing connected to SharePoint list.

We now have our Visio drawing ready, which is using SQL Server, Excel Services, and SharePoint Foundation List as an external data source. The next section explains how you can save this web drawing to a SharePoint document library.

> **NOTE**
>
> Under the Data tab on the top menu there is a button named Automatic Link. After you click it, it will start the Automatic Link Wizard. The Automatic Link enables you to quickly link rows of data to shapes in your diagram if existing values in the shape equal values in the row.

Publish a Drawing to a SharePoint 2010 Document Library

The Visio web drawing (VDW file) is a new Visio file type that allows diagrams to be rendered in the browser using Visio Services on SharePoint 2010. To save your Visio drawing as a web drawing file in a SharePoint 2010 document library, follow these steps:

1. Click **File, Save, Send**. You will see an option to Save to SharePoint in the right pane as shown in the Figure 12.24.

FIGURE 12.24   Save to SharePoint.

2. Click **Save to SharePoint, Browse for a Location**. Under file types, select **Web Drawing**, and then click **Save As**. You can provide the path for the exact location on your SharePoint server where you want to save this file and then click **Save**. You can also manually upload this file to your SharePoint directory.

After your Visio web drawing file has been saved to the SharePoint document library, you can continue to work on it in Visio. You can edit Visio web drawing files using the complete set of features provided by Visio and then save again. When the file appears in your document library, you can open it in a browser by clicking it.

Browsing a Visio Web Drawing Online

A Visio diagram saved to a SharePoint document library as a Visio web drawing can be viewed in any web browser by just clicking its filename in the document library.

The diagram renders in the browser if the viewer has Silverlight installed on his or her machine. Visio Services renders seamlessly anything you can draw in Visio (see Figure 12.25).

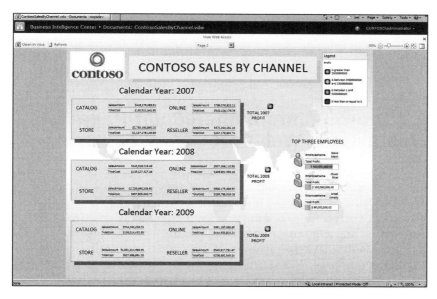

FIGURE 12.25   Visio web drawing in a browser.

Visio Services enables you to navigate diagrams using easy-to-use control features for panning, zooming, switching pages, following hyperlinks, and discovering shape data. You can also open a drawing in Visio directly from the browser with one click using the **Open in Visio** button.

Because Visio web drawings are stored in a SharePoint document library, users get a variety of useful document management features, such as access control using permission management and change control using version management. Drawings can also be integrated with SharePoint workflows.

By default, Visio web drawings open in their own web page for a full-screen viewing experience. Visio Graphics Service allows Visio web drawings to be embedded in other

SharePoint pages using Visio Web Access web parts. Using the Visio Web Access web part, you can embed Visio web drawings in SharePoint pages. By putting all relevant information onto one page, you save viewers time and enable them to understand the information fully. You will learn more about Visio Web Access web parts in later sections.

The next section covers options available for refreshing data in Visio web drawings.

Refreshing Data in a Visio Web Drawing

Visio Graphics Service has taken Visio's data refresh features to the browser. When Visio Graphics Service renders a data-driven drawing in a browser, it fetches the linked external data from the data source. After you publish your drawing to the SharePoint document library, your diagram will always visually represent the most up-to-date data. You can also refresh data manually by clicking the **Refresh** button. Visio Graphics Service supports refresh on open, manual refresh and automatic periodic refresh.

The next section explains how the ContosoSalesByChannel.vdw drawing can be presented using the Visio Web Access web part.

Embedding a Drawing into a SharePoint Page Using the Visio Web Access Web Part

There are multiple ways to share your Visio web drawings with viewers online. One of the options is to upload the drawing file (.vdw file) to the document library. Users can then open it in a browser by clicking on the actual file name. Another option is to embed your web drawing directly into a SharePoint page using the Visio Web Access web part. This is helpful when you are developing a dashboard page. Contribute, Approve, Manage Hierarchy, Design, or Full Control level permissions let you embed your Visio web drawings into an existing SharePoint page. This section will provide you step-by-step guidelines on how to embed drawings in a SharePoint page using Visio Web Access web part. To do so, follow these steps:

1. Create a New Visio Web Access web part page by clicking **New Page** under Site Actions.
2. Click the **Insert** tab and then click the **Web Part** button.
3. Select the **Business Data** category as shown in Figure 12.26, select the **Visio Web Access** web part, and then click the **Add** button.
4. At this point, an empty Visio Web Access web part should appear on your page. To assign an existing web drawing to display in this web part, follow the **Click Here to Open the Tool Pane** link (Figure 12.27).
5. Type in the URL to the web drawing you want to display in the text box, or use the **Browse** button to navigate the SharePoint folders to find the drawing. Figure 12.28 shows the window you see when you use the browse button to search for your web drawing file.

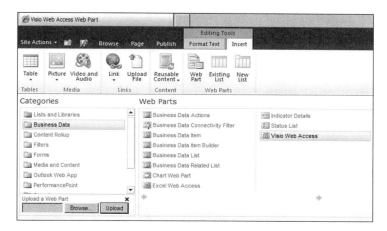

FIGURE 12.26   Visio Web Access web part.

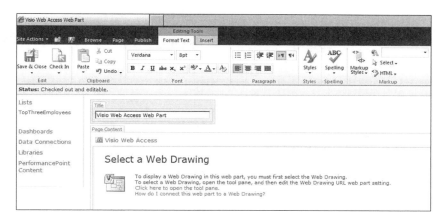

FIGURE 12.27   Tool Pane link.

6. After the URL is in the Input field, click either the **Apply** or **OK** button at the bottom of the configuration panel. You will notice the drawing is embedded in the page after you click **Save and Close** (Figure 12.29). You can click **Page** on the top ribbon bar and then click **Make Homepage** to use this Visio web part page your home page.

NOTE

You can only embed web drawings that are hosted within the same SharePoint farm as the site hosting the web part. Also note that Visio Services checks the permissions of page viewers before it renders a web drawing. If the viewer does not have at least View permissions, Visio Services will not render the web drawing.

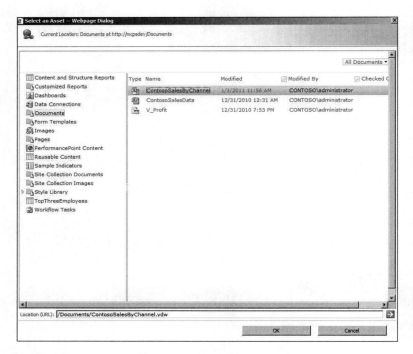

FIGURE 12.28   Select an asset: Web Page Dialog.

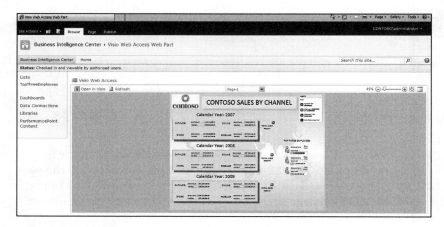

FIGURE 12.29   Visio Web Access web part home page.

Table 12.1 lists other settings options to further customize your Visio Web Access web part page.

TABLE 12.1   Further Customizing Your Visio Web Access Web Part Page

Property Label	Description
Override the web drawing's default initial view using the web part's current page, pan and zoom	By default, when the web part displays a drawing, it maintains the same zoom level and pan coordinates as when the drawing was saved last. You can override this setting by checking this box and manipulating the diagram directly in the web part.
Force faster rendering	If the person viewing the drawing has Silverlight 3.0 or later installed, the web drawing is rendered using Silverlight. If the viewer does not have Silverlight, the drawing is rendered as an image file in PNG format. If you prefer that the web part never use the Silverlight, even if it is installed on the viewer's computer, you can select this option for faster rendering.
Automatic Refresh Interval	If the web drawing is connected to an external data source, you can have the web part check the data source periodically to get the latest data. Type the number of minutes you would like for the interval between data refresh attempts. Leave this at 0 if you prefer that users refresh the data manually by clicking the Refresh button on the Visio Web Access web part. The value should be Integer and greater or equal to 1.
Expose the following shape data items to web part connections	If you have linked the Visio Web Access web part to another web part via the Send Shape Data To web part connection, the data fields that you specify in this box are sent to the other web part on each shape click. Make sure to separate data field names you want to send with semicolons.
Toolbar and User Interface check boxes	The options available in this section are pretty much self-explanatory. You can enable or disable them by checking and unchecking the check boxes.
Web Drawing Interactivity	The options available in this section are pretty much self-explanatory. You can enable or disable them by checking and unchecking the check boxes. They let you control features you want to share with your web drawing viewers.
Appearance, Layout, and Advanced	Visio Web Access web part inherits the settings found in the Appearance, Layout, and Advanced sections of the web part configuration panel. You can customize them based on what works for your solution.

12

* Source: http://blogs.msdn.com/b/visio/archive/2009/11/05/embedding-a-web-drawing-into-a-sharepoint-page.aspx

Interaction with Other SharePoint 2010 Applications

In this section, we review how the Visio Web Access web part can interact with other SharePoint 2010 web parts. We use our previously created web drawing to set up an interaction with other web parts. You have to make sure the ContosoSalesByChannel.vdw drawing is published in a SharePoint 2010 document library. Also verify whether you have the Visio Web Access web part working on your home page. After confirming such, you can set up an interaction as follows:

1. Create a new custom list in SharePoint and add a new column called **Shapes to Highlight**. Choose **Single Line of Text** as the column data type.

2. Create a new item in your list for each group of shapes you want to highlight. In the Shapes to Highlight field, enter a comma-delimited list of the names of the shapes you want to highlight as shown in Figure 12.30, with no spaces (for example, Sheet.23,Sheet.69).

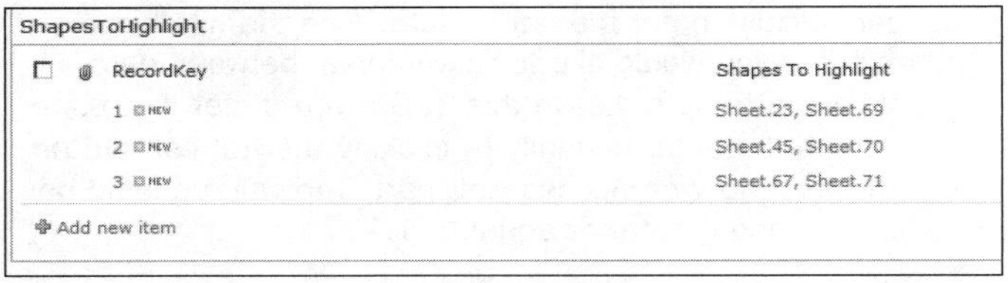

FIGURE 12.30   Custom list.

3. On the web part page, add the List View web part for the list that you created at the bottom of the page. The name of the list should show up as a web part once you select List and Libraries from the categories as shown in Figure 12.31.

4. In the corner of the Visio Web Access web part, click the arrow to open the Visio Web Access web part menu.

5. Click **Edit Web Part**. In Edit mode, click the arrow to open the Visio Web Access web part menu again, point to Connections, choose **Get Shapes to Highlight From**, and then choose the List web part (**ShapesToHighlight**) you added to the page as shown in Figure 12.32

6. The Configure Connection dialog pops up asking you to map a field from the Provider web part to a field in the Consumer web part. Visio Web Access is the consumer web part because it is receiving a list of shape names from the List View web part. Choose **Shape Names** for the Consumer field and **Shapes to Highlight** for the Provider field as shown in Figure 12.33.

7. Click **Finish**. Now your two web parts are connected, and when you select a row in your List web part, Visio highlights the shapes that are specified in that row.

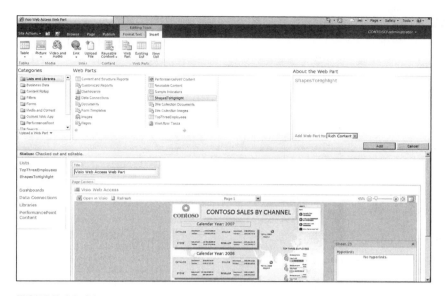

FIGURE 12.31   List View web part.

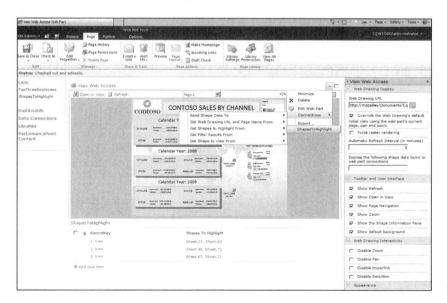

FIGURE 12.32   Visio Web Access web part menu.

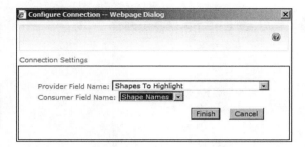

FIGURE 12.33   Configure Connection window.

Just as with Get Shapes to Highlight From, you can use a few more connection actions. Table 12.2 describes each possible connection action.

TABLE 12.2   Possible Connection Actions

Connection Action	Description
Send Shape Data To	This connection action lets you send data embedded with shapes to another web part. When a shape is selected in the drawing, data from that shape is sent as a comma-delimited row. By default, the shape name, shape ID, URL of the drawing, and name of the page that the selected shape is on is always sent with rest of the data items.
Get Web Drawing URL and Page Name From	This connection action enables you to load a web drawing or switch the displayed page. It takes the drawing URL and page name as parameters.
Get Filter Results From	This connection action enables you to filter a Visio diagram that is connected to a SharePoint list. The connected web part must be connected to a SharePoint list as a data source. When the SharePoint list is filtered, the diagram highlights the shapes connected to the filtered value.
Get Shape to View From	This connection action enables you to change the view and zoom of the diagram displayed in the Visio Web Access web part. The connection takes the shape name and zoom level as parameters.

Custom Data Providers

When you want to use an external data source that is not compatible with Visio Graphics Service, you can create a custom data provider using steps shared at http://msdn. microsoft.com/en-us/library/ff394595.aspx.

This MSDN article shares the most important classes and methods available in the Visio Services class library to create and deploy a custom data provider. The custom data provider in this article reads data from an XML file and then displays the same data in a Visio web drawing file.

Summary

Microsoft Visio 2010 integration with SharePoint 2010 has opened a whole new way to display Visio diagrams more effectively. Visio developers can now create interactive, dynamic, data-driven Visio web drawings using Microsoft Visio 2010 Premium and Professional editions. They can publish their drawings online in a SharePoint document library for others to view without having Visio installed on their local machines.

This chapter walked through the process of developing each piece of Visio Graphics Service content. It explained you how you can access data from different external data sources. In addition, the chapter explained how to set up an interaction between the Visio Web Access web part and other SharePoint web parts. In later chapters, a complete end-to-end solution shows how Visio Graphics Service fits into the overall BI stack and how the components from this chapter are used to build the complete solution.

Best Practices

The following are best practices from this chapter:

▶ It is important to understand how much space you need to store your web drawings and how many users will be simultaneously accessing your web drawings. You can access an article about capacity planning for Visio Graphics Service at http://www.microsoft.com/downloads/en/details.aspx?FamilyID=fd1eac86-ad47-4865-9378-80040d08ac55&displaylang=en.

▶ For large diagrams, use the **Get Shape to View From** connection setting to configure the zoom settings.

▶ Most data providers are already listed with Visio Graphics Service, but if not, make sure all your external data sources are listed as a trusted data provider.

▶ Make sure ODC files, SharePoint lists, and Excel sheets are stored on the same SharePoint site as your drawing, if used as an external data source.

CHAPTER **13**

Visio Graphics Service Security

IN THIS CHAPTER

- ▶ Internal Data Sources
- ▶ External Data Sources
- ▶ Adding a New Trusted Data Provider
- ▶ Data Source Delegation
- ▶ Publishing an ODC file to SharePoint 2010 with Secure Store Service Security Model

Accessing data from any data source requires that a user should be authenticated by that data source first. In the case of data driven Visio web drawings, Visio Graphics Service authenticates the data source on behalf of the web drawing viewer. It either uses viewer's SharePoint server credential or Secure Store Service account to setup a connection to the data source. Visio web drawings can be connected to both internal and external data sources as long as you are using a trusted data provider. If the provider is not registered with SharePoint 2010 then drawing will not attempt to setup a connection with the data source. This chapter discusses different aspects of data level security when dealing with Visio Graphics Service on SharePoint 2010. Visio web drawings (.VDW files) must be published to a SharePoint document library to be opened in a browser. By setting the document library permissions correctly you can limit access to a particular drawing for your viewers. This helps you with securing your content on user interface/SharePoint level. In this chapter, we will not focus on content level security but keep our focus on data level security. To learn more about content or site level security, review article shared at http://technet.microsoft.com/en-us/library/cc288189.aspx.

Internal Data Sources

If Visio web drawing is accessing data from an internal data source such as a SharePoint list or Excel workbook, Visio Graphics Service connects to it by using the viewer's SharePoint server credentials. To use an Excel workbook as a data source, Excel Services must be started, and the workbook or list must be hosted on the same SharePoint farm as the web drawing. You can verify whether Excel Services is running by completing the following steps on the Central Administration home page: Click the **Manage Service Applications** link on the Central Administration home page. This will take you to Manage Service Applications page as shown in Figure 13.1. Confirm that Excel Services Application Service is already started.

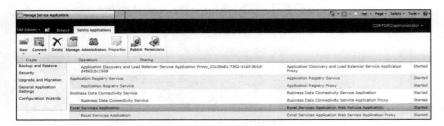

FIGURE 13.1   Manage service applications.

External Data Sources

Visio Graphics Service can connect to external data sources such as SQL Server, IBM DB2, Oracle, other OLEDB/ODBC providers, and custom data sources. When Visio Graphics Service is loading data in a web drawing, the service checks the connection information stored in the web drawing to determine whether the specified data provider is on a trusted data provider list. If the provider is on the trusted list, a connection is tried; otherwise, the connection request is ignored. By default, the data providers shared in the Table 11.1 in Chapter 11 are already included on the list.

Adding a New Trusted Data Provider

If you are trying to use a data provider which is not registered with the trusted data provider list then you can add a new trusted data provider through the SharePoint Central Administration home page using following steps:

1. Click the **Manage Service Applications** link on the Central Administration home page and then click the **Visio Graphics Service** link.
2. Click the **Trusted Data Providers** link.
3. To add a new provider, click the **Add a New Trusted Data Provider** link.

NOTE

To edit or remove an existing data provider, select the actual data provider you want to edit or remove and choose the required action from the drop-down menu.

When adding a new data provider, you are asked for following parameter values as shown in Figure 13.2:

▶ **Trusted Data Provider ID:**The data provider ID must be the same ID used to reference the data provider in the connection string.

▶ **Trusted Data Provider Type:**The data provider type must be one of the following values:

Number	Type
1	OLE DB
2	SQL
3	ODBC
4	ODBC with DSN
5	SharePoint Lists
6	Custom Data Provider

▶ **Trusted Data Provider Description:**The data provider description is a friendly name that appears on the Trusted Data Providers page.

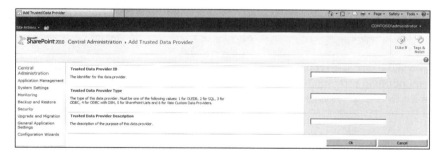

FIGURE 13.2   Adding new trusted data provider.

TIP

You can also add, edit or delete trusted data providers using Windows PowerShell command prompt. Detailed steps are shared at http://technet.microsoft.com/en-us/library/ee524056.aspx.

Data Source Delegation

Visio Graphics Service supports two types of data connections for a web drawing: embedded connection and external connection using an *Office Data Connectivity* (ODC) file. When creating a data connection in Microsoft Visio 2010, choose Previously Created Connection option on data selector window to provide location for an ODC file.

When using the Integrated Windows authentication model with either embedded or external connection, the Visio Graphics Service uses the viewer's Windows credentials to authenticate with the database. Integrated Windows authentication with constrained Kerberos delegation provides the stronger security setup.

When you are using Secure Store Service model, the Visio Graphics Service uses the Secure Store Service to map the viewer's credential to a credential with access to the database. The Secure Store Service supports mappings for both Integrated Windows authentication and other forms of authentication such as SQL Server authentication. The Secure Store Service model is supported only when the drawing uses an ODC file to connect to the data source. The ODC file specifies the Secure Store Service target application that will be used for credential mapping.

For ease of configuration, a farm administrator can also map all users to a single unattended service account with database access. This unattended service account must be a low-privilege Windows domain account that is given access to databases. The Visio Graphics Service impersonates this account if no other authentication method is specified.

> **NOTE**
>
> When using Secure Store Service security model or an Unattended Service account, this approach does not help with auditing of database calls by individual user. Creating the Secure Store Service Target Application.

In this section we will create the Secure Store Service target application for Visio Graphics Service and then later use the same application id to connect to an external data source using an ODC file:

1. Before you start, verify that you are the member of the farm administrators group.
2. On the Central Administration Home page, in the Application Management section, click the **Manage Service Applications** link and then click the **Secure Store Service** link.
3. Click the **New** button on the top ribbon. Doing so brings you to the Target Application Settings page as shown in Figure 13.3.

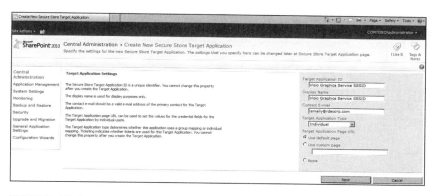

FIGURE 13.3   Target Application Settings page.

4. Click the **Next** button after providing values for the following parameters:

  ▶ **Target Application ID:** The Secure Store target application ID is a unique identifier. You cannot change this property after you create the target application. Enter **Visio Graphics Service SSSID** in the Target Application ID text box.

  ▶ **Display Name:** The display name is used for display purposes only. Enter **Visio Graphics Service SSSID** in the Display Name text box.

  ▶ **Contact Email:** The contact email should be a valid email address of the primary contact for this target application. Enter your email address for now.

  ▶ **Target Application Type:** The target application type determines whether this application uses a group mapping or individual mapping. Ticketing indicates whether tickets are used for this target application. You cannot change this property after you create the target application. For now, select **Individual** from the drop-down menu.

  ▶ **Target Application Page URL:** The target application page URL can be used to set the values for the credential fields for the target application by individual users. You can leave it to use the default page for now.

5. Click the **Next** button after configuring the credential field types for your target application. You can choose from multiple different field types. For now, though, we can go with default values as shown in Figure 13.4, which are Windows Username and Password.

6. Click the **OK** button after configuring the target application administrator. The target application administrator is the user (or users) who has access to manage the target application settings. The farm administrator has access by default. For now, you can enter **Administrator** in the text box and click the **Check Names** icon. After you click Check Names icon, the system will resolve the domain name for the Administrator account as shown in Figure 13.5.

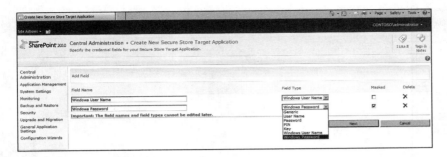

FIGURE 13.4   Credential Field Type Settings page.

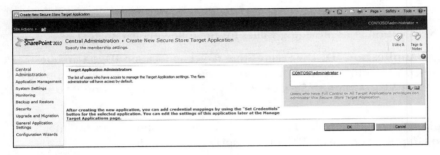

FIGURE 13.5   Target application administrator settings.

Now that you have configured the Secure Store Service application for Visio Graphics Service, our next step is to set the credentials for this Secure Store Service application:

7. Click the **Visio Graphics Service SSSID** link and then click the **Set Credentials** link in the drop-down menu.

8. You will now see the window where you can set credentials for this service as shown in Figure 13.6. Type the username and password of the credentials to be stored. If this is an individual application ID, you also have to type the username of the credential owner. The credential owner should be a user or claim that must have permissions to access these credentials. Group application IDs already have had the credential owner specified during the application ID creation step. For now, you can use CONTOSO\Administrator account to associate with Visio Graphics Service SSSID. Click OK once your provide all the information as shared in the Figure 13.6.

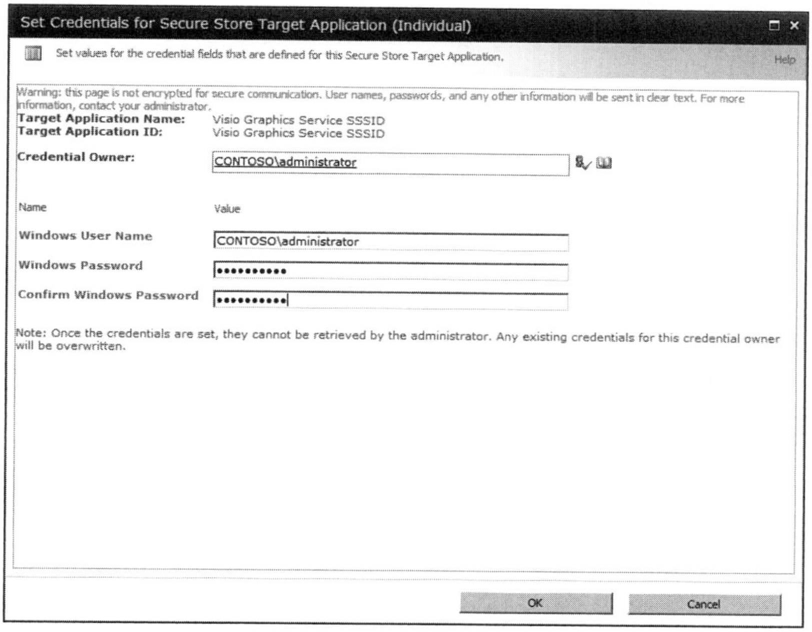

FIGURE 13.6   Set up Windows credentials for Visio Graphics Service SSSID.

We are now ready to create an ODC file which will use the same Secure Store Service Application ID which we just created to connect to ContosoRetailsDW SQL database. Refer to our next section to accomplish this task.

Publishing an ODC File to SharePoint 2010 with Secure Store Service Security Model

As shared earlier Visio web drawings can connect to an external data source using office data connectivity (ODC) files. You can simply create one ODC file for your external data source and then publish it on your SharePoint data connection library. All Excel and Visio based reports/drawing files under document library can use the same ODC file which you will be publishing in your data connection library. This is very helpful when you have to make changes to your data connection string in future. If for example, your server location changes in future then you can simply update this ODC file with new location and all reports will be directed to the new location without making any changes to the actual report/drawing file.

In this section we will create and publish an ODC file using Microsoft Excel 2010. Use the following steps to accomplish this task:

1. Open Microsoft Excel 2010 and click the **Data** tab from the top menu bar. Then click the **From Other Source** link on the ribbon and select the **From SQL Server** option from the drop-down menu. Doing so displays the Data Connection Wizard window.

2. Type the server name and then click **Next**. You can choose to connect to your (local) SQL Server. On the Select Database and Table screen, choose the **ContosoRetailDW** database. You can uncheck the **Connect to a Specific Table** check box to avoid selecting any table for now. Click the **Next** button.

3. Click on the **Authentication Settings** button. This will bring up the Excel Service Authentication Settings window as shown in Figure 13.7. Refer to step 4 of the previous topic to identify the name of your Secure Store Service Application ID. We will be using the same SSS ID to connect to ContosoRetailDW database via this ODC file.

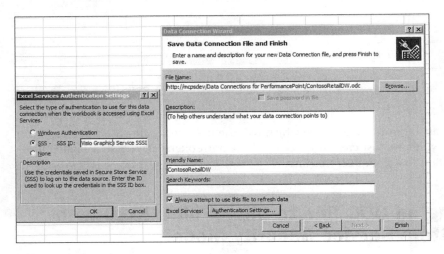

FIGURE 13.7 ODC file settings.

4. In the **File Name** text box provide the complete address of the data connection library where you would like to store this ODC file. You can choose any data connection library on your SharePoint site but just keep in mind that you have to save this ODC file on a same SharePoint site as your Visio web drawing.

5. Click **Finish** when you have configured File Name and Authentication settings using the directions provided in steps 3 and 4.

6. A Web File Properties window opens. Provide settings as shown in Figure 13.8 and then click the **OK** button.

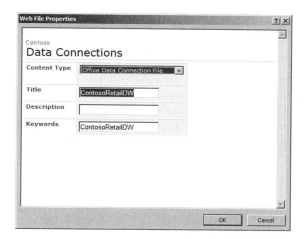

FIGURE 13.8   Web file properties.

You have now successfully configured and published the ODC file to SharePoint 2010 under the Data Connections library of your choice. This ODC file is connecting to the SQL Server database using the Secure Store Service application you created earlier for Visio Graphics Service. You can now use this ODC file to develop data-driven Visio web drawings. Review Chapter 12, "Visio Graphics Service Development," to learn more about developing Visio web drawings using ODC files.

Summary

This chapter explained how Visio web drawings can connect to internal or external data sources. It also provided the steps to add a trusted data provider in SharePoint 2010. This chapter also explained how to create an ODC file to connect to SQL Server data sources with a Secure Store Service security model. It also provided a detailed summary of data source delegation methods available when working with Visio Graphics Service on SharePoint 2010.

Best Practices

The following are best practices from this chapter:

- ▶ For stronger and enterprise-level security solutions, use Kerberos delegation and ensure that all servers reside in the same domain to be used for per-user identity data source connections.

- ▶ Most of the data providers are already listed in SharePoint 2010 Visio Graphics Service settings. Always review the existing list before adding a new data service provider.

▶ Keep only those data providers in the Trusted Data Providers list that you think you will use with Visio web drawings.

▶ Use low-privileged accounts when configuring unattended service accounts to connect to an external data source.

▶ If using windows authentication then External data sources must reside within the same domain as the SharePoint Server 2010 farm or Visio Graphics Services must be configured to use the Secure Store Service. For more information, review planning documentation at http://technet.microsoft.com/en-us/library/cc560988.aspx.

PART VI

End-to-End Solutions

IN THIS PART

Building a Management Dashboard Solution

The most common requirement within a *business intelligence* (BI) solution is to provide a management dashboard filled with scorecards, reports, charts, and graphs. This chapter provides an end-to-end solution for building out the presentation of BI information within a management dashboard.

Preparing the Management Console

The first step in building out the solution is laying down the BI foundation within your SharePoint environment. This includes several areas covered previously in this book.

Creating the Site Collection and Sites

Several planning questions need to be answered to build out the solution properly. Because the management dashboard will use PerformancePoint Services, the obvious location of the solution is within a Business Intelligence Center site collection.

However, you need to decide whether this is the main solution that will be hosted within the site collection or if this solution is one of many that will be contained within the site collection. You might want to provide overall results within the BI Center site collection but then have specific pages or subsites that focus on particular areas or departments within your organization.

Nonetheless, you need to create the main BI Center site collection first and then create any specific pages or sites below it if required. Figure 14.1 shows an example of this.

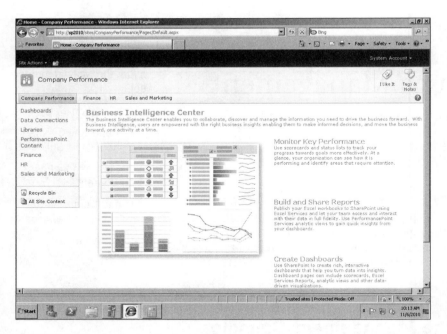

FIGURE 14.1   Company Performance site collection with departmental pages.

The solution details in this chapter do not depend on this structure, but the example involves a main site collection named Company Performance along with departmental pages below it using the Business Intelligence Center site templates.

The steps outlined at this point using the example are as follows:

1. Create a Business Intelligence Center site collection named **Company Performance**.
2. Create pages (or sites) for functional areas (for example, Finance, HR, Sales & Marketing).

NOTE

Typically, creating pages for the functional areas within the BI site collection should suffice. Creating subsites adds overhead and might not be warranted based on requirements.

Customizing the Navigation

The Quick Launch (left-side navigation) displays several links within the site that may or may not be necessary for all users. In addition, when using pages to segregate functional areas, these pages do not appear in the Quick Launch or the top navigation. Therefore, the navigation of the site collection should be customized to provide a friendlier interface.

To customize the navigation, follow these steps:

1. From the BI site collection, select **Site Settings** from the Site Actions menu.

2. Under the Look and Feel section, click the **Navigation** link. The Navigation Settings page appears.

3. Within the Global Navigation and the Current Navigation sections, check the **Show Pages** option, as shown in Figure 14.2.

FIGURE 14.2   Modifying the global and current navigation to show pages.

4. Scroll down to the Navigation Editing and Sorting section.

5. Under the Current Navigation node, select the **Dashboards** entry and then click **Delete** from the menu bar in the window.

6. Repeat the deletion for **Data Connections**, **Libraries**, and **PerformancePoint Content**.

7. Select each sample page shown within the navigation and then click **Hide** from the menu bar in the window. (Optionally, you may navigate to the Pages library of the site collection and delete these pages as done for this example.)

8. Select **Current Navigation** and click **Add Heading**. The Navigation Heading dialog appears.

9. Enter the name of the main site into the Title field (**Company Performance** in this example).

10. In the URL field, enter the root location of the site collection (for example, /sites/CompanyPerformance) or just click the **Browse** button (which defaults to the root location) and then click **OK**.

11. Click **OK** within the Navigation Heading dialog. This action creates an entry in the Quick Launch for the main site; it already appears in the top navigation. The cleaned up navigation should now look similar to Figure 14.3.

12. Click **OK**.

13. Click **Company Performance** in the top or left navigation to return to your main site page. The modified navigation should look similar to Figure 14.4.

FIGURE 14.3   Refined navigation structure settings.

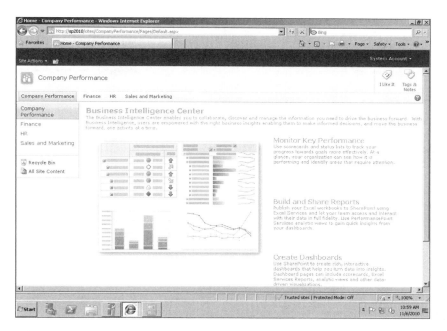

FIGURE 14.4   Modified navigation results.

Configuring Reporting Services

Because this solution requires Reporting Services, at this point Reporting Services needs to be installed and configured in SharePoint Integration mode if it has not been already. See Chapter 3, "Reporting Services Setup and Installation," for specific instructions.

Configuring PerformancePoint Services

PerformancePoint Services is used in this solution. Therefore, the service application needs to be configured properly if it has not been already. See Chapter 6, "PerformancePoint Services Configuration," for specific instructions on configuring PerformancePoint Services.

Deployed Solution

For the sample solution, the premise of the solution is to answer a high-level requirement of providing an answer to the Contoso management about the health of the company and identify areas that can be improved. The answer for this requirement is to build a dashboard that contains the information in a clean and concise manner. The sample dashboard built for the deployed solution displays information about Category Sales, Returns, and Trend information using the different BI components explained in earlier chapters of this book. Figure 14.5 shows the final solution.

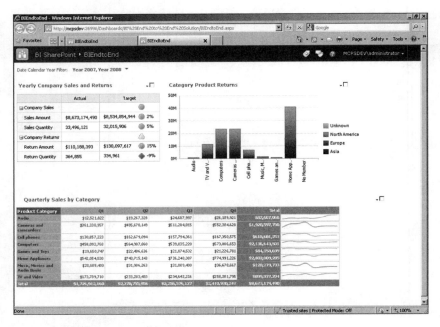

FIGURE 14.5   Deployed BI solution.

The dashboard built is composed of several different BI components coming together to form the dashboard: Scorecard, Analytic Chart, and a SQL Server Reporting Services Report. In addition, the dashboard contains a filter on the Calendar Year that then filters and interacts with each of the dashboard components. The remaining parts of this chapter walk through the steps to build these components, create the dashboard to contain the content, connect the components filter, and then deploy and interact with the BI solution within the SharePoint site.

Creating a Reporting Services Report with Report Builder 3.0

Report Builder 3.0 is a user-friendly tool for developing reports. It is a component that was released along with SQL Server 2008 R2 and is available for download from the SQL Server 2008 R2 Feature Pack website. A report developed with Report Builder 3.0 can be rendered on a PerformancePoint Services dashboard. This is a convenient way of reusing existing reports while packaging them up as a component within a dashboard. To create a report from scratch using Report Builder 3.0, follow these steps:

1. Create a data source, which defines where the data for the report will be retrieved (for example, a SQL Server Analysis Services cube or a SQL Server relational database).

2. Create a dataset, which defines the query used to retrieve the report data from the data source.

3. Create a report that renders the dataset.

This section covers creating a report from scratch with Report Builder 3.0. The report is then rendered in a PerformancePoint Services dashboard within SharePoint. Figure 14.6 shows the sample report layout.

Product Category	Q1	Q2	Q3	Q4	Total	
Audio	$13,531,935	$17,590,586	$18,868,875	$18,955,900	$68,947,296	
Cameras and camcorders	$142,792,873	$161,847,325	$168,992,918	$167,792,909	$641,426,024	
Cell phones	$57,886,862	$70,313,114	$72,787,061	$72,564,975	$273,552,011	
Computers	$230,350,640	$297,168,106	$267,888,349	$277,376,545	$1,072,783,640	
Games and Toys	$14,979,686	$15,835,042	$17,165,767	$17,357,266	$65,337,762	
Home Appliances	$245,686,501	$292,162,569	$290,819,161	$292,059,271	$1,120,727,502	
Music, Movies and Audio Books	$9,021,074	$9,709,643	$9,188,784	$9,605,472	$37,524,973	
TV and Video	$92,293,408	$117,391,631	$126,474,204	$124,024,668	$460,183,911	
Total	$806,542,979	$982,018,016	$972,185,119	$979,737,005	$3,740,483,119	

FIGURE 14.6   Sample report.

The report shows quarterly sales by product category for a given year. In addition, the report includes a sparkline that shows the sales figures in a line chart within a single cell. The sparkline is one of the new visualizations available in SQL Server Reporting Services 2008 R2.

Create a Data Source

It is a best practice to create shared data sources; that is, define a data source, store it in a SharePoint library, and then reference the data source from multiple reports. A data source can also be defined within a report, but then it is available only to that report. Follow these steps to create a shared data source:

1. Navigate to a SharePoint library.

2. Click the **Documents** tab under Library Tools and then click the **New Document** icon on the ribbon bar, as shown in Figure 14.7.

FIGURE 14.7   Create a data source.

3. Select **Report Data Source** from the drop-down menu. See the "Add Content Types to a Document Library" section in Chapter 3 for the configuration required to see Report Data Source in the New Document drop-down menu.

4. Fill in the data source Properties dialog, as shown in Figure 14.8. As an example, this data source is for a SQL Server Analysis Services cube. In the following example, SharePoint2010 is the name of the server running Analysis Services. The connection string must be entered as text; there is no help available that prompts for the individual components of the connection string.

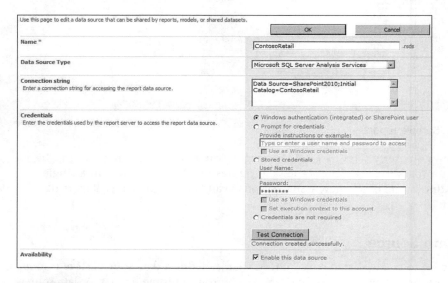

FIGURE 14.8   Data source properties.

5. Click the **Test Connection** button to make sure that it works.
6. Check **Enable This Data Source** to make the data source available for use.

TIP

Because there is no built-in support for locating your data sources, your Information Systems staff should create the shared data sources in the appropriate SharePoint library.

Create a Dataset

A dataset is simply a query that retrieves information from a data source. The query includes the data columns that you want to render on your report. It is a best practice to create shared datasets. As the name implies, a shared dataset can be used in multiple reports. Follow these steps to create a shared dataset:

1. Launch Report Builder 3.0 and click **New Dataset** on the Getting Started dialog, as shown in Figure 14.9.

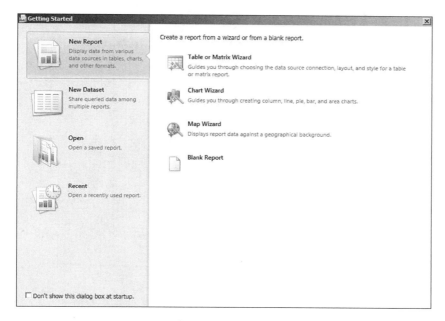

FIGURE 14.9   Report Builder Getting Started dialog.

2. Choose a data source from the available list, as shown in Figure 14.10. To browse for a data source, click the **Browse Other Data Sources** hyperlink and then navigate to a document library that contains data sources. Click the **Create** button after selecting a data source.

3. After you select a data source, the query designer is displayed, as shown in Figure 14.11.

4. Choose the query parameters to filter the dataset.

5. Choose the measures and dimensions and add them to the query fields.

Figure 14.11 has the following annotations:

▶ **Select Cube:** Click the ellipsis button to select the cube for the query. An Analysis Services database can contain one or more cubes.

▶ **Query Fields:** Drag and drop fields from the Measures and Dimensions onto this area. These fields will be returned in the query results.

▶ **Query Parameters:** Drag and drop fields from the Measures and Dimensions onto this area to filter the query.

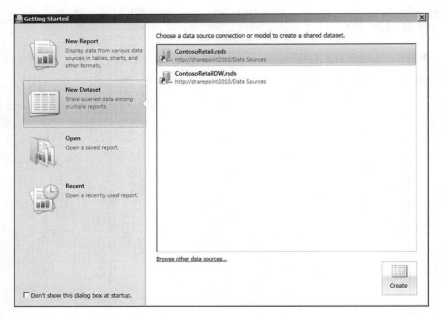

FIGURE 14.10   Choose a data source.

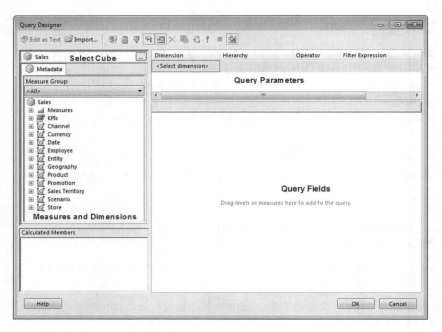

FIGURE 14.11   Query designer.

Figure 14.12 shows the query designer completed for the sample report along with a portion of the query results.

Save the shared dataset by clicking the disk icon near the top left of the window shown in Figure 14.12. Specify **SalesByCategory** as the name of the query. This query will be used in the next section to create the report.

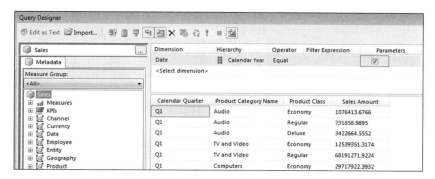

FIGURE 14.12   Report query.

Create a Report

After creating a data source and a dataset, you are now ready to create a report. Report Builder 3.0 provides wizards and a WYSIWYG designer that makes the report authoring process very easy. You should have Report Builder 3.0 already open from the prior steps; if not then open it from the Microsoft SQL Server 2008 R2 Report Builder program group. Follow these steps to create a report:

1. Select **New Report** from the Getting Started dialog.
2. Select **Table** or **Matrix Wizard**, as shown in Figure 14.13. The wizard is launched and will guide you through the remaining steps to create your report.
3. Choose a dataset as shown in Figure 14.14. The options are to choose an existing dataset, click the Browse button to navigate to a shared dataset in a SharePoint library, or create a dataset. Creating a dataset will store the dataset definition in the report, and it will not be available to any other report. Choose the **SalesByCategory** dataset from the list of datasets or click Browse to navigate to the SharePoint library that contains your dataset.
4. Specify row groups, column groups, and values on the Arrange Fields page of the wizard as shown in Figure 14.15. Drag and drop the available fields into the row group, column group, or value as appropriate.
5. Select a layout from one of the available options on the Choose the Layout page of the wizard, as shown in Figure 14.16.

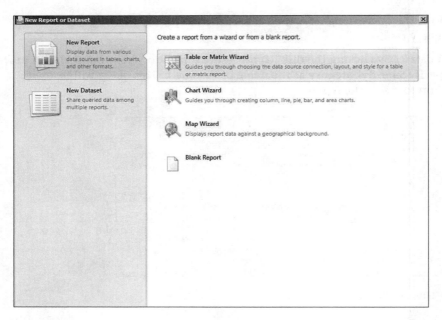

FIGURE 14.13   Table or Matrix Wizard.

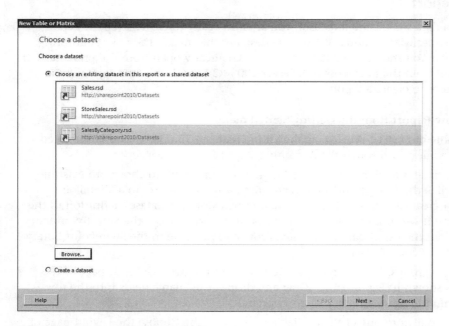

FIGURE 14.14   Choose a dataset.

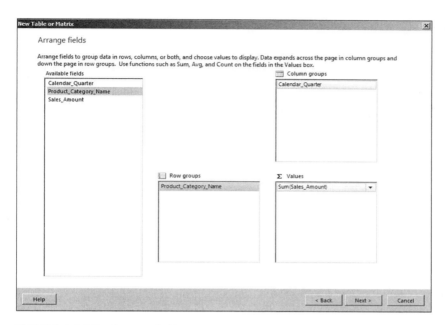

FIGURE 14.15   Arrange fields.

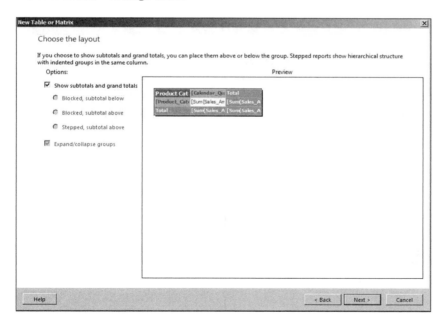

FIGURE 14.16   Choose a layout.

6. Select a style from one of the available options on the Choose a Style page of the wizard, as shown in Figure 14.17.

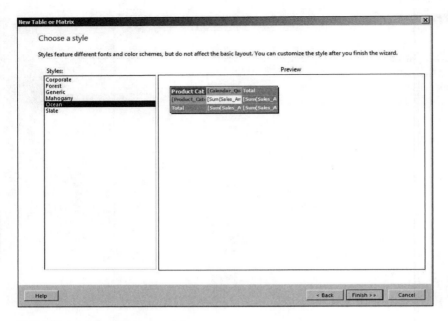

FIGURE 14.17   Choose a style.

TIP

The Getting Started dialog is displayed when you open Report Builder 3.0 if the option **show the getting started dialog on startup** is checked. If you do not see the Getting Started dialog, click the icon in the top left corner of the Report Builder window and select New to display it. You can also click the icon in the top left corner of the Report Builder window and click the Options button to change the **show the getting started dialog on startup** setting.

After you complete the New Table or Matrix Wizard, the report layout will look like Figure 14.18.

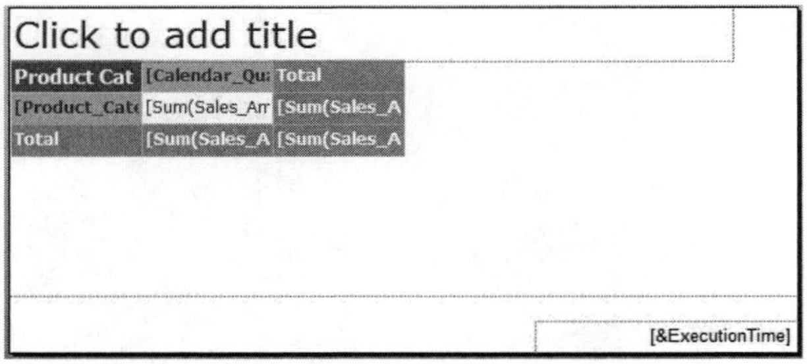

FIGURE 14.18   Report layout.

At this point the tabular section of the report is complete. Let's add a sparkline to the report which will render a chart of the quarterly sales figures in a column within each row. Follow these steps to add the sparkline to the report:

1. Right-click the **Total** column and then select **Insert Column, Right** from the drop-down menu to add a column to the report.

2. Click the **Insert** tab and then click the sparkline icon on the ribbon bar, as shown in Figure 14.19.

FIGURE 14.19   Insert a sparkline.

3. Click the middle row of the report layout in the column just added to place the sparkline there. Select the sparkline type from the dialog, as shown in Figure 14.20.

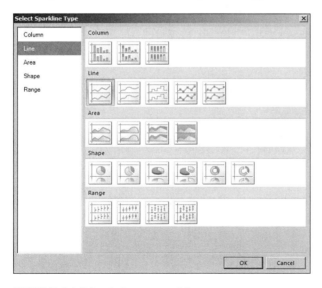

FIGURE 14.20   Select a sparkline type.

4. Figure 14.21 shows the final report layout.

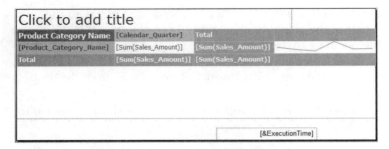

FIGURE 14.21   Final report layout.

5. Click in the cell that contains the sparkline and then fill in the chart data, as shown in Figure 14.22.

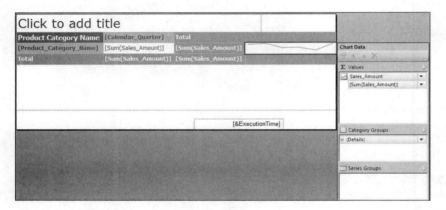

FIGURE 14.22   Sparkline settings.

This completes the report layout; the sparkline will plot the sales total for each calendar quarter.

Creating PerformancePoint Content

Using the Dashboard Designer, the following PerformancePoint Services objects are created for use in the solution:

- ▶ Analysis Services data connections
- ▶ *Key performance indicators* (KPIs)
- ▶ Scorecards
- ▶ Analytic chart reports
- ▶ SQL Server Reporting Services reports
- ▶ Filters

For help in starting the Dashboard Designer, refer to Chapter 7, "PerformancePoint Services Development."

Creating the Analysis Services Data Connection

Before creating any of the additional PerformancePoint Services content items, you create an Analysis Services data connection.

To create an Analysis Services data connection, follow these steps:

1. Click the **Data Connections** folder within Dashboard Designer and select the **Create** tab.

2. Click the data source icon and select the Analysis Services template and click **OK**.

3. Enter the server name.

4. Select **SSAS Database** from the Database drop-down.

5. Select **SSAS Cube** from the Cube drop-down.

   For this solution, we are going to use the unattended service account that was configured for PerformancePoint Services in Chapter 6, "PerformancePoint Services Configuration."

6. Click the **Test Data Source** button.

   Figure 14.23 displays the populated values on the Editor tab.

7. Click the **Properties** tab and supply a name for the data connection.

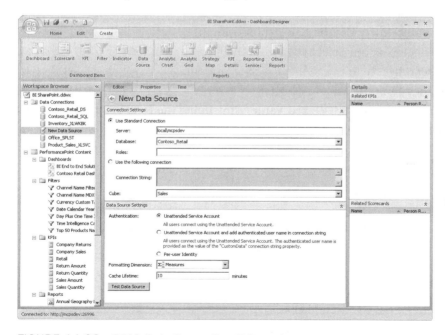

FIGURE 14.23   SSAS Data Connection Editor tab.

Creating the Scorecard and KPIs

Sales and Returns KPIs are going to be created for the solution comparing total dollars to expected dollars and comparing total quantities to expected quantities. Objective KPIs are created for organizing Sales and Returns information. After the KPIs are developed, you create a scorecard as the container for the KPIs. The following processes show how to create these objects for the BI solution.

To create the Sales Amount KPI, follow these steps:

1. Click the **PerformancePoint Content** folder within Dashboard Designer and select the **Create** tab.

> **NOTE**
>
> If running Dashboard Designer for the first time, you might need to click on Add Lists from the Home ribbon in order to add the PerformancePoint Content folder to the current workspace.

2. Click the **KPI** icon and select **Blank KPI** and click **OK**.
3. On the Actual line, click the **1 (Fixed Values)** link under the Data Mappings column.
4. Click the **Change Source** button.
5. Select **SSAS Data Connection** and click **OK**.
6. Select **Sales Amount** from the list of measures and click **OK**.
7. Click the **Default** link under the Calculation column.
8. On the Calculation screen, select **Data** from the list and click **OK**.
9. Click the **(Default)** link in the Number Format column.
10. Select **Currency** from the list and click **OK**.
11. On the Target line, click the **1 (Fixed Values)** link under the Data Mappings column.
12. Click the **Change Source** button.
13. Select **SSAS Data Connection** and click **OK**.
14. Select **Adjusted Sales Quota** from the list of measures and click **OK**.

> **NOTE**
>
> If your version of the Sales Cube does not contain Adjusted Sales Quota measure, use the Sales Quota Amount measure instead.

15. Click the **(Default)** link in the Number Format column.
16. Select **Currency** from the list and click **OK**.
17. Click the **Set Scoring Pattern and Indicator** button.

18. Select the default of **Increasing Is Better** as the scoring pattern and **Band** by **Normalized Value of Actual\Target** as the banding method and click **Next**.

19. Select the **Stoplight** indicator and click **Next**.

20. Enter the worst value of **0** and click **Finish**.

21. Update the thresholds as shown in Figure 14.24.

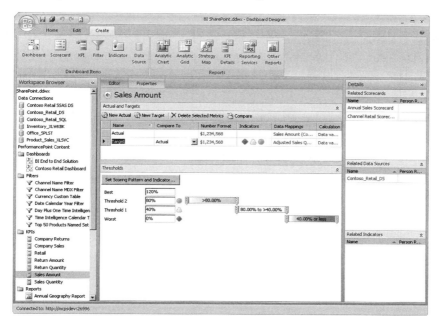

FIGURE 14.24   Sales Amount KPI.

22. Click the **Properties** tab and supply a name for the KPI: **Sales Amount**.

23. Click **Save**.

To create the Sales Quantity KPI, follow these steps:

1. Click the **PerformancePoint Content** folder within Dashboard Designer and select the **Create** tab.

2. Click the **KPI** icon and select **Blank KPI** and click **OK**.

3. On the Actual line, click the **1 (Fixed Values)** link under the Data Mappings column.

4. Click the **Change Source** button.

5. Select **SSAS Data Connection** and click **OK**.

6. Select **Sales Quantity** from the list of measures and click **OK**.

7. Click the **Default** link under the Calculation column.

8. On the Calculation screen, select **Data** from the list and click OK.

9. Click the **(Default)** link in the Number Format column.

10. Select **Number** from the list and click **OK**.

11. On the Target line, click the **1 (Fixed Values)** link under the Data Mappings column.

12. Click the **Change Source** button.

13. Select **SSAS Data Connection** and click **OK**.

14. Select **Adjusted Sales Quota Quantity** from the list of measures and click **OK**.

NOTE

If your version of the Sales Cube does not contain the Adjusted Sales Quota Quantity measure, use the Sales Quota Quantity measure instead.

---

15. Click the **(Default)** link in the Number Format column.

16. Select **Number** from the list and click **OK**.

17. Click the **Set Scoring Pattern and Indicator** button.

18. Select the default of **Increasing Is Better** as the scoring pattern and **Band by Normalized Value of Actual\Target** as the banding method and click **Next**.

19. Select the **Stoplight** indicator and click **Next**.

20. Enter the worst value of **0** and click **Finish**.

21. Update the thresholds as shown in Figure 14.25.

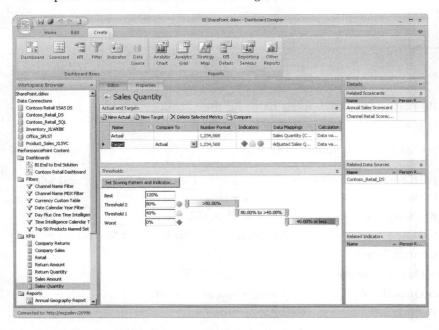

FIGURE 14.25   Sales Quantity KPI.

22. Click the **Properties** tab and supply a name for the KPI: **Sales Quantity**.

23. Click **Save**.

To create the Return Amount KPI, follow these steps:

1. Click the **PerformancePoint Content** folder within Dashboard Designer and select the **Create** tab.

2. Click the **KPI** icon, select **Blank KPI**, and click **OK**.

3. On the Actual line, click the **1 (Fixed Values)** link under the Data Mappings column.

4. Click the **Change Source** button.

5. Select **SSAS Data Connection** and click **OK**.

6. Select **Sales Return Amount** from the list of measures and click **OK**.

7. Click the **Default** link under the Calculation column.

8. On the Calculation screen, select **Data** from the list and click **OK**.

9. Click the **(Default)** link in the Number Format column.

10. Select **Currency** from the list and click **OK**.

11. On the Target line, click the **1 (Fixed Values)** link under the Data Mappings column.

12. Click the **Change Source** button.

13. Select **SSAS Data Connection** and click **OK**.

14. Select **Return Quota Amount** from the list of measures and click **OK**.

> **NOTE**
>
> If your version of the Sales Cube does not contain the return amount measures mentioned in these steps, select other measures for example purposes.

15. Click the **(Default)** link in the Number Format column.

16. Select **Currency** from the list and click **OK**.

17. Click **Set Scoring Pattern** and the **Indicator** button.

18. Select **Decreasing Is Better** as the scoring pattern and **Band by Stated Score (Advanced)** as the banding method and click **Next**.

19. Select the **Stoplight** indicator and click **Next**.

20. Click the **Specify Data Mapping** button.

21. Click the **Change Source** button.

22. Select **SSAS Data Connection** and click **OK**.

23. Select the **Return Amount Variance** measure from the list of measures and click **OK**.

24. Click the **Finish** button.

25. Update the thresholds as shown in Figure 14.26.

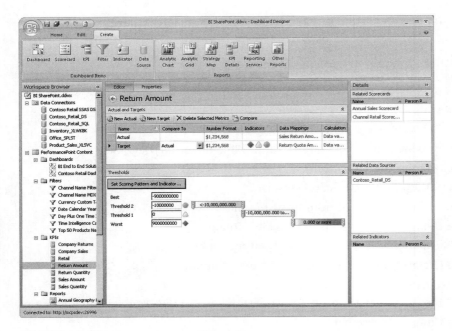

FIGURE 14.26   Return Amount KPI.

26. Click the **Properties** tab and supply a name for the KPI: **Return Amount**.

27. Click **Save**.

To create the Return Quantity KPI, follow these steps:

1. Click the **PerformancePoint Content** folder within Dashboard Designer and select the **Create** tab.

2. Click the **KPI** icon, select **Blank KPI**, and click **OK**.

3. On the Actual line, click the **1 (Fixed Values)** link under the Data Mappings column.

4. Click the **Change Source** button.

5. Select **SSAS Data Connection** and click **OK**.

6. Select **Sales Return Quantity** from the list of measures and click **OK**.

7. Click the **Default** link under the Calculation column.

8. On the Calculation screen, select **Data** from the list and click **OK**.

9. Click the **(Default)** link in the Number Format column.

10. Select **Number** from the list and click **OK**.

11. On the Target line, click the **1 (Fixed Values)** link under the Data Mappings column.

12. Click the **Change Source** button.

13. Select **SSAS Data Connection** and click **OK**.

14. Select **Return Quota Quantity** from the list of measures and click **OK**.

15. Click the **(Default)** link in the Number Format column.

16. Select **Number** from the list and click **OK**.

17. Click the **Set Scoring Pattern and Indicator** button.

18. Select **Decreasing Is Better** as the scoring pattern and **Band By Stated Score (Advanced)** as the banding method and click **Next**.

19. Select the **Stoplight** indicator and click **Next**.

20. Click the **Specify Data Mapping** button.

21. Click the **Change Source** button.

22. Select **SSAS Data Connection** and click **OK**.

23. Select the **Return Quantity Variance** measure from the list of measures and click **OK**.

24. Click the **Finish** button.

25. Update the thresholds as shown in Figure 14.27.

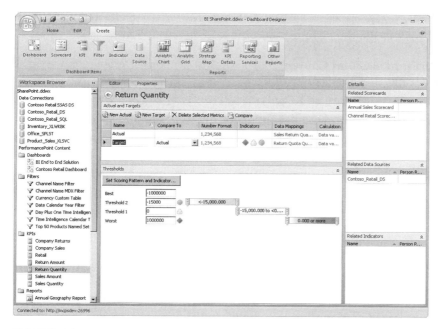

FIGURE 14.27   Return Quantity KPI.

NOTE

If your version of the Sales Cube does not contain the return amount measures mentioned in these steps, select other measures for example purposes.

---

26. Click the **Properties** tab and supply a name for the KPI: **Return Quantity**.

27. Click **Save**.

To create the Company Sales Objective KPI, follow these steps:

1. Click the **PerformancePoint Content** folder within Dashboard Designer and select the **Create** tab.
2. Click the **KPI** icon and select **Objective KPI** and click **OK**.
3. Supply a name for the KPI: **Company Sales**.
4. Click **Save**.

To create the Company Returns Objective KPI, follow these steps:

1. Click the **PerformancePoint Content** folder within Dashboard Designer and select the **Create** tab.
2. Click the **KPI** icon, select **Objective KPI**, and click **OK**.
3. Supply a name for the KPI: **Company Returns**.
4. Click **Save**.

After creating the KPIs, create the PerformancePoint scorecard, as follows:

1. Click the **PerformancePoint Content** folder within Dashboard Designer and select the **Create** tab and click the **Scorecard** icon.
2. Click the **Microsoft Category and Analysis Services** template and click **OK**.
3. Click the Analysis Services data source to use for the scorecard and click **Next**.
4. On the Select a KPI Source screen, keep the default of **Create KPIs from SQL Server Analysis Services Measures** and click **Next**.
5. Click the **Select KPI** button to import KPIs from the workspace or SharePoint site.
6. Select each KPI to import (**Sales Amount**, **Sales Quantity**, **Return Amount**, **Return Quantity**, **Company Sales**, and **Company Returns**), click **OK**, and then click the **Next** button.
7. No Measure filters will be added. Click the **Next** button.
8. No Column Members will be selected. Click **Finish**.
9. Supply a name for the scorecard: **Yearly Company Sales and Returns**.

    The initial wizard brings over the KPIs in a nonformatted order. So, now you must format the scorecard to assign the numeric KPIs to the object KPIs.

10. Click the **Edit** tab.
11. Click the **Company Sales** KPI, and in the Header section of the Edit tab, click the **Up** arrow until the Company Sales KPI is on top.
12. Click the **Sales Amount** KPI and move the KPI using the same method for the Company Sales KPI until it is below the Company Sales KPI.
13. Click the **Sales Quantity** KPI and move the KPI until it is below the Sales Amount KPI.

14. Highlight both the **Sales Amount** and **Sales Quantity** KPIs, and then click the **Increase Indent** icon in the Header section of the Edit menu to move the KPIs as belonging to the Company Sales KPI. The Company Sales KPI should now have a plus sign because a tree has now been created.

15. Perform the same steps for the Company Returns, Return Amount, and Return Quantities KPIs, making the Return Amount and Return Quantity KPIs belong to the Company Returns KPI.

16. Click the **Update** icon in the View section of the Edit menu to see the data for the KPIs come across in the scorecard.

17. Click **Save**.

Figure 14.28 displays the newly created scorecard.

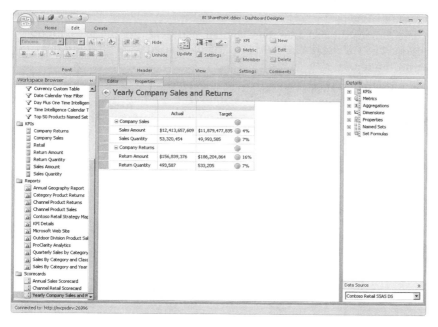

FIGURE 14.28   Yearly Company Sales and Returns scorecard.

Creating Reports

For the BI solution, two types of reports are going to be created in PerformancePoint Services: analytic charts and Reporting Services reports. The analytic chart is created from scratch by dragging dimensions and measures onto a new report. The Reporting Services report references a SharePoint integrated Reporting Services report.

To create an analytic chart report, follow these steps:

1. Click the **PerformancePoint Content** folder within Dashboard Designer and select the **Create** tab.

2. Click the **Analytic Chart** icon.

3. Select **SSAS Data Connection** and click **Finish**.

4. Type in the name of the report: **Category Product Returns**.

5. Expand the Dimensions and Geography dimension on the right side in the Details section and drag the Continent Name field into the Series area of the report.

6. Expand the Product dimension and drag the Category Name field into the Bottom Axis area of the report.

7. Expand the Measures section and drag the Sales Return Amount field into the Background area of the report.

8. Expand the Date dimension and drag the Calendar Year field into the Background area of the report. The Calendar Year field is going to be used for a filter but not displayed within the report.

9. For the solution, the report type is going to use the Stacked Bar Chart. Click the **Edit** tab and click the **Report Type** icon and select **Stacked Bar Chart** from the list.

   The report should populate with data automatically. The report is displayed in Figure 14.29.

10. Click **Save**.

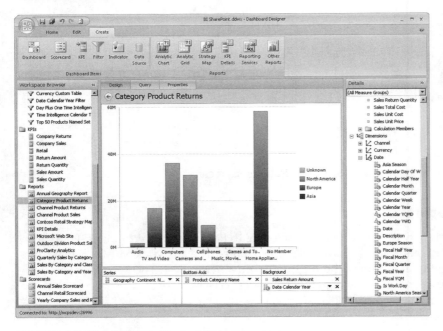

FIGURE 14.29   Category Product Returns report.

To connect to the Reporting Services report, follow these steps:

1. Click the **PerformancePoint Content** folder within Dashboard Designer and select the **Create** tab.
2. Click the **Reporting Services** icon.

> **NOTE**
>
> Dashboard Designer within SharePoint 2010 requires the Microsoft Report Viewer 2008. If you do not have Microsoft Report Viewer 2008 installed you will be prompted as such. Use the link in the message box to download and install Microsoft Report Viewer 2008. Restarting Dashboard Designer after installation allows the report form to be opened.

3. Select **SharePoint Integrated** from the Server Mode drop-down.
4. In the Report Server URL textbox, type in the report server URL.
5. In the Report URL textbox, type in the report URL pointing to the Quarterly Sales by Category and Year.rdl path.
6. Uncheck the **Show Toolbar** and **Show Parameters** icons.
7. Select **75** for the Zoom value.

   The DateCalendarYear parameter of the report should be shown in the Parameters list.

8. For reports that require a default value in the parameter in order to display the report, update the Report parameters section to add a default value for each parameter in the report. Click the **Edit** button to change the default value. For the report, the default value is Year 2007.
9. Click the **Preview** button.

   The report will display in the Preview section.

10. Click the **Properties** tab and type in the name of the report: **Quarterly Sales by Category**.
11. Click **Save**.

Figure 14.30 shows the configuration of the report.

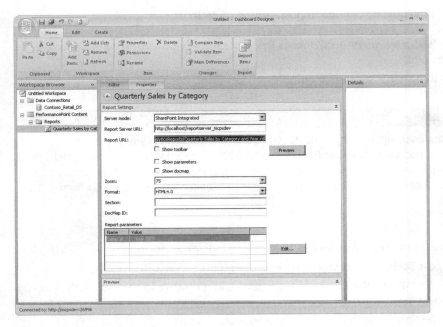

FIGURE 14.30   Quarterly Sales by Category Reporting Services report.

Creating the Filter

Filters provide the ability for a user to interact with the dashboard. The dashboard is set up to connect each of the dashboard's report items to the filter itself; this creates a similar view of data across the different analytical components of the dashboard.

To create a filter, follow these steps:

1. Click the **PerformancePoint Content** folder within Dashboard Designer and select the **Create** tab.
2. Click the **Filter** icon and select the **Member Selection** template and click **OK**.
3. Select **SSAS Data Connection** and click **Next**.
4. Click the **Select Dimension** button.
5. Select **Date.Calendar Year** and click **OK**.
6. Click the **Select Members** button.
7. Right-click the **All Date** member and choose **Select Children** from the menu and click **OK** and then click **Next**.
8. Click **Multi-Select Tree** and click **Finish**.
9. Click the **Properties** tab and add a name to the Name textbox. For this filter, type in **Date Calendar Year Filter**.
10. Click **Save**.

Building and Deploying the PerformancePoint Dashboard

After building the components that make up the dashboard, you then develop them by creating multiple zones for the dashboard, dragging the content items into the zones, and then connecting the filters to the items for user interaction.

To build the dashboard, follow these steps:

1. Click the **PerformancePoint Content** folder within Dashboard Designer and select the **Create** tab.

2. Click the **Dashboard** icon and select the **3 Rows** template and click **OK**.

3. Provide a name for the Dashboard: **BI End to End Solution**.

4. In the Pages section, provide a name for the page: **BIEndtoEnd**.

5. Expand the Filters tree and drag the Date Calendar Year Filter into the Top Row zone.

6. Expand the Scorecards tree and drag the Yearly Company Sales and Returns scorecard into the Center Row zone.

7. Expand the Reports tree and drag the Category Product Returns report into the Center Row zone to the right of the Yearly Company Sales scorecard.

8. From the Reports tree, drag the Quarterly Sales by Category report to the Bottom Row zone.

9. Now that the items have been created onto the dashboard, connect the content items to the Date Calendar Year filter.

10. Click the drop-down arrow for the Yearly Company Sales and Returns scorecard in the Center Row zone and select **Create Connection**, as shown in Figure 14.31.

11. On the Items tab, select the **Get Values From** as the Top Row – (1) Date Calendar Year filter.

12. Click the **Values** tab and leave the default **Page** in the Connect To field.

13. Select **Source Value** as the member unique name and click **OK**.

    The Values tab should be configured as shown in Figure 14.32.

14. Click the drop-down arrow for the Category Product Returns item in the Center Row zone and select **Create Connection**.

15. On the **Items** tab, select the **Get Values From** as the Top Row – (1) Date Calendar Year filter.

16. Click the **Values** tab and select **Date.Calendar Year** from the Connect to drop-down.

17. Select **Source Value** as the member unique name and click **OK**.

18. Click the drop-down arrow for the Quarterly Sales by Category report in the Bottom zone and select **Create Connection**.

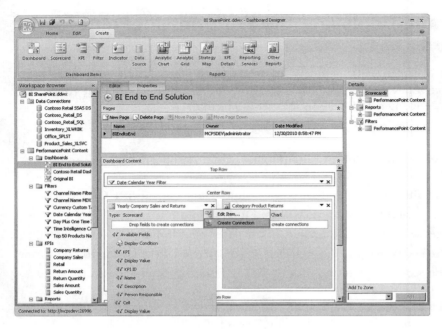

14

FIGURE 14.31   Create Connection menu.

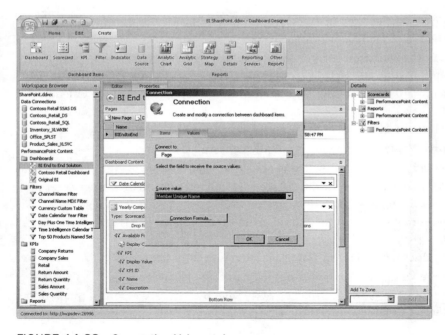

FIGURE 14.32   Connection Values tab.

19. On the Items tab, select the **Get Values From** as the Top Row – (1) Date Calendar Year filter.

20. Click the **Values** tab and the DateCalendarYear parameter is selected in the Connect To drop-down.

21. Select **Source Value** as the member unique name and click **OK**.

As shown in Figure 14.33, all items within the dashboard should now have a connection item pointing to the Date Calendar Year filter.

22. Click the **Properties** tab and click the **Browse** button on the **Document Library** entry and select the **Dashboard** library.

23. For the Master Page drop-down, select the **Minimal** master page.

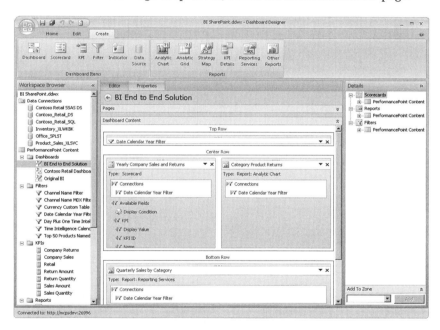

FIGURE 14.33   Dashboard layout.

> **NOTE**
>
> The default v4 master page that comes with SharePoint 2010 PerformancePoint Services inserts the dashboard into a standard SharePoint page, which eliminates real estate and introduces scrollbars to PerformancePoint content items.

24. Click **Save**.

After building the dashboard, the dashboard is ready for deployment. To deploy the dashboard, just click the **Office** icon in the upper-left of the Dashboard Designer and select **Deploy** from the menu, as shown in Figure 14.34.

An Internet Explorer window displays the BI Solution dashboard within the SharePoint site.

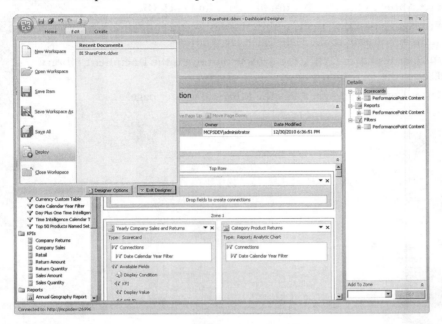

FIGURE 14.34   Dashboard deployment.

Interacting with the BI Dashboard

After you deploy the BI End to End Solution dashboard, users can interact with its data.

The initial interaction is to apply a different date value from the Date Calendar Year filter than is on the dashboard. When the filter is being applied, all items that are connected to the filter display an Updating message, as shown in Figure 14.35.

Because the dashboard contains an analytic chart, users can right-click a chart item and select Decomposition Tree from the menu, as shown in Figure 14.36.

NOTE

The Show Details and Decomposition Tree menu items are only available if you are using a measure that is not a calculated measure in the cube. If the measure is calculated, Show Details is disabled and the Decomposition Tree menu item will not appear.

FIGURE 14.35   Dashboard filter updates.

FIGURE 14.36   Decomposition Tree menu.

Clicking Decomposition Tree from the menu brings up a new window that enables users to interact with the data by clicking through different dimensions within the cube and following the trail from the original view of the data to the details that are making up the aggregated values. Figure 14.37 shows a sample Decomposition Tree interaction with the Contoso Retail cube.

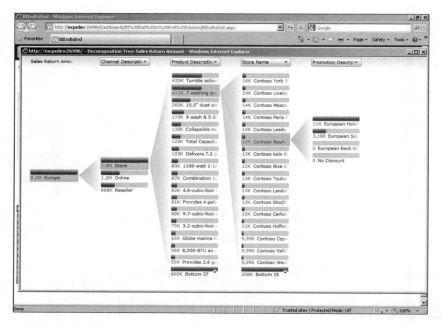

FIGURE 14.37   Decomposition Tree window.

In the Yearly Company Sales and Returns scorecard, the KPIs that were developed earlier in this chapter changed the calculation from Default to Data Value. By changing the KPI's calculation property in the design, users interacting with the KPI in a dashboard can then drill into the aggregated value using the Decomposition Tree menu item or by viewing the details by right-clicking the value and selecting the Show Details in the menu. Figure 14.38 displays sales amount detail from the Contoso Retail cube.

In addition to the previous examples, users can change the analytic chart type to a different report type, add additional measures to the chart, filter values within the scorecard, export report values to Excel, and perform many other PerformancePoint actions that come with the PerformancePoint toolset.

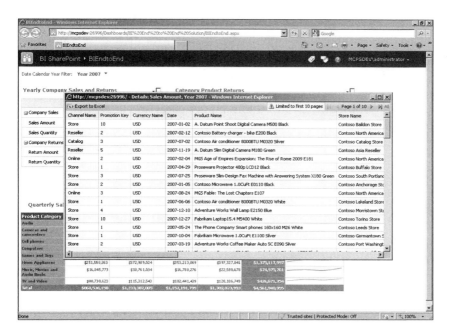

FIGURE 14.38   Scorecard value details.

Summary

This chapter stepped through the end-to-end process of creating and deploying a management dashboard console. The process detailed the initial creation of a SharePoint site, the development of a Reporting Services report using Report Builder, the building of PerformancePoint content, the connecting of all content items on a dashboard via a filter and how a user interacts with the solution. The solution utilizes PerformancePoint Services and Reporting Services within SharePoint 2010 to provide a visualization of business performance using the Microsoft Business Intelligence toolset.

Best Practices

The following are best practices from this chapter:

- ▶ Typically, creating pages for the functional areas within the BI site collection should suffice. Subsites add additional overhead and might not be warranted based on requirements.

- ▶ The navigation of the BI site collection should be customized to provide a friendlier interface.

▶ Create shared data sources and shared datasets instead of embedding these in reports. Doing so frees business users from having to deal with these details and enables them to make some changes without editing individual reports.

▶ Out of the box, a minimal PerformancePoint master page is available to use for the dashboard formatting. In order to customize the look and feel of the dashboard to conform with the rest of the site, create custom master pages and apply that master page during the deployment of the dashboard.

CHAPTER 15

Integrating Visio and Excel Services

In Chapter 14, "Building a Management Dashboard
Solution," we developed a management dashboard using
SQL Reporting Services and PerformancePoint Services. In
this chapter, we create a new dashboard to display Contoso
sales data using Excel and Visio Graphics Services. Before
we move forward with this chapter, make sure these
services are installed and configured correctly on your
SharePoint farm.

> **NOTE**
>
> Review Chapter 2, "Excel Services in SharePoint 2010,"
> and Chapter 11, "Visio Graphics Service Configuration,"
> to learn more about how to install and configure Visio
> and Excel Services on your SharePoint farm.

Deployed Solution

In Chapter 14, the dashboard we developed was composed
of several different *business intelligence* (BI) components.
Performance Point Service Scorecard, Analytic Chart, and a
SQL Server Reporting Services Report were used to prepare
the dashboard. In addition, the dashboard contained a filter
on the Calendar Year connected to each of the dashboard
components. This new dashboard will use the Visio Web
Access web part to display a Visio web drawing on a dashboard page. Drawing will be using an Excel Services data
sheet as a back-end data source.

NOTE

Note that this new Visio dashboard is not a replacement of the dashboard we created in Chapter 14. This exercise was done to explain how Visio web drawings can be integrated with SharePoint 2010.

Creating a Visio Web Drawing with Microsoft Visio 2010 Premium Edition

Before we start, we need to prepare an Excel sheet that we will deploy on a SharePoint 2010 document library. We will use this Excel sheet as an external data source for our web drawing. You can either create this sheet manually by executing a shared SQL query against ContosoRetailDW database or access this sheet from the book's resource material. This Excel sheet shows annual sales data, by continent, for all years:

```
SELECT  C.ContinentName
    , D.CalendarYearLabel
    , SUM(A.SalesAmount) AS SalesAmount
    , SUM(A.ReturnAmount) AS ReturnAmount
    , SUM(A.DiscountAmount) AS DiscountAmount
    , SUM(A.TotalCost) AS TotalCost
    , SUM(A.SalesAmount)-SUM(A.TotalCost) AS Margin
FROM        dbo.FactSales A
INNER JOIN    dbo.DimStore B
ON    A.StoreKey = B.StoreKey
INNER JOIN    dbo.DimGeography C
ON    B.GeographyKey = C.GeographyKey
INNER JOIN    dbo.DimDate D
ON    A.DateKey = D.Datekey
GROUP BY   C.ContinentName
        , D.CalendarYearLabel
ORDER BY   C.ContinentName
        , D.CalendarYearLabel
```

When the Excel sheet is ready, publish it on a SharePoint document library. Also, verify that you can open this Excel sheet in the browser by clicking the sheet name in the document library.

Start Microsoft Visio Premium Edition and create a blank drawing with landscape page orientation. Page orientation can be changed from the Design tab on the top menu bar. When you have a blank drawing page up, follow these steps to connect your drawing to the SalesByContinent.xlsx Excel sheet:

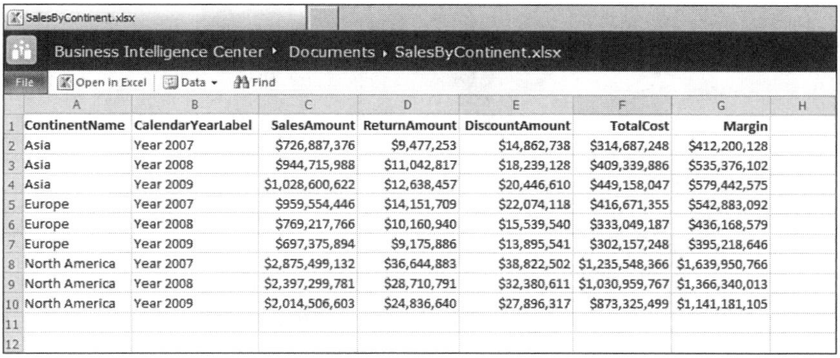

	A	B	C	D	E	F	G	H
1	ContinentName	CalendarYearLabel	SalesAmount	ReturnAmount	DiscountAmount	TotalCost	Margin	
2	Asia	Year 2007	$726,887,376	$9,477,253	$14,862,738	$314,687,248	$412,200,128	
3	Asia	Year 2008	$944,715,988	$11,042,817	$18,239,128	$409,339,886	$535,376,102	
4	Asia	Year 2009	$1,028,600,622	$12,638,457	$20,446,610	$449,158,047	$579,442,575	
5	Europe	Year 2007	$959,554,446	$14,151,709	$22,074,118	$416,671,355	$542,883,092	
6	Europe	Year 2008	$769,217,766	$10,160,940	$15,539,540	$333,049,187	$436,168,579	
7	Europe	Year 2009	$697,375,894	$9,175,886	$13,895,541	$302,157,248	$395,218,646	
8	North America	Year 2007	$2,875,499,132	$36,644,883	$38,822,502	$1,235,548,366	$1,639,950,766	
9	North America	Year 2008	$2,397,299,781	$28,710,791	$32,380,611	$1,030,959,767	$1,366,340,013	
10	North America	Year 2009	$2,014,506,603	$24,836,640	$27,896,317	$873,325,499	$1,141,181,105	
11								
12								

FIGURE 15.1 Excel sheet in a browser.

1. Click the **Data** tab (available in the top menu bar).
2. Click **Link Data to Shapes**.
3. Select **Microsoft Excel Workbook** in the Data Selector window and then click **Next**.
4. Provide the complete path of your Excel workbook stored at your SharePoint document library (for example, http://sp2010bi/Documents/SalesByContinent.xlsx) and then click **Next**.
5. Choose the actual worksheet that has data from among the names on the drop-down menu, and then click **Next**. You can also provide a range of data instead of an entire worksheet.
6. Choose your unique identifiers in the dataset. For SalesByContinent, select **ContinentName** and **CalendarYearLabel** as unique identifiers and then click **Finish**.

   You will see your sales data at the bottom of your blank drawing. We will use this data now to link it to actual shapes.
7. Change the background of your drawing page to the world background by using the **Background** option under the Design menu.
8. Rename your drawing page **2007**. For each year, we will create a separate page. In total, we will have three pages, named 2007, 2008, and 2009.
9. Drop the shape of your choice on your Visio web drawing. I have used the building 1 shape available under Landmark Shapes. You can access Landmark Shapes from the More Shapes menu available on left side of the window (More Shapes, Maps and Floor Plans, Maps, Landmark Shapes (US Units)). You will need three shapes on each page for three different continents. Place the shape in such a way that they represent continents on your drawing.
10. Link shapes to the data rows by dragging rows to actual shapes. Doing so links data in Excel to actual shapes on your drawing. For example, the Data row for Asia 2007 will be linked to the building 1 Shape on page 2007 placed over Asia. (See Figure 15.2)

15

FIGURE 15.2   Visio web drawing in a browser.

11. By default, not every measure will appear when you create a link between shapes and data rows. You will need to use **Edit Data Graphic** option on the Data menu to add the rest of the measure items to your drawing (if required) and update their formatting.

12. Add a text header on each page to explain to users what data they are presenting.

13. Publish the drawing to your SharePoint document library as a Visio web drawing. When the sheet is published, it will look something like Figure 15.2.

At this point, we have our Visio web drawing ready. Our next task is to create the dashboard page, which we will use to display this drawing using the Visio Web Access web part. To create a new dashboard page, follow these steps:

1. Click **Dashboard** link from the menu bar on left of your Business Intelligence Center home page.

2. Click the **Document** button under Library Tools. Click the **New Folder** button. Type **Visio Dashboard** in the Name text box and click **Save**.

3. Click the **Visio Dashboard** folder, and then click the **New Document** button. An option to create a web part page appears on the menu. Click **Web Part Page** to create a new web part page.

4. Name your web part page **Sales By Continent**. For layout, choose **Header, Left Column, Body**, choose Dashboards from the document library drop-down menu, and then click **Create**.

5. Click the **Add a Web Part** link available in the Body of the Page. Select **Business Data** from the Categories menu and then select **Visio Web Access** from the Web Parts menu. Click the **Add** button to add the Visio Web Access web part to the body of the page.

6. Click the **Click Here to Open the Tool Pane** link to open your SalesByContinent.vdw Visio web drawing as a web part in the body of your dashboard page. The drawing will look like Figure 15.3.

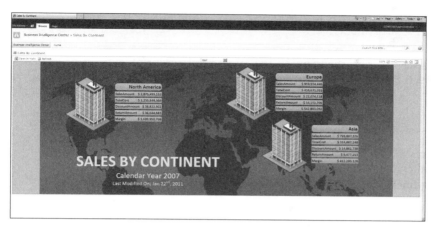

FIGURE 15.3   Visio Web Access web part.

7. Click the Stop Editing button on the top ribbon bar to stop editing the page.

At this point, we have our Visio Web Access web part page. Now we will add a custom list to our site and connect that list item to the shapes in our Visio web drawing:

1. Select **More Options** from the Site Actions menu. Create a custom list called **Calendar Year**.

2. Create a **Year** column in your list, and then add this list to your Visio web part drawing page, as shown in Figure 15.4. Insert 2007, 2008, and 2009 as list items to the Calendar Year list.

FIGURE 15.4   Custom SharePoint Foundation list.

Our next step is to link our SharePoint Foundation list with the Visio Web Access web part:

1. Click **Page, Edit Page**.
2. Select **Connections** from the menu in the upper-right corner of your Visio web part. Select **Get Web Drawing URL and Page Name From** and click the **Calendar Year** custom list.
3. Select **Year** from the Provider Field Name and **Page Name** from the Consumer Field Name drop-down menu. Then click **Finish**.

After you click Finish, a Select column appears on your Calendar Year custom list with a Link icon. You can click that Link icon to pass the associated year value to your web drawing. Drawing filters the page based on the year value you pass to the drawing.

We will now create another SharePoint Foundation list for continents. This time when we will select a continent, the actual continent shape will be highlighted in our web drawing:

1. Create a custom list called **Continents**. Create two columns in this list: **Continent** and **ShapeName**. Continent will have values such as Asia, Europe, and North America. ShapeName will have corresponding shape names (for example, Building 1). Enable the **Shape Information** window and then click the actual shape to identify each shape name.

FIGURE 15.5   Custom SharePoint Foundation list: Calendar Year.

2. Now link your drawing to this new list. This time choose **Get Shapes to Highlight** from the Connection menu. Select the Continent list to pass the value of the ShapeName field from the SharePoint Foundation list to your web drawing.
3. Click **Finish**. A red border appears around the shape whose value is selected on the Continents list.

FIGURE 15.6   Custom SharePoint Foundation list: Continents.

At this point, we have a dashboard that displays sales data by continent for three years. This dashboard is using data from an Excel sheet hosted on the same SharePoint site. It is also using SharePoint Foundation lists to interact with a Visio web drawing on the same dashboard page.

Summary

This chapter showed how you can use data-driven Visio web drawings on a dashboard page using Visio Web Access web parts. This chapter also covered how to use SharePoint Foundation list items to either select the page on your drawing or highlight the shapes on your drawing using values passed from the list. This technique can be used as a filter.

The Visio web drawing we created displays sales data by continent. The solution utilizes the Visio Graphics Service and Excel Services to provide the proper visualization of business performance data by continent.

Best Practices

The following are best practices from this chapter:

▶ To open a Visio drawing in a browser via SharePoint site, you must save your drawing file as a web drawing (.vdw file).

▶ When connecting to a SQL Server database from a Visio web drawing, use an ODC file stored on the same SharePoint site as your Visio web drawing. This helps you with maintaining a single connection file for all Visio web drawings.

▶ The Automatically Link button under the Data menu lets you quickly link your data rows to shapes. It is handy when dealing with many data rows.

▶ It is important to use legends when defining data as nontext. You can create a legend quickly by using the Insert Legend button under the Data menu.

▶ You can copy and paste shapes to quickly create shapes of the same size on your drawing.

PART VII

Troubleshooting

IN THIS PART

CHAPTER 16

Reporting Services Issues

A number of configuration settings can affect running
Reporting Services in SharePoint Integrated mode. This
chapter covers some of the common settings that you
might need to tweak to provide the desired user experience.
In addition this chapter will touch on a few other areas of
which you need to be aware to get Reporting Services
running smoothly in SharePoint Integrated mode.

How Do I Create a Shared Dataset in Report Builder?

SQL Server Reporting Services 2008 R2 has a new shared
dataset feature that provides for creating a dataset and
reusing it in multiple reports. Report Builder 3.0 provides
the Report Data window that is used to access built-in
fields, parameters, images, data sources, and datasets, as
shown in Figure 16.1. Right-clicking **Datasets** allows you to
add a shared dataset to the current report or create a new
dataset that will be embedded in the current report. It does
not allow you to create a new shared dataset. There are two
ways to create a shared dataset in Report Builder 3.0:

- ▶ Click **New** right below Report Data as shown in Figure
  16.1 and then select Dataset from the popup menu.

- ▶ Select the **New Dataset** option on the Getting Started
  dialog, as shown in Figure 16.2. For a detailed walk-
  through of the steps required to create a shared
  dataset, see the "Creating a Report with Report Builder
  3.0" section in Chapter 14," Building a Management
  Dashboard Solution."

IN THIS CHAPTER

- ▶ How Do I Create a Shared
  Dataset in Report Builder?

- ▶ Report Builder Getting Started
  Dialog Not Displayed

- ▶ Enable Report Builder to Create
  or Edit Reports

- ▶ Is the Reporting Services
  Add-In Installed?

- ▶ How Do I Activate the Report
  Server Integration Feature?

- ▶ How Do I Create Report
  Artifacts in a SharePoint
  Library?

- ▶ Checking Report Project
  Settings

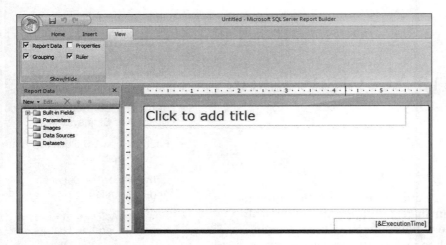

FIGURE 16.1   Report data.

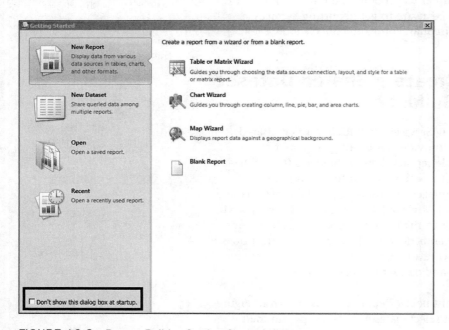

FIGURE 16.2   Report Builder Getting Started dialog.

Report Builder Getting Started Dialog Not Displayed

By default, Report Builder 3.0 shows the Getting Started dialog on startup, as shown in
Figure 16.2. This dialog provides an easy way to get started with a task in Report Builder.
When the Don't Show This Dialog at Startup check box in the lower-left area of the dialog

is checked, the Getting Started dialog will no longer display automatically when you launch Report Builder.

To restore this functionality, follow these steps:

1. Click the **Reporting Services** icon in the upper-left corner of the Report Builder window and then click the **Options** button.

2. Check the **Show the Getting Started Dialog Box at Startup** check box, as shown in Figure 16.3.

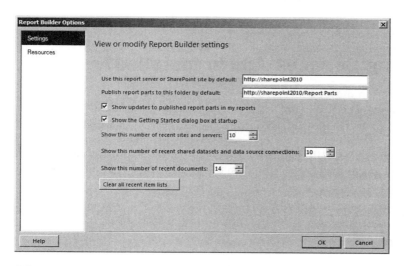

FIGURE 16.3   Report Builder Options dialog.

Enable Report Builder to Create or Edit Reports

Report Builder is a click-once application, which allows it to be launched from a SharePoint library to create or edit a report without having to perform a local installation. Report Builder is simply launched on demand. However, this capability is controlled by the Enable Report Builder Download setting in the Reporting Services Server Defaults. Follow these steps to check this setting:

1. Open SharePoint Central Administration from the Microsoft SharePoint 2010 Products program group.

2. Select **General Application Settings**.

3. Select **Set Server Defaults** in the Reporting Services section. The pertinent portion of the page is shown in Figure 16.4.

4. Make sure **Enable Report Builder Download** is checked to allow Report Builder to be launched on demand.

Report Builder Download	☐ Enable Report Builder download
Enable clients to download Report Builder from sites in this SharePoint farm.	
Custom Report Builder Launch URL	
Specify a custom URL for this property when the report server does not use the default Report Builder URL.	

FIGURE 16.4   Enable Report Builder Download option.

5. In addition, note the Custom Report Builder Launch URL setting shown in Figure 16.4. This setting enables you to specify the location of the Report Builder click-once application. You only need to do this if you want to use a URL that is different than the default.

Is the Reporting Services Add-In Installed?

The Reporting Services add-in must be installed for Reporting Services to run in SharePoint Integrated mode. The Reporting Services add-in is included in the SharePoint prerequisite installer; it can also be downloaded from the SQL Server 2008 R2 feature pack site. As a general rule you should run the SharePoint prerequisite installer to install the components that are required by SharePoint. To check whether the Reporting Services add-in has been installed, go to the Control Panel and look at the installed programs, as shown in Figure 16.5.

Uninstall or change a program

To uninstall a program, select it from the list and then click Uninstall, Change, or Repair.

Organize ▼   Uninstall   Change   Repair

Name ▲	Publisher	Install...	Size	Version
Microsoft Chart Controls for Microsoft .NET Framework 3.5	Microsoft Corporation	8/29/2010	3.45 MB	3.5.0.0
Microsoft Filter Pack 2.0	Microsoft Corporation	8/29/2010	6.76 MB	14.0.4763.1000
Microsoft Office 2003 Web Components	Microsoft Corporation	8/29/2010	29.8 MB	12.0.6213.1000
Microsoft Report Viewer Redistributable 2008 SP1	Microsoft Corporation	8/29/2010		
Microsoft Report Viewer Redistributable 2008 SP1	Microsoft Corporation	11/9/2010		
Microsoft Server Speech Platform Runtime (x64)	Microsoft Corporation	8/29/2010	5.21 MB	10.0.7135.0
Microsoft Server Speech Recognition Language - TELE (en-US)	Microsoft Corporation	8/29/2010	29.6 MB	10.0.7135.0
Microsoft SharePoint Server 2010	Microsoft Corporation	8/29/2010		14.0.4763.1000
Microsoft SQL Server 2005 Analysis Services ADOMD.NET	Microsoft Corporation	8/29/2010	1.78 MB	9.00.1399.06
Microsoft SQL Server 2008 Analysis Services ADOMD.NET	Microsoft Corporation	8/29/2010	171 KB	10.1.2531.0
Microsoft SQL Server 2008 R2 (64-bit)	Microsoft Corporation	8/29/2010		
Microsoft SQL Server 2008 R2 Books Online	Microsoft Corporation	8/29/2010	177 MB	10.50.1600.1
Microsoft SQL Server 2008 R2 Native Client	Microsoft Corporation	8/29/2010	6.06 MB	10.50.1600.1
Microsoft SQL Server 2008 R2 Policies	Microsoft Corporation	8/29/2010	984 KB	10.50.1600.1
Microsoft SQL Server 2008 R2 Report Builder 3.0	Microsoft Corporation	12/4/2010	78.0 MB	10.50.1600.1
Microsoft SQL Server 2008 R2 Setup (English)	Microsoft Corporation	8/29/2010	43.6 MB	10.50.1600.1
Microsoft SQL Server 2008 Setup Support Files	Microsoft Corporation	8/29/2010	24.8 MB	10.1.2731.0
Microsoft SQL Server Browser	Microsoft Corporation	8/29/2010	8.99 MB	10.50.1600.1
Microsoft SQL Server Compact 3.5 SP2 ENU	Microsoft Corporation	8/29/2010	3.39 MB	3.5.8080.0
Microsoft SQL Server Compact 3.5 SP2 Query Tools ENU	Microsoft Corporation	8/29/2010	4.63 MB	3.5.8080.0
Microsoft SQL Server System CLR Types (x64)	Microsoft Corporation	8/29/2010	1.12 MB	10.50.1600.1
Microsoft SQL Server VSS Writer	Microsoft Corporation	8/29/2010	3.59 MB	10.50.1600.1
Microsoft Sync Framework Runtime v1.0 (x64)	Microsoft Corporation	8/29/2010	802 KB	1.0.1215.0
Microsoft Sync Services for ADO.NET v2.0 (x64)	Microsoft Corporation	8/29/2010	532 KB	2.0.1215.0
Microsoft Visual Studio 2008 Shell (integrated mode) - ENU	Microsoft Corporation	8/29/2010	162 MB	9.0.30729
Microsoft Visual Studio Tools for Applications 2.0 - ENU	Microsoft Corporation	8/29/2010	208 MB	9.0.35191
SQL 2008 R2 Reporting Services SharePoint 2010 Add-in	Microsoft Corporation	8/29/2010	15.7 MB	10.50.1600.1

FIGURE 16.5   Installed programs.

For the installation details, see the "Reporting Services Add-In for SharePoint" section in Chapter 3, "Reporting Services Setup and Installation."

TIP

There are several versions of the Reporting Services Add-In. Make sure to match the version that you install with your version of SQL Server and SharePoint.

How Do I Activate the Report Server Integration Feature?

Report Server Integration is the name of the SharePoint feature that must be activated to run Reporting Services in SharePoint Integrated mode. The feature is installed by the Reporting Services add-in for SharePoint and should be activated during the installation. The feature is activated at the site collection level. To activate the feature, follow these steps:

1. Click **Site Actions**.
2. Click **Site Settings**.
3. Click **Site Collection Features** (in the Site Collection Administration group).
4. Click **Activate** next to the Report Server Integration feature.

Beginning with SQL Server Reporting Services 2008 R2 version of the Reporting Services add-in for SharePoint, the Report Server Integration feature is automatically activated in every site collection when installed. In addition, the feature is activated in any new site collections that are created.

How Do I Create Report Artifacts in a SharePoint Library?

Clicking New Document in a SharePoint library displays a drop-down menu with the options Report Builder Model, Report Builder Report, and Report Data Source. However, for these menu options to be displayed, the library must be configured to allow multiple content types, and the appropriate content types must be added to the list of content types for the library. For the complete details on setting this up, see the "Add Content Types to a Document Library" section in Chapter 3, "Reporting Services Setup and Configuration."

16

Checking Report Project Settings

There are two report authoring tools available for designing and deploying reports in SharePoint Integrated mode for SharePoint 2010: Report Builder 3.0 and Business Intelligence Development Studio (BIDS). Both of these tools have their own property settings that must be specified correctly in order to successfully deploy reports to a SharePoint document library.

The most important setting for a BIDS report project is the TargetServerURL. The URL that you specify must be the root site in a site collection. When you install and configure SharePoint, a default site collection is created for you. The URL of the root site in the default site collection is typically the name of the server; for example http://SharePoint2010. If you create an additional site collection, the URL of the root site might look like this: http://SharePoint2010/sites/BI. You can go back to the "Deploy Report from BIDS" section of Chapter 4, "Report Management," for the complete details on setting the BIDS report project properties.

The most important setting in Report Builder 3.0 is **Use This Report Server or SharePoint Site by Default.** The URL that you specify must be the root site in a site collection, same as what you specified in a BIDS report project. You can go back to the "Save from Report Builder" section of Chapter 4 for the complete details on setting Report Builder properties for SharePoint Integrated mode.

Summary

Getting Reporting Services and Report Builder working correctly in SharePoint Integrated mode is not too difficult. The main task is installing and configuring the Reporting Services add-in for SharePoint. There are also a couple of important settings to be aware of in BIDS, Report Builder, and SharePoint Central Administration. This chapter covered a couple of areas that might require some attention to get things running smoothly.

Best Practices

The following are best practices from this chapter:

- ▶ Pay close attention to the installation and configuration of the Reporting Services add-in for SharePoint. This is the key requirement for getting Reporting Services running in SharePoint Integrated mode.

- ▶ Make sure to become familiar with the Report Builder settings, because this is the end-user tool for developing reports.

- ▶ Make sure to become familiar with the BIDS project settings for deploying reports to a SharePoint document library.

- ▶ Remember to configure a SharePoint library with the appropriate content types to support developing reports, models, and data sources.

CHAPTER 17

PerformancePoint Services Issues

With every development tool, you can expect development roadblocks from time to time. These might require you to change tool settings or perhaps to consider a different angle to create a workaround and successful resolution. This chapter covers how to get around some of these roadblocks when developing in PerformancePoint Services.

PerformancePoint Services Is Not Configured Correctly

When creating a data source for Analysis Services, you must set the server name, select the SSAS database, pick a role, and select the *SQL Server Analysis Services* (SSAS) cube from the available list. However, when you click the Cube dropdown, a message appears stating that the data source cannot be used because PerformancePoint Services is not configured correctly, as shown in Figure 17.1.

In addition to the error message, a Windows Application Log message states the following:

> The PerformancePoint Services Unattended Service Account is not set. The setting is located in "Manage service applications" in SharePoint Central Administration under the PerformancePoint Services management page.

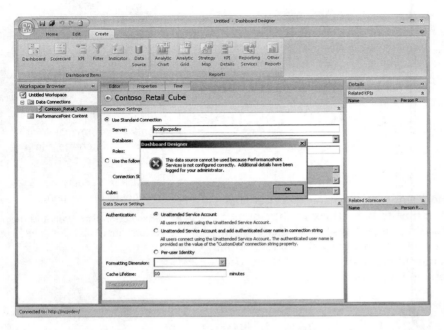

FIGURE 17.1   Improper configuration of PerformancePoint Services.

The resolution is to navigate to Central Admin, Applications Management, Manage Service Applications, PerformancePoint Service Application, PerformancePoint Service Application Settings to add the service account. However, when adding the service account to the PerformancePoint Services Application Settings page, a message might appear stating that the Unattended Service Account cannot be set for the service application. The message is shown in Figure 17.2

The resolution is to set up the Secure Store Service first before entering the unattended service account information on the PerformancePoint Service Application Settings page.

See Chapter 6, "PerformancePoint Services Configuration," for the steps to set up the Secure Store Service and set the unattended service account on the PerformancePoint Services Application Settings page.

FIGURE 17.2   Secure Store Service not set for PerformancePoint Services.

Dashboard Connection Formula

In most instances, the filter on a dashboard is pretty straightforward. The standard steps are to create a Member Selection filter, select values to be used in the Selection criteria, and then drag the filter onto a dashboard. After adding the filter to the dashboard, a report or scorecard then creates a connection to pull in the member unique name to a value on the reporting object.

However, in some cases, a manipulation needs to occur between the filtered value and how the reporting object will interpret the value, which is where the connection formula is used to translate the filter value. To understand what to code within the Connection Formula screen, though, you must understand what is being sent to the SSAS server for the translation. For any code being placed into the text, PerformancePoint Services will wrap the code with the following syntax:

```
SELECT { StrToSet("DISTINCT({USER CODE})") } DIMENSION PROPERTIES MEMBER_TYPE on 0
FROM [Cube Name]
```

User code is the code that is placed within the connection formula, which provides insight on how to code within the text box. Also, the connection formula will translate the <<UniqueName>> code as the unique name of the member selected from the filter.

Figure 17.3 illustrates a simple connection formula, and Figure 17.4 displays the Profiler trace that shows what was sent to the SSAS server.

FIGURE 17.3   Connection formula example.

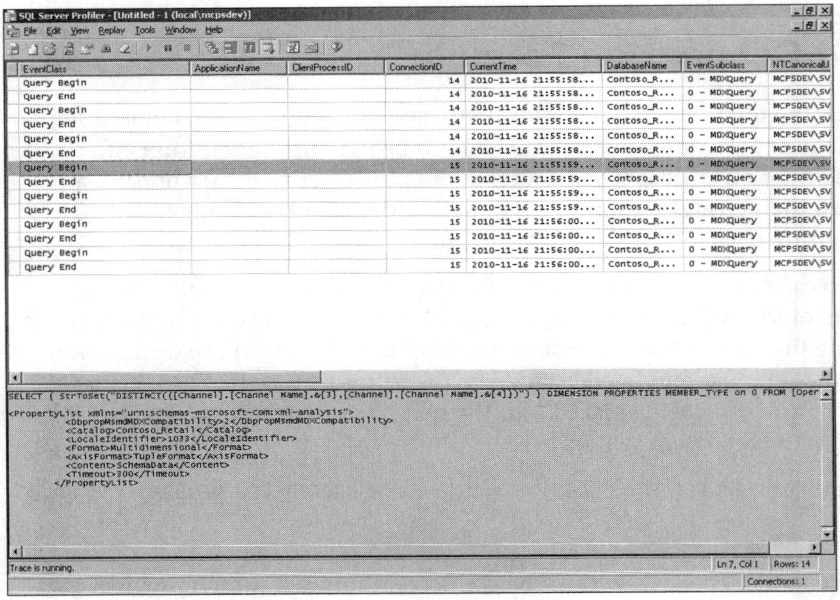

FIGURE 17.4   SSAS Profiler trace for basic a connection formula.

A simple example is all well and good, but here is an advanced example where a dimension called Date Ref is used as a filter and then translated to a Date Dimension value based on other calculations within the cube:

```
STRTOMEMBER(case when '<<UniqueName>>' = '[DATE REF].[DATE REF TYPE].&[YESTERDAY]'
  then '[CREATION DATE].[Date].[Date].&' + [measures].[yesterday value]
  when '<<UniqueName>>' = '[DATE REF].[DATE REF TYPE].&[WTD]'
  then '[CREATION DATE].[Week Ending Date].&' + [measures].[WTD value]
 when '<<UniqueName>>' = '[DATE REF].[DATE REF TYPE].&[MTD]'
  then '[CREATION DATE].[Fiscal Period].&' + [measures].[MTD value]
 when '<<UniqueName>>' = '[DATE REF].[DATE REF TYPE].&[QTD]'
  then '[CREATION DATE].[Fiscal Qtr].&' + [measures].[QTD value]
 when '<<UniqueName>>' = '[DATE REF].[DATE REF TYPE].&[YTD]'
  then '[CREATION DATE].[Fiscal Year].&' + [measures].[YTD value]
 else
  '[CREATION DATE].[Date].[Date].&' + [measures].[yesterday value]
 end)
```

Figure 17.5 contains the trace example of how this calculation formula is then wrapped and sent to the SSAS server.

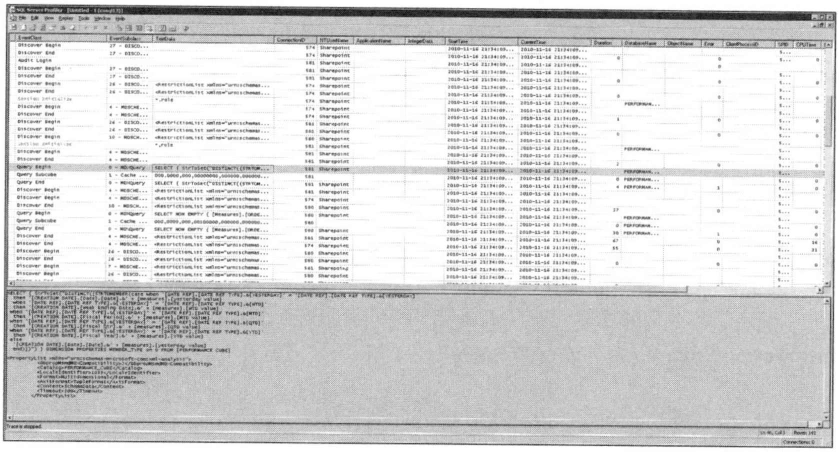

FIGURE 17.5   SSAS Profiler trace for the advanced connection formula.

Knowing that PerformancePoint Services is going to wrap the query with a StrToSet function allows for creative solutions for piecing together the string to be interpreted.

Other examples on using *multidimensional expressions* (MDX) to extend the connection formula are found in Table 17.1.

TABLE 17.1   Connection Formula MDX Examples

Description	Syntax
Children of the selected member	`<<UniqueName>>.Children or <<SourceValue>>.Children`
Parent of the selected member	`<<UniqueName>>.Parent`
Descendants of the member at level 2	`Descendants(<<UniqueName>>,2)`
Top 10 descendants of the member at level 2 for the "Internet Sales Amount" measure for Quarter 3 of 2008	`TopCount({Descendants(<<UniqueName>>,2)}, 10, ([Date].[Calendar].[Calendar Quarter].&[2008]&[3],[Measures].[Internet Sales Amount]))`
The **Hierarchize** function, which lets you compare several countries or regions and select the top two members (cities) in each region	`Hierarchize(Union(<<UniqueName>>, Generate(<<UniqueName>>, TopCount(Descendants([Geography].[Geography].CurrentMember, [Geography].[Geography].[City]), 2, ([Measures].[Sales Amt], [Time].[FY Year].&[2006]) )) ))`
Nonempty values function	`NONEMPTY(EXISTS([Dimension].[Hierarchy - Dimension].[Level number].members,<<SourceValue>>,'Measure Group'))`

* Source: http://technet.microsoft.com/en-us/library/ff535784.aspx

Creating PerformancePoint Content Items in a Nontrusted Location

When PerformancePoint Services is initially configured, the default for trusted locations is to trust all locations. Although this is great for the developer, the administrator might not want to grant such wide open permissions on the SharePoint site. If you are trying to create a PerformancePoint content item in a nontrusted location, a message will appear stating that the query could not complete because the report is in a nontrusted location, as shown in Figure 17.6.

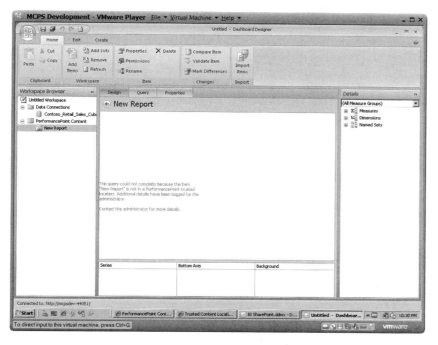

FIGURE 17.6   Nontrusted content location.

In addition to the message in the Dashboard Designer, events are written to the Application log. The following message is an example of an event in the Application log where PerformancePoint content is being saved in a list called PerformancePoint Content but the list itself is a Nontrusted Location:

> The shared service administrator must configure the following content locations as "trusted":

> /Lists/PerformancePoint Content

To set the list that the Dashboard Designer is going to use for storage of the PerformancePoint content items, refer to steps detailed in Chapter 6 in the "PerformancePoint Services Configuration in the Trusted Content Locations" section.

Insufficient Security for Dashboard Deployment

A developer is able to create PerformancePoint Services content, including a dashboard, and save the items to the SharePoint site. However, when attempting to deploy the dashboard, a message appears, as shown in Figure 17.7.

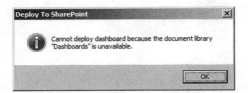

FIGURE 17.7   Unable to deploy dashboard.

To solve the problem, ensure that the developer has the proper permission level in the SharePoint site. To develop content, the developer needs the Contributor permission level, but the actual deployment of the dashboard requires the Designer permission level. Adding the Designer permission level to the SharePoint user or group the developer belongs to will allow for the deployment of the dashboard.

Cube Action Not Available on a PerformancePoint Services Report

In the SSAS cube development, a custom action is created to allow for displaying details about the data within Excel or some other front-end application. The action is displayed in the menu when the user right-clicks a cell to drill into and selects additional account. In Figure 17.8, two actions are available for the Operation cube: Row_Action and Sales Details.

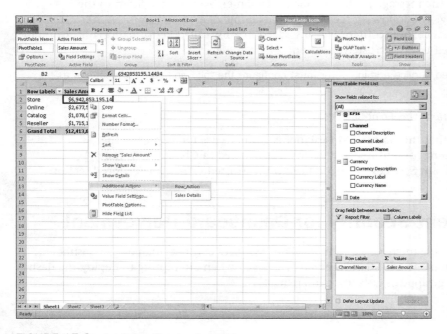

FIGURE 17.8   Available Excel cube actions.

When using the PerformancePoint Services Dashboard, as shown in Figure 17.9, right-clicking an Analytic Grid cell and selecting Additional Actions displays just one available action: Sales Details.

FIGURE 17.9   Available PerformancePoint Services cube actions.

You might be wondering why the Row_Action is not displayed. The answer is in the type of action that is developed. For PerformancePoint Services, only a drillthrough action will display in an Analytic content item. For this example, the Row_Action was created via a new action in SSAS with a target type of Cells and an MDX statement as the action expression. Although this specific action is essentially creating a drillthrough action in nature, because the type is not a drillthrough action the action will not display within the PerformancePoint Services\Additional Actions menu.

Summary

PerformancePoint Services has many different parts that need to be set up correctly from within SharePoint or the data sources themselves for functionality to be exposed as expected. This chapter showed the different behaviors and messages that are displayed to the developer or end user if the underlying settings have not been properly configured. In addition to what PerformancePoint sends back to the user, this chapter covered the steps necessary to resolve configuration issues.

Best Practices

The following are best practices from this chapter:

▶ Ensure that PerformancePoint Services is set up in conjunction with the Secure Store Service before starting development.

▶ To deploy a dashboard, the user must have the Designer permission level assigned for the SharePoint web application.

▶ To use SSAS cube actions within a PerformancePoint Services dashboard, ensure that the cube action was created as a drillthrough action.

CHAPTER 18

PowerPivot Issues

Because PowerPivot is an add-in to Excel with a complementary service in SharePoint, troubleshooting PowerPivot issues essentially comes down to troubleshooting Excel and SharePoint.

Those familiar with SharePoint will know that the *Unified Logging Service* (ULS) logs are the best place to look for issues with *web front-end servers* (WFEs), service problems, and so on.

Those familiar with troubleshooting databases will know that tracing the interaction with the database is the best place to look for data issues. In addition, because PowerPivot for Excel can serve as a sort of database, Microsoft has added tracing capabilities to Excel to aid with troubleshooting.

This chapter explores how to use these tools and also identifies some common PowerPivot issues.

Troubleshooting PowerPivot for Excel

Tracing the interaction between an application and a database is typically performed from a database server. However, because PowerPivot for Excel can connect to multiple data sources, including traditional and nontraditional ones, it would be useful to be able to trace this interaction from within Excel. Thankfully, Microsoft has included the ability to generate trace files from within the PowerPivot add-in for Excel.

Enabling Tracing from PowerPivot for Excel

Tracing is enabled from the Settings menu of the PowerPivot tab on the Excel ribbon toolbar, as shown in Figure 18.1.

FIGURE 18.1   Accessing the PowerPivot Settings menu.

Enabling a trace is as simple as opening the **Settings** menu and selecting the **Enable PowerPivot Tracing for the Current Excel Session** check box on the Support and Diagnostics tab. However, there's a slight catch. For the trace to begin, the PowerPivot database engine, known as the VertiPaq engine, needs to be instantiated into memory. Because the Excel file could be used to simply view the existing data, the VertiPaq engine is not automatically loaded. As a result, if you enable tracing before the VertiPaq engine is instantiated, the check box will now state "Client Tracing will begin soon. Waiting for the Server to respond," as shown in Figure 18.2.

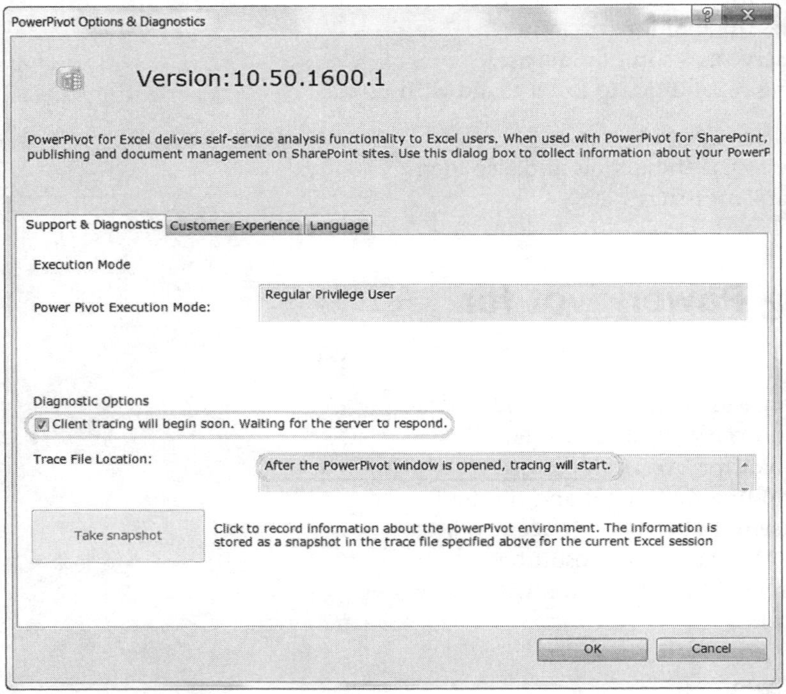

FIGURE 18.2   Tracing enabled, but the VertiPaq engine is not loaded.

You will also notice that there is a Snapshot button, but it is disabled. The Snapshot button captures the current state of the database as part of the trace file. This can be useful for troubleshooting, and it is considered a best practice to snapshot at the beginning of the trace. However, because the VertiPaq engine has not started yet, this snapshot cannot be created yet. At this point, the user would have to click OK to close the Diagnostics screen, load the database into memory, and then return to this Diagnostics screen to take the snapshot. For this reason, it is simpler to load the database into memory before beginning the trace process.

To load the VertiPaq database engine into memory, just click the pivot table data region, which opens the PowerPivot field list. Alternatively, open the PowerPivot window. After doing either of those two actions, once tracing is enabled in the PowerPivot Settings screen, the trace filename will be displayed and the Snapshot button will be enabled and can be selected.

The trace file is placed onto the current user's desktop by default, and there is no option to change that setting. This is likely not a problem because trace files are usually generated only to solve an immediate problem and the desktop is a convenient location for the file.

Disable Tracing from PowerPivot for Excel

Because trace files are verbose and can grow in size quickly, it is a good idea to stop the trace after the issue has been captured. To stop the trace from continuing to build, you should open the Settings window and clear the check box that was selected earlier. Note that in the initial release of PowerPivot (build 10.50.1600.1), there were reports of the trace file not stopping even after clearing the check box. In fact, if you clear the check box and close the Settings window, and then reopen the Settings window, you might notice that the check box is still checked. If this occurs, the tracing activity can only be stopped by closing the Excel file. This is believed to be a bug and may have been fixed by the time you read this, however you should watch out for this behavior.

In summary, when creating a trace file to troubleshoot PowerPivot for Excel, the following steps are recommended:

1. Open the file in question.
2. Either click a data region or open and then close the PowerPivot window to instantiate the VertiPaq engine in memory.
3. Open the Settings window from the PowerPivot tab of the ribbon, enable the trace, and then take a snapshot.
4. Close the Settings window and perform whatever analysis that you want to capture in the trace file.
5. Close the Excel file to terminate the trace (Note that the Excel file does *not* need to be saved to save the trace file.)
6. Analyze the trace file or provide it to someone who can.

18

Analyze Traces from PowerPivot for Excel

The trace file produced from Excel with PowerPivot is the same type of trace file produced by SQL Server Profiler. As a result, the best tool to analyze these trace files is SQL Server Profiler. However, only Profiler from SQL Server 2008 R2 can read these trace files because the trace definitions needed to be updated to support the VertiPaq engine.

Because the PowerPivot VertiPaq database engine is essentially an in-memory Analysis Services cube, the information in the trace files will be similar to what is produced when tracing Analysis Services queries, including connection information and the actual *multidimensional expression* (MDX) being used to query the data.

If a snapshot is created in the trace file, it will result in trace entries of "Server State Discover Begin," followed by several "Server State Discover Data:" entries, and then end with a "Server State Discover End" entry, as shown in Figure 18.3.

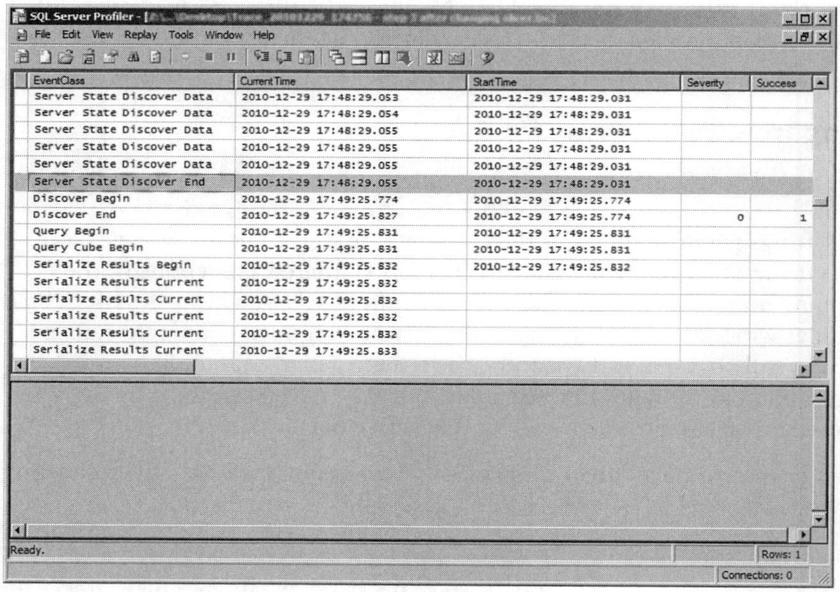

FIGURE 18.3   Snapshot entries in a trace file.

Troubleshooting PowerPivot for SharePoint

PowerPivot applications that are loaded into SharePoint present a bigger challenge for troubleshooting because there are many layers involved including SQL Server, SharePoint Services, the SharePoint web application, the network layer, and so on. Each of these layers has different tools for troubleshooting.

After a PowerPivot application is uploaded into SharePoint, its data becomes part of the Analysis Services in VertiPaq Mode instance on the database server. As such, if users are having problems with applications in the PowerPivot Gallery on SharePoint, SQL Server Profiler should be used to generate trace files from the PowerPivot instance on the database server. Because the PowerPivot databases are actually Analysis Services databases, the trace files produced will be similar to traces produced against standard Analysis Services databases.

If users are having issues with SharePoint itself, the SharePoint *Unified Logging Service* (ULS) logs can prove useful for troubleshooting, because the SharePoint WFEs and application servers write to the ULS logs. This is the best way to troubleshoot issues with Excel Services and the PowerPivot System Service. The default location for the logs is C:\Program Files\Common Files\Microsoft Shared\Web Server Extensions\14\LOGS.

Keep in mind that in a multiserver farm environment, logs from several servers might have to be analyzed to troubleshoot a particular problem.

The logs are not very readable in their raw format but can be opened with one of the ULS log viewers available on CodePlex. Figure 18.4 is an example using Stephan Gordon's ULS Log Viewer and filtering a log file to only PowerPivot entries.

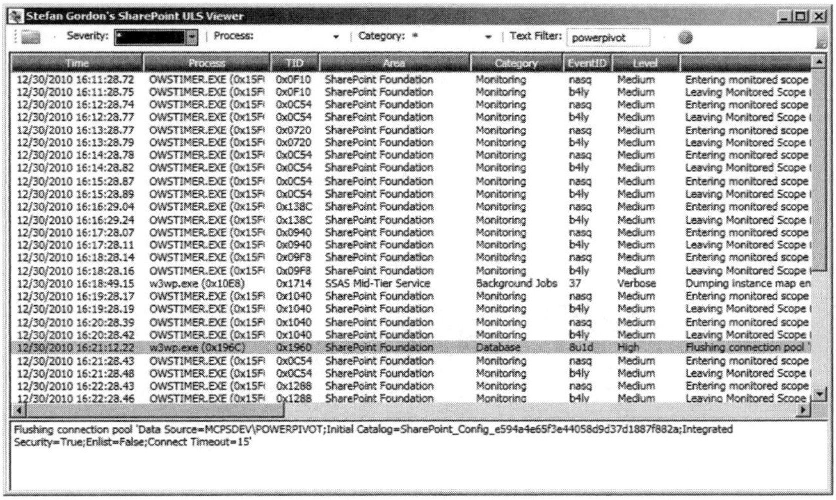

FIGURE 18.4   ULS Log Viewer for troubleshooting PowerPivot on SharePoint.

Log files by their very nature are verbose, and it can be difficult to locate the relevant issues. For this reason, it is important to narrow down when the error occurred or, if possible, to re-create the issue and then look at the most recent log files.

Common Issues

Some of the more common issues encountered during PowerPivot installation and usage are covered here. You can find many more issues and solutions online from Microsoft and several PowerPoint-specific websites, including the great PowerPivot Twins of Dave Wickert and Denny Lee at http://www.powerpivottwins.com.

Installing PowerPivot

▶ The PowerPivot for Excel add-in is available in both 32-bit and 64-bit versions. Ensure that the bit level of the add-in matches the bit level of the Excel installation. You can determine this by launching Excel and selecting **File**, **Help** and checking the version number under About Microsoft Excel.

▶ The PowerPivot for Excel add-in uses the *Visual Studio Tools for Office* (VSTO). These need to be installed as part of the Excel 2010 installation. If the VSTO were not installed with Excel 2010, Excel will need to be uninstalled and reinstalled with the VSTO option selected. Only then can the PowerPivot add-in be installed successfully into Excel.

▶ If installing PowerPivot for Excel on Windows XP, be sure to have SP3 installed and .NET3.5 SP1.

▶ Installing PowerPivot in an existing SharePoint farm is a complex process that can raise numerous issues. The best way to avoid these issues is to carefully follow a step-by-step installation guide. General installation steps are provided in Chapter 10, "PowerPivot for SharePoint." If necessary, you can find more detailed installation steps at http://msdn.microsoft.com.

Using PowerPivot

▶ **Relationships:** PowerPivot can scan the tables and automatically create relationships. However, if the relationship is from one dimension to another (that is, not from a dimension to a fact table), it might not be automatically detected and you should manually create it.

▶ **Hierarchies:** The initial version of PowerPivot does not support hierarchies (also known as drill paths, such as from Year to Quarter to Month to Day).

▶ **SharePoint list data in PowerPivot:** Using a SharePoint list as a data feed is supported but requires the Data Services Update for .NET Framework 3.5 SP1.

▶ **Excel Web Access warning in SharePoint:** Because PowerPivot applications require Excel Services to query external data, the Excel Web Access warning will pop up frequently. This is designed behavior with Excel Services, but should be disabled to avoid annoying PowerPivot users. To disable, open Central Administration, select **Manage Service Applications**, and select the Excel service application (that is, **ExcelServiceApp1**). Then click **Trusted File Locations**, **Trusted File Locations** and select **http://**. On the Settings page, under the External Data section, clear the **Warn on Refresh** check box.

▶ **User credential delegation error in SharePoint:** Users familiar with the MOSS 2007 double-hop scenario that requires Kerberos might think that this is a Kerberos issue, but SharePoint 2010 uses the Claims to Windows Token service, and both Excel and PowerPivot are Claims to Windows Token aware. If getting an error regarding user credential delegation, this is likely due to the Claims to Windows Token service not running. To check this, go to Central Administration and navigate to

System Settings, Manage Services on server. Select the correct server from the Server drop-down list and confirm that the Claims to Windows Token Service is started.

Summary

Troubleshooting PowerPivot essentially comes down to troubleshooting Excel and SharePoint. The ULS logs are the best place to start troubleshooting SharePoint issues. Data issues are best investigated by tracing the path to the data using SQL Server Profiler and the Excel trace capability provided with the PowerPivot add-in.

Visio Services Issues

This chapter explains how to deal with some of the known challenges that plague Visio Graphics Services. The issues discussed in this chapter (including their various symptoms) and their resolutions derive from TechNet (source: http://technet.microsoft.com/en-us/library/ee513129.aspx).

Visio Graphics Service Data Refresh Failed (Event ID 8037, 8038, 8062, 8063)

Microsoft Visio diagrams can be connected to an external data source, such as Excel Service. This error usually occurs when the data schema in a file changes. Users might observe the following errors in the event log:

▶ **Event ID: 8037 Description:** Invalid data type found in Published File cache for file *<FileName>* Exception : *<ExceptionCode>*.

▶ **Event ID: 8038 Description:** Invalid data type found in Rendered File cache for file *<FileName>* Exception : *<ExceptionCode>*.

▶ **Event ID: 8063 Description:** Invalid data type found in ODC cache for file %1.

▶ **Event ID: 8062 Description:** Primary key column deleted.

According to Microsoft, the following might cause errors:

▶ External data source, such as a Microsoft Excel workbook no longer exists or is inaccessible.

▶ The primary key is changed, and Visio Graphics Service cannot update the data in the Visio diagram.

▶ Data provider is not valid or trusted.

Fixing these issues can help you resolve this error. Make sure your data providers are trusted, your primary keys are set up correctly, and both source and drawing are hosted on the same SharePoint site.

Visio Configuration Database Not Found (Event ID 8040)

Visio Graphics Service stores its application configuration settings in the configuration-a12-n database. It is very important that service has access to this database at all times to function properly. Users will observe the following symptoms if this issue occurs:

▶ Visio Diagrams will not render.

▶ Event ID: 8040 will appear in the event log. The description "Can't find configuration manager" will display.

According to Microsoft, this issue might be caused by the following:

▶ The configuration database is not accessible.

▶ The configuration database is not responding or responding extremely slowly due to heavy network activity.

Microsoft recommends that to resolve this issue you confirm that the SQL Server configuration database is functioning correctly. You can do so as follows:

1. On the SharePoint Central Administration website, in the System Settings section, click **Manage Servers in This Farm**.

2. In the Farm Information section, note the configuration database server name and the version.

3. Start SQL Server Management Studio and connect to the same configuration SQL database server you noted in step 2.

4. If you can't connect to the database server then run the SharePoint Products and Technologies Configuration Wizard to fix this issue.

If this resolution does not work, identify whether the SQL Server network connection has any issues. To confirm connectivity, follow these steps:

1. On the Central Administration page, in the System Settings section of the reading pane, click **Manage Servers in This Farm**.

2. In the Farm Information section, note the configuration database server name.

3. Open a command prompt window and type **ping** *<server name>*. Confirm if you get the response back from the server.

   If you do not receive a reply back from the server then it indicates a problem with the network connection or another problem that prevents a response from the server.

4. Log on to the server and troubleshoot the connectivity issue.

Visio Graphics Service Untrusted Data Provider Request (Event ID 8041)

This error occurs when the data provider your drawing is using is not on the list of trusted data providers. Users might see the following symptoms when this issue happens:

▶ Data is not refreshing.

▶ Event ID: 8041 appears in the event log with a "Trusted data provider error. *<error name>*" description.

According to Microsoft, this issue might happen because the data provider is not registered as a trusted data provider. Follow the guidelines in Chapter 11, "Visio Graphics Service Configuration," to add your data source to a trusted data provider list.

Visio Graphics Service Failed to Generate Diagram (Event ID 8060, 8042, 8043)

This error occurs when the service is unable to generate the diagram. Users might observe the following symptom because of this issue:

▶ Event ID: 8060, Event ID: 8042, and Event ID: 8043 will appear in the event log.

According to Microsoft, the following could be the reasons:

▶ If this error appears together with another error, the diagram might fail to render because of the causes specified in the corresponding error that is triggered.

▶ If only this error is appearing in the log, Visio Graphics Service in SharePoint might have failed to generate a diagram for an unknown reason.

▶ Another reason could be because Visio Graphics Service is configured incorrectly.

You need to review all three of these potential reasons to identify what is really causing this issue.

Visio Proxy Initialization Failed (Event ID 8044)

This error appears in the log if Proxy is not configured correctly. The Visio Graphics Service application and its corresponding web parts use a proxy to connect to the back-end service. Users might observe following symptoms:

19

▶ Diagrams will not render.

▶ Event ID: 8044 will appear in the event log with an "Unable to initialize Visio service proxy" description.

Microsoft suggests the following as possible causes:

▶ The application proxy for the Visio Graphics Service is not running or is incorrectly configured.

To resolve this issue, we need to verify whether the Visio Graphics Service application proxy is configured correctly. To do so, follow these steps:

1. On the SharePoint Central Administration page, click **Manage Service Applications**.

2. Verify that a service application proxy is associated with each of your Visio Graphics Service application. If a service application has a proxy configured then it should appear in the next line with increased indent and "Proxy" word should be used in the description provided in the Type column on Manage Service Application page.

If no service application proxy corresponds to the Visio Graphics Service application that fails, create a new one by using Windows PowerShell 2.0. To create a new one, follow these steps:

1. Click **Start, All Programs, Microsoft SharePoint 2010 Products, SharePoint Management Shell**.

2. Create a new Visio Graphics Service application proxy by entering the Windows PowerShell cmdlet `New-SPVisioServiceApplicationProxy` at the command prompt in the SharePoint Management Shell.

Create a new service application if the preceding steps don't resolve your issue. To create a new service application, follow these steps:

1. On the Central Administration page, click **Manage Service Applications**.

2. In the Name column, select the Visio Graphics Service application proxy that is failing and then on the ribbon click **Delete**.

3. Select the parent Visio Graphics Service application of the application proxy that you deleted and then on the ribbon click **Delete**.

4. Create a new Visio Graphics Service application. On the Service Applications tab of the ribbon, click **New, Visio Graphics Service**. Make sure that the Create Service Application Proxy check box is selected.

5. In a command prompt window, use the command `ping <serverAddress>` to verify the connectivity.

Visio Application Proxy Has Invalid Endpoint (Event ID 8049)

The application for Visio Graphics Service uses a proxy to set up communication between the front-end and back-end service. For Visio Graphics Service to function properly, the front-end service must be connected to the application server that is returned by the application proxy. Users might observe the following symptoms:

- ▶ The Visio Graphics Service fails to render diagrams.

- ▶ Event ID: 8049 appears in the event log with an "Application proxy invalid endpoint for *<descriptive text>*" description.

Microsoft suggests that the following might be the cause:

- ▶ The specified SharePoint Server application server is inaccessible.

- ▶ The specified application server is responding slowly because of heavy network activity or load on the specific server.

To resolve this issue, we first need to check error logs. To review the log, follow these steps:

1. Open the Windows Event Viewer.
2. Search for Event ID 8049 in the Windows Application Event log.
3. In the event description, note the application server that is failing.

Verify whether the application server connection is working correctly as follows:

1. From the failing application server, open the SharePoint Central Administration website.
2. If you cannot access the Central Administration site from the failing server, check that the network settings are correct and that the server has appropriate permissions to join the SharePoint farm.

Verify whether the Visio Graphics Service is running on the failing server as follows:

1. On the Central Administration page, click **Manage Servers in This Farm**.
2. Verify that the Visio Graphics Service runs on the failing application server.
3. If there is a service application proxy for the failing service application, create a new service application.

One possible resolution is to just restart the Visio Graphics Service. You can do that as follows:

1. On the Central Administration page, click **Manage Servers in This Farm**.
2. In the Server column, click the name of the failing application server. The Services on Server page opens.
3. In the Service column, locate Visio Graphics Service, click **Stop** and then click **Start**.

You might have to create a new Visio Graphics Service application if restart does not resolve your issue. To do so, follow these steps:

1. On the Central Administration page, click **Manage Service Applications**.
2. In the Type column, click the name of the Visio Graphics Service application that has the failing service instance.
3. On the ribbon, click **Delete**.

4. In the Delete Service Application dialog box, click **OK**.

5. Create a new Visio Graphics Service application.

Visio Graphics Service Data Provider Not Found (Event ID 8050)

Visio web drawings connect to external data sources, such as Excel Services. It is possible that users might observe the following symptoms when trying to connect to an external data source:

▶ Refresh data does not work.

▶ Event ID: 8050 appears in the event log with a "Data provider connection failed with connection string *<descriptive text>*" description.

According to Microsoft this might happen because of Visio Graphics Service being unable to connect to a data provider. Make sure the data provider is in the trusted data provider list.

Visio Graphics Service File Loading Error (Event ID 8051, 8061)

Visio web drawings can be uploaded to a document library and then embedded in a SharePoint page by using the Visio Web Access web part. This error usually occurs when the web part is unable to access the file. Users might observe following symptoms:

▶ The file might not load.

▶ Event ID: 8061 appears in the event log with a "File not found at this location: *<file location>*" description.

▶ Event ID: 8051 appears in the event log with an "Unable to parse file at location: *<file location>*" description.

Microsoft identifies the following as possible causes:

▶ A Visio web access web part references a file that no longer exists or is invalid.

▶ A corrupted Visio web diagram.

▶ An invalid Visio web drawing.

Summary

It is very important to read through the directions available at Microsoft website for installing SharePoint 2010 with Visio Graphics Service. Sometimes we miss small configuration settings and then end up with an unstable environment. Visio Graphics Service has many components that need to be configured properly to ensure proper functionality. This chapter covered various behaviors and messages that are displayed to the developer or end user if Visio Graphics Services have not been properly configured.

Best Practices

The following are best practices from this chapter:

▶ Ensure that the Visio Graphics Service is set up in conjunction with the Secure Store Service before starting development. Unattended Service Account will only work when Secure Store Service Application is created. Unattended Service Account helps with refreshing data from an external data source.

▶ To avoid all possible configuration issues, pay careful attention to the Visio configuration chapter (Chapter 11). Do not delete any web drawing from your SharePoint site until you are sure that web drawing is not configured to be accessed from a Visio Web Access web part.

▶ Make sure the data provider you are using in your web drawing is listed in a trusted data provider list.

▶ Monitor network activities to make sure there are no connectivity issues between all servers used to configure your SharePoint farm.

19

INDEX

A

B

How can we make this index more useful? Email us at indexes@samspublishing.com

Maximum Private Bytes setting (ECS Memory Utilization), 20

Maximum Recalc Duration setting (Visio Graphics Service), 190

Maximum Request Duration setting (Excel Services), 22-23

Maximum Size of Workbook Cache setting (Excel Services), 21

Maximum Unused Object Age setting (ECS Memory Utilization), 21

Maximum Web Drawing Size setting (Visio Graphics Service), 189

MDX Query filter, 127

MDX tuple formulas, 111

Member Selection filter, 127

memory, configuring in Excel Services, 20-21

Memory Cache Threshold setting (ECS Memory Utilization), 20-21

Microsoft BI website, 3

Microsoft Office Developer Center, 3

Microsoft scorecard templates, 114

Microsoft SharePoint 2010 website, 3

Minimum Cache Agesetting (Visio Graphics Service), 189

monitoring PowerPivot for SharePoint, 182

multiple pages, creating in dashboards, 134

multiserver farm install (PowerPivot for SharePoint), 171-175

N

Named Set filter, 127

native mode web parts, 81-85

navigation, customizing, 237-239

non-Business Intelligence Center sites, enabling with PerformancePoint Services, 92-95

nontrusted content location, 292-293

O

Objectives, creating, 111

ODC files, publishing, 229-231

office data connectivity files. *See* ODC files

opening Dashboard Designer, 100

P

Page Field Filter, 78

parameters (report), 64-65

PerformancePoint Content category (Dashboard Designer), 101-102

PerformancePoint Services, 84-89, 97-99, 250-251, 261

  adding, 89-90

  application settings, 91-92

  configuring, 239

  connecting to Reporting Services reports, 261

  Dashboard Designer, 99-102

    objects, 101-102

    opening, 100

    redirecting to from content list, 100

  dashboards

    building, 263

    connecting filters to dashboard content objects, 130

    creating, 127-130

    deploying to SharePoint, 135

    interacting with, 266-268

    linking KPI Details reports to scorecards, 133-134

    multiple pages in, 134

  data connection libraries, creating, 92-95

  data connections

    Analysis Services data connections, 102-104, 251

How can we make this index more useful? Email us at indexes@samspublishing.com

data exposure, controlling, 181-182

data refresh options, 179-180

hardware and software requirements, 168

installing, 168

multiserver farm install, 171-175

single-server install, 169-171

monitoring, 182

overview, 162-168

PowerPivot Gallery, 175-177

PowerPivot Management Dashboard, 183-184

snapshots, 179-180

spreadmarts, 181-182

troubleshooting, 300-301

Excel Web Access warning, 302

hierarchies, 302

installation, 302

relationships, 302

SharePoint list data, 302

user credential delegation errors, 302-303

workbooks, publishing, 180-181

PowerPivot Gallery, 175-177

PowerPivot Management Dashboard, 183-184

PowerShell, configuring Visio Graphics Service with, 190

processing

data refresh options, 58-59

data snapshot options, 59

processing timeout, 59

reports, 58-59

ProClarity Analytics Server Page reports, 123

properties

report project properties, 51

Report Viewer web part properties, 75-77

workbook properties, configuring in Excel Services, 23

proxy initiation failure, troubleshooting, 306

publishing

ODC files, 229-231

Visio web drawings, 211-213

workbooks with PowerPivot for SharePoint, 180-181

Q-R

Query String (URL) Filter, 78

RDA BI/SQL Server Practice Group Blog, 3

redirecting to Dashboard Designer from content list, 100

refresh options. *See* **data refresh options**

relationships

creating between tables, 159

in PowerPivot, 302

Report Builder, 45

creating reports with, 240-250

deploying reports from, 51-53

enabling, 283

Report Explorer web part, 81-85

Report Library template, 28-29

Report Server Integration, enabling, 285

Report Viewer web part, 81-85

configuring, 71-75

connections, 77-81

native mode web parts, 81-85

properties, 75-77

Reporting Services, 32-38, 283-285. *See also* **reports**

configuring, 239

connecting to, 261

Content Types, adding to document libraries, 42-45

installing, 38-39

Report Builder, enabling, 283

security

    Excel Services, 19

    insufficient security for dashboard deployment, troubleshooting, 293-294

    PerformancePoint Services, 137-141

        data source delegation, 141-144

        SharePoint permissions, 144-145

    Visio Graphics Service, 220-223

        external data sources, 224

        internal data sources, 223-224

Select a Scorecard Template screen, 114

Select an Item dialog, 72

Select Measure Control setting (PerformancePoint Services), 92

Send Shape Data To connection action, 220

services

    Excel Services. *See* Excel Services

    PerformancePoint Services. *See* PerformancePoint Services

    Reporting Services, 32-38

        configuring, 239

        installing, 38-39

        Reporting Services Add-In for SharePoint, 39-42

        SharePoint integration, 40-42

    Secure Store Service, 288

    Usage and Health Data Collection, 182

    Visio Graphics Service. *See* Visio Graphics Service

session management (Excel Services), 20

Session Timeout setting (Excel Services), 22

shared datasets, 62-64, 281

shared schedules, 55-58

SharePoint Central Administration

    PerformancePoint Services, adding, 89-90

    Reporting Services integration, configuring, 40-42

trusted content locations, configuring, 97

trusted data source locations, configuring, 96

SharePoint List data connections, 107-108

SharePoint list data, in PowerPivot, 302

SharePoint List Filter, 78

SharePoint List template, 107

SharePoint Unified Logging Service (ULS) logs, 300-301

Show Details setting (PerformancePoint Services), 92

Silverlight, 175

single-server install (PowerPivot for SharePoint), 169-171

site collection, 92-94, 235-236

site groups, 145

Site Settings page, 55-57

site templates. *See* templates

sites, enabling with PerformancePoint Services, 92-95

snapshots

    PowerPivot for SharePoint, 179-180

    reports, 59

sparklines, 249-250

spreadmarts, 181-182

SQL Server Analysis Services (SSAS)

    data sources, delegating, 142

    Filter, 78

SQL Server Table data connections, 108-109

SQL Server Table template, 108

SSAS (SQL Server Analysis Services)

    data sources, delegating, 142

    Filter, 78

Standard scorecard templates, 114

Stop When Refresh on Open Fails setting (Excel Services), 24-25

stopping Excel Calculation Services (ECS), 175

Strategy Map reports, 121-122

How can we make this index more useful? Email us at indexes@samspublishing.com

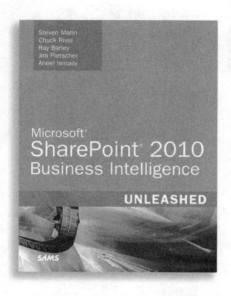